Prentice Hall
LITERATURE
Timeless Voices, Timeless Themes

Selection Support:
Skills Development
Workbook

THE AMERICAN EXPERIENCE

Prentice
Hall

Upper Saddle River, New Jersey
Glenview, Illinois
Needham, Massachusetts

ISBN 0-13-054828-6

14 15 16 17   10 09 08

Prentice
Hall

CONTENTS

UNIT 1: BEGINNINGS (TO 1750)

UNIT 2: A NATION IS BORN (1750–1800)

UNIT 5: DISILLUSION, DEFIANCE, AND DISCONTENT (1914–1946)

"The Earth on Turtle's Back" (Onondaga), **"When Grizzlies Walked Upright"** (Modoc), **from *The Navajo Origin Legend*** (Navajo), **from *The Iroquois Constitution*** (Iroquois)

Build Vocabulary

Spelling Strategy When adding the suffix *-tion* to a word that ends in *te*, drop the *te*: *deliberate* + *-tion* = *deliberation*.

Using the Suffix *-tion*

A. Directions: The suffix *-tion*, which means "the act, state, or quality of," turns words into nouns. For example, the verb *deliberate* + *-tion* becomes the noun *deliberation*. On the lines after each word, write the noun form ending in *-tion* and a definition of the new word.

1. create _____

_____

2. relate _____

_____

3. inflate _____

_____

Using the Word Bank

ablutions	confederate	deliberation
protruded	disposition	

B. Directions: On the line, write the letter of the definition before the word it defines.

____ 1. disposition   a. inclination to believe, do, or choose something

____ 2. deliberation   b. ritual washings or cleansings of the body

____ 3. confederate   c. careful consideration

____ 4. ablutions   d. stuck out

____ 5. protruded   e. united with others for a common purpose

C. Directions: On the line, write the letter of the word that is most similar in meaning to the word in capital letters.

____ 1. PROTRUDED: a. jutted   b. curved   c. stood   d. reversed

____ 2. DISPOSITION: a. gain   b. size   c. tendency   d. teamwork

____ 3. ABLUTIONS: a. rinsings   b. dyeings   c. heatings   d. coolings

____ 4. DELIBERATION: a. anger   b. belief   c. action   d. thought

____ 5. CONFEDERATE: a. disorganized   b. allied   c. imprisoned   d. nonviolent

"The Earth on Turtle's Back" (Onondaga), **"When Grizzlies Walked Upright"** (Modoc), **from** *The Navajo Origin Legend* (Navajo), **from** *The Iroquois Constitution* (Iroquois)

Grammar and Style: Compound Sentences

Writers often link related ideas in compound sentences. A **compound sentence** consists of two or more main clauses joined by a semicolon or a coordinating conjunction (usually *and*, *but*, or *or*). A **main clause** is a clause that can stand alone as a sentence. It expresses a complete thought and contains a **subject** (who or what the sentence is about) and a **predicate** (what the subject is or does).

| subj. | pred. | subj. | pred. |

She swam deeper and deeper; her lungs felt ready to burst.

| subj. | pred. | subj. | pred. |

Her lungs felt ready to burst, but she swam deeper still.

A. Practice: Use the method indicated in parentheses to combine each pair of sentences into a compound sentence. Write the compound sentences on the lines provided. Put one line under each subject and two lines under each predicate.

1. The grizzlies looked like they do today. They walked on two feet. (use *but*)

   _____

2. The Chief of the Sky Spirits brought his family down to earth. The mountains of snow and ice became their lodge. (use a semicolon)

   _____

   _____

3. The daughter looked for the ocean. She fell out of the mountain. (use *and*)

   _____

4. The little girl could have died. The grizzlies could save her. (use *or*)

   _____

B. Writing Application: Create your own compound sentences by adding a second main clause to each clause that follows. Use the combining method indicated in parentheses, and write the sentence on the lines provided.

1. The tiny bit of Earth fell on Turtle's back (use *and*) _____

   _____

2. The Spirit Chief climbed back up the mountain (use a semicolon) _____

   _____

3. The lords of the Confederacy must not be dishonest (use *but*) _____

   _____

4. The wind could bring the ears of corn to life (use *or*) _____

   _____

"The Earth on Turtle's Back" (Onondaga), **"When Grizzlies Walked Upright"** (Modoc), **from *The Navajo Origin Legend*** (Navajo), **from *The Iroquois Constitution*** (Iroquois)

Reading Strategy: Recognize Cultural Details

Literature reflects the culture that produces it. While you read a piece of literature, pay attention to cultural details—such as references to objects, animals, or practices that signal how people live, think, or worship—to gain cultural insight. For example, the cultural details in the three Native American myths and the Iroquois Constitution indicate how the Native Americans lived as well as what they valued in life.

DIRECTIONS: Read the following excerpts from the selections. Then answer the questions that follow.

"The Earth on the Turtle's Back"

There was an ancient chief in the Skyland. His young wife was expecting a child, and one night she dreamed that she saw the Great Tree uprooted. The next day she told her husband the story.

He nodded as she finished telling her dream. "My wife," he said, "I am sad that you had this dream. It is clearly a dream of great power and, as is our way, when one has such a powerful dream we must do all we can to make it true. The Great Tree must be uprooted."

"When Grizzlies Walked Upright"

The Sky Spirit broke off the small end of his giant stick and threw the pieces into the rivers. The longer pieces turned into beaver and otter; the smaller pieces became fish. When the leaves dropped from the trees, he picked them up, blew upon them, and so made the birds.

from *The Navajo Origin Legend*

The white ear of corn had been changed into a man, the yellow ear into a woman. It was the wind that gave them life. It is the wind that comes out of our mouths now that gives us life. When this ceases to blow we die. In the skin at the tips of our fingers we see the trail of the wind; it shows us where the wind blew when our ancestors were created.

from *The Iroquois Constitution*

We now do crown you with the sacred emblem of your lordship. You shall now become a mentor of the people of the Five Nations. The thickness of your skin shall be seven spans—which is to say that you shall be proof against anger, offensive actions and criticism. Your heart shall be filled with peace and good will and your mind filled with a yearning for the welfare of the people of the confederacy.

1. What can you infer about the Native American's attitude toward nature? Support your opinion with evidence from the excerpts.

_____

2. Explain what you can infer about the place of dreams in Native American culture from the excerpt from "The Earth on Turtle's Back."

_____

3. What does the excerpt from *The Iroquois Constitution* tell us about the ideals of the Iroquois people?

_____

4. Explain the significance of the words "the thickness of your skin" found in *The Iroquois Constitution*. What does it mean today to be "thick-skinned"?

_____

"The Earth on Turtle's Back" (Onondaga), **"When Grizzlies Walked Upright"** (Modoc), **from *The Navajo Origin Legend*** (Navajo), **from *The Iroquois Constitution*** (Iroquois)

Literary Analysis: Origin Myths

Origin myths are traditional stories that recount the origins of earthly life. Passed down from generation to generation, these myths often explain such phenomena as the beginning of human life, the customs and religious rites of a people, the creation of natural landmarks, and events beyond a people's control.

DIRECTIONS: Complete the chart below by explaining in the right column how each phenomenon in the left column came into being. Review each selection for help.

Selection and Phenomenon	Explanation
"The Earth on Turtle's Back": the world	
"When Grizzlies Walked Upright": Mount Shasta, beaver, otter, fish, birds, grizzly bears	
from *The Navajo Origin Legend*: man, woman	

"A Journey Through Texas" from *The Journey of Alvar Núñez Cabeza de Vaca*
by Alvar Núñez Cabeza de Vaca
"Boulders Taller Than the Great Tower of Seville" by García López de Cárdenas

Build Vocabulary

Spelling Strategy When adding a prefix to a word, keep all the letters of the original word: *mortality + im- = immortality; spell + mis- = misspell.*

Using the Root -*mort*-

A. DIRECTIONS: The Latin root -*mort*- means "death." For each sentence that follows, use the context clues and your knowledge of the root -*mort*- to help you define the word in italics. Write your definitions on the lines provided.

1. The explorer fell halfway down the canyon and lay *mortally* wounded.

   mortally _____

2. Were they subject to death like all human beings, or were they *immortal*?

   immortal _____

3. Following the tragedy, the airport hangar served as a temporary *mortuary* until the bodies could be identified.

   mortuary _____

4. The wake will be held in the parlor of the local *mortician* after he has prepared the body.

   mortician _____

5. Despite her death, she remains alive for many of us because she has been *immortalized* in song and verse.

   immortalized _____

Using the Word Bank

entreated	feigned	mortality	subsisted	traversed	dispatched

B. DIRECTIONS: On the line, write the letter of the word that is most nearly *opposite* in meaning to the word in capital letters.

____ 1. ENTREATED: a. purchased b. refused c. asked d. begged

____ 2. MORTALITY: a. death b. life c. illness d. weakness

____ 3. SUBSISTED: a. survived b. perished c. hid d. helped

____ 4. FEIGNED: a. smirked b. avoided c. pretended d. revealed

____ 5. TRAVERSED: a. crossed b. assisted c. stopped d. silenced

____ 6. DISPATCHED: a. received b. sent c. broke d. repaired

"A Journey Through Texas" from *The Journey of Alvar Núñez Cabeza de Vaca*
by Alvar Núñez Cabeza de Vaca
"Boulders Taller Than the Great Tower of Seville" by García López de Cárdenas

Grammar and Style: Past and Past Perfect Verb Tenses

Verb tenses help show in what sequence events unfolded. The **past tense**, often formed by adding *-ed* or *-d* to a verb, shows an action or condition that began and ended at a given time in the past. The **past perfect tense**, formed by using *had* before the past participle of the verb, shows a past action or condition that ended before another past action or condition began.

> **Past:** We *reached* the Tizón River.

> **Past Perfect:** We reached the Tizón River much closer to its source than where Melchior Díaz and his men *had crossed* it.

A. Practice: In the following sentences, underline the verbs in the past tense and circle the verbs in the past perfect tense.

1. The women whom we had sent out returned.

2. At the end of three days Castillo returned to where he had left us.

3. He told how he had found permanent houses and that he had also seen maize.

4. Then we saw something that astonished us very much.

5. When they had marched for twenty days, they came to gorges of the river.

B. Writing Application: Expand these sentences to show the order in which events unfolded. If the verb in the given clause is in the past tense, add another clause using a verb in the past perfect tense. If the verb in the given clause is in the past perfect tense, add another clause using a verb in the past tense. Write your expanded sentences on the lines provided.

1. He had walked only twelve paces

_____

2. After the guide had told them of the danger

_____

3. Empty gourds riddled the path

_____

4. They struggled to make their meaning clear

_____

5. The Indians led the explorers over the distant mountains

_____

"A Journey Through Texas" from *The Journey of Alvar Núñez Cabeza de Vaca*
by Alvar Núñez Cabeza de Vaca
"Boulders Taller Than the Great Tower of Seville" by García López de Cárdenas

Reading Strategy: Signal Words

One way to make sense of a writer's work is to look for signal words that point out relationships among the ideas and events presented. Signal words may place events in time, indicate reasons or cause-and-effect relationships, or set up a contrast between ideas.

Time: *On that same day* many fell sick, and *on the next day* eight of them died.

Reason: We called them "of the cows," *because* most of the cows die near there.

Contrast: What from the top seemed easy was, *on the contrary*, rough and difficult.

DIRECTIONS: After reading each numbered passage in the first column, write the signal word or words it contains and the type of relationship that each signal word indicates.

Passage	Signal Words	Relationship
1. They entreated us not to be angry any longer, because, even if it was their death, they would take us where we chose.		
2. The next morning all those who were strong enough came along, and at the end of three journeys we halted.		
3. The people who heard of our approach did not come out to meet us, but we found them at their homes.		
4. Although this was the warm season, no one could live in this canyon because of the cold.		
5. They returned about four o'clock in the afternoon, as they could not reach the bottom because of the many obstacles they met.		

"A Journey Through Texas" from *The Journey of Alvar Núñez Cabeza de Vaca*
by Alvar Núñez Cabeza de Vaca
"Boulders Taller Than the Great Tower of Seville" by Garcia López de Cárdenas

Literary Analysis: Exploration Narratives

"A Journey Through Texas" and "Boulders Taller Than the Great Tower of Seville" are both **exploration narratives**—explorers' firsthand accounts of their experiences. Such narratives generally focus on the difficulties that the explorers faced and the specific discoveries they made. Though generally factual and meant to be informative, exploration narratives nevertheless express viewpoints and reactions that are sometimes distinctly personal. In addition to providing factual information, the writers may aim to impress others or perhaps to inspire them to follow in their footsteps.

DIRECTIONS: Read the following passages from "A Journey Through Texas." Then, on the lines that follow, identify the elements of exploration narratives that you find in each passage.

1. On that same day many fell sick, and on the next day eight of them died! All over the country, where it was known, they became so afraid that it seemed as if the mere sight of us would kill them. They besought us not to be angry nor to procure the death of any more of their number, for they were convinced that we killed them by merely thinking of it. In truth, we were very much concerned about it, for, seeing the great mortality, we dreaded that all of them might die or forsake us in their terror, while those further on, upon learning of it, would get out of our way hereafter. We prayed to God our Lord to assist us, and the sick began to get well. Then we saw something that astonished us very much, and it was that, while the parents, brothers and wives of the dead had shown deep grief at their illness, from the moment they died the survivors made no demonstration whatsoever, and showed not the slightest feeling; nor did they dare to go near the bodies until we ordered their burial. . . .

_____

_____

_____

_____

2. In doubt as to what should be done, and which was the best and most advantageous road to take, we remained with them for two days. They gave us beans, squashes, and calabashes. Their way of cooking them is so new and strange that I felt like describing it here, in order to show how different and queer are the devices and industries of human beings. They have no pots. In order to cook their food they fill a middle-sized gourd with water, and place into a fire such stones as easily become heated, and when they are hot to scorch they take them out with wooden tongs, thrusting them into the water of the gourd, until it boils. As soon as it boils they pull into it what they want to cook. . . .

_____

_____

_____

_____

_____

from *The Interesting Narrative of the Life of Olaudah Equiano*
by Olaudah Equiano

Build Vocabulary

Spelling Strategy *In-*, a common prefix meaning "not," changes to *im-* when added to words that begin with *b, m,* and *p*: *imbalanced, immortal, improvident.*

Using the Root *-vid-*

A. DIRECTIONS: The word root *-vid-*, from the Latin *videre*, means "to see." On the lines provided, explain how each word that follows conveys the meaning of the root.

1. videotape _____

_____

2. evident _____

_____

Using the Word Bank

loathsome	copious	pacify
pestilential	improvident	avarice

B. DIRECTIONS: On the line, write the letter of the definition before the word it defines.

____ 1. copious   a. disgusting; offensive

____ 2. avarice   b. abundant

____ 3. pacify   c. greed

____ 4. pestilential   d. lacking thrift or foresight

____ 5. improvident   e. to make peaceful

____ 6. loathsome   f. causing infection

C. DIRECTIONS: On the line provided, write the word from the Word Bank that best completes each sentence. Use each word only once.

1. Smith's sin was _____, for he pursued wealth with single-minded devotion.

2. The old sailors told horror tales of a _____ sea monster.

3. Given their lack of resources, making a long journey seemed _____.

4. The newcomers fell ill, the strange climate proving _____ to them.

5. They hoped their gifts would _____ any hostile natives they encountered.

6. The island was lush, with _____ natural resources.

from *The Interesting Narrative of the Life of Olaudah Equiano*
by Olaudah Equiano

Grammar and Style: Active and Passive Voice

A verb is in the **active voice** when the subject of the sentence or clause performs the action. A verb is in the **passive voice** when the action is performed on the subject. The passive voice consists of a form of the helping verb *be* plus the past participle of the main verb.

Active Voice: I *expected* every hour to share the fate of my companions.

Passive Voice: We *were conducted* immediately to the merchant's yard.

The passive voice is suitable when the performer of the action is unknown, unimportant, or best concealed. Otherwise, use the active voice to make your writing more forceful and effective.

A. Practice: On the line before each number, write *A* if the verb is in the active voice and *P* if it is in the passive voice. Then, on the long line provided, rewrite the sentence using a verb in the opposite voice, adding or dropping words as necessary.

_____ 1. The ship took in all the cargo.

_____

_____ 2. The groans of the dying turned the scene into almost inconceivable horror.

_____

_____ 3. Two of the wretches were drowned.

_____

_____ 4. Eventually we were landed on Barbados.

_____

B. Writing Application: In the following sentences based on the selection by Equiano, the verbs are all in the passive voice. Decide if each would be more effective in the active voice. If so, rewrite the sentence on the lines provided, adding or dropping words as necessary. If not, explain your reasons for leaving the verb in the passive voice.

1. Equiano and his sister were kidnapped from their home in West Africa.

_____

_____

2. During the journey across the ocean, Equiano was separated from his sister.

_____

_____

3. At the merchant's in Barbados, the captives were confined to a yard.

_____

_____

4. Eventually, they were purchased.

_____

_____

from *The Interesting Narrative of the Life of Olaudah Equiano*
by Olaudah Equiano

Reading Strategy: Summarizing

When you **summarize** a passage or a selection, you state briefly in your own words its main ideas and most important details. A good way of checking your understanding of a text, summarizing is especially helpful when you read material written in another time period or in an unfamiliar style.

A. DIRECTIONS: As you read or reread the selection by Olaudah Equiano, fill out this chart to help you keep track of the main ideas and key details you need to include in your summary. One sample entry has been done for you.

Main Ideas	Details
The slaves on the ship were kept in close confinement under terrible conditions.	terrible stench; crowded; filthy; shrieks and groans; many perish; Equiano thinks death would be a relief

B. DIRECTIONS: Use the chart you completed to write a summary of the selection on the lines provided.

_____
_____
_____
_____
_____
_____
_____
_____
_____
_____

from *The Interesting Narrative of the Life of Olaudah Equiano*
by Olaudah Equiano

Literary Analysis: Slave Narratives

A **slave narrative** is an autobiographical account of life as a slave. Often written to expose the horrors of human bondage, it documents a slave's experiences from his or her own point of view. The selection from Equiano's narrative provides an especially grim description of the long voyage from Africa to Barbados that Equiano was forced to endure when he was only eleven years old.

Among the indignities that Equiano put up with while a slave was the unwelcomed changing of his name. During his lifetime, Equiano was known by three different names. His African name was Olaudah Equiano. His American master from Virginia decided to change Equiano's name to Jacob. A short time later, an English merchant purchased "Jacob," took him to England, and renamed him again.

DIRECTIONS: Read the following excerpt from Equiano's autobiography. Then answer the questions on the lines provided.

Some of the people of the ship used to tell me they were going to carry me back to my own country and this made me very happy. I was quite rejoiced at the sound of going back, and thought if I should get home what wonders I should have to tell. But I was reserved for another fate and was soon undeceived when we come within sight of the English coast. While I was on board this ship, my captain and master named me Gustavus Vassa. I at that time began to understand him a little, and refused to be called so, and told him as well as I could that I would be called Jacob; but he said I should not, and still called me Gustavus; and when I refused to answer to my new name, which at first I did, it gained me many a cuff; so at length I submitted and was obliged to bear the present name, by which I have been known ever since.

1. Slave narratives contain vivid accounts of oppression. What examples of oppression appear in the passage above?

   _____

   _____

2. In what way was Equiano's response to the change in his name different from his response to the oppression he suffered on his voyage from Africa? How do you account for the difference?

   _____

   _____

3. Why might Equiano have asked the captain to call him Jacob rather than Olaudah?

   _____

   _____

4. Look up Gustavus I in an encyclopedia. Then write who Equiano was named after. Was this name an appropriate choice? Why?

   _____

   _____

"Diamond Island: Alcatraz (Allisti Ti-Tanin-Miji)" by Darryl Babe Wilson

Build Vocabulary

Using Signal Words

A. DIRECTIONS: Signal words can serve as valuable narrative links that help you distinguish events in the present, the near past, and the more distant past. In these sentences from "Diamond Island: Alcatraz," circle the words that show you when the events occurred.

1. Thanksgiving weekend, 1989. It is this time of the year when I think about Grandfather and his ordeal.

2. He told me the story one winter in his little one-room house in Atwam.

3. The old person in the old house under the old moon began to tell the story of his escape from "the rock" long ago.

4. Grandfather has been within the earth for many snows now.

Using the Word Bank

expended	redolence	autonomous

B. DIRECTIONS: On the line provided, write the word from the Word Bank that best completes the meaning of each sentence.

1. I _____ a great deal of energy swimming in that cold water.

2. To survive as an _____ people is difficult in the modern world.

3. The _____ of the room reminded me of my grandmother's house.

C. DIRECTIONS: On the line before each item, write S if the two words are synonyms. Write A if they are antonyms.

____ 1. autonomous, dependent

____ 2. redolence, aroma

____ 3. expended, conserved

"Diamond Island: Alcatraz (Allisti Ti-Tanin-Miji)" by Darryl Babe Wilson

Thematic Connection: Meeting of Cultures

One way to conserve the past is by gathering oral histories from older members of a community, as Wilson does in Diamond Island: Alcatraz. Not only can oral-history interview provide facts and details about the past, but it can also show how someone with a different mindset or different cultural values views contemporary life.

DIRECTIONS: Work with a group of classmates to plan, execute, and compile a series of oral-history interviews of older people in your community. Use the list below to help you plan and organize the interviews.

Name of Interviewer: _____

Date of Interview: _____

Name of Person Interviewed: _____

Biographical Information on Person Interviewed: _____

_____

_____

_____

_____

Topics or Experiences to Explore in Interview: _____

_____

_____

Interview Questions: _____

_____

_____

_____

_____

_____

_____

_____

_____

_____

_____

_____

_____

from *Journal of the First Voyage to America* by Christopher Columbus

Build Vocabulary

Spelling Strategy To form the plural of a word that ends in a consonant plus *y*, change the *y* to *i* and add *es*: *ambiguity, ambiguities*.

Using the Root *-flict-*

A. DIRECTIONS: The word root *-flict-* means "to strike." On the line, write the letter of the word that best completes each statement.

____ 1. A cruel person is likely to *inflict* _____.

    a. harm   b. joy   c. sympathy   d. quality

____ 2. A *conflict* between nations most likely involves _____.

    a. alliances   b. disputes   c. roadways   d. passports

____ 3. A person *afflicted* with measles probably is _____.

    a. happy   b. healthy   c. ill   d. recovering

Using the Word Bank

indication	exquisite	affliction	abundance

B. DIRECTIONS: On the line provided, write the word from the Word Bank that best completes the meaning of each sentence. Use each word only once.

1. The voyage was miserable, with the crew facing grave _____.

2. For many weeks there was no _____ of land.

3. The sailors would never forget the _____ beauty of the new land.

4. Columbus hoped to find gold or spices in _____.

C. DIRECTIONS: On the line, write the letter of the pair of words that expresses a relationship most similar to the relationship of the pair of words in capital letters.

____ 1. INDICATION : SIGN ::
    a. normality : strangeness
    b. cloud : weather
    c. murmur : whisper
    d. walk : run

____ 2. ABUNDANCE : EXCESS ::
    a. busy : occupied
    b. crowded : overcrowded
    c. doubtful : certain
    d. discovered : explored

____ 3. AFFLICTION : HARDSHIP ::
    a. poverty : wealth
    b. ignorance : bliss
    c. contentment : happiness
    d. calories : diet

____ 4. PRETTY : EXQUISITE ::
    a. bad : horrible
    b. knowledgeable : uneducated
    c. delicate : broken
    d. calm : peaceful

from _Journal of the First Voyage to America_ by Christopher Columbus

Grammar and Style: Action Verbs and Linking Verbs

Action verbs express physical or mental action. **Linking verbs** express a state of being and are followed either by a noun or pronoun that renames the subject or by an adjective that describes it.

    Action Verb: I went ashore.

    Linking Verb: Everything _looked_ green.

While writers must make use of both action and linking verbs, action verbs generally make writing more lively.

A. Practice: Underline the verb in each sentence. Then, on the line before the sentence, write AV if the verb is an action verb or LV if it is a linking verb.

_____ 1. Groves of lofty trees were abundant.

_____ 2. At one of the lakes, I saw a snake.

_____ 3. We followed it for some distance.

_____ 4. The water did not look deep.

_____ 5. We dispatched it with our lances.

B. Writing Application: Read each sentence, and determine if it contains an action verb or a linking verb. Then, on the lines provided, write a related sentence with the type of verb that does _not_ appear in the first sentence. An example has been completed for you.

    Example: The melody of the birds _was_ exquisite. [_Was_ is a linking verb.]

    Related: The birds _chirped_ an exquisite melody. [_Chirped_ is an action verb.]

1. Columbus's journal is a marvelous document.

    _____

    _____

2. His descriptions capture the lush splendor of the Caribbean islands.

    _____

    _____

3. His long time at sea seems particularly tense.

    _____

    _____

4. Columbus made several subsequent journeys to the "new" world.

    _____

    _____

5. Of course, to the native inhabitants their world was not new at all!

    _____

    _____

from *Journal of the First Voyage to America* by Christopher Columbus

Reading Strategy: Author's Purpose

Recognizing an author's purpose for writing can help you understand why certain words, details, and events are included in a piece of writing. Columbus kept a journal for the purpose of persuading Queen Isabella and King Ferdinand to give him more financial backing for his explorations. As a result, his language puts his explorations in the best possible light. For example, he talks about the beauty of the island:

> This island even exceeds the others in beauty and fertility. Groves
> of lofty and flourishing trees are abundant, as also large lakes, sur-
> rounded and overhung by the foliage, in a most enchanting manner. . . .
> The melody of the birds was so exquisite that one was never willing
> to part from the spot, and the flocks of parrots obscured the
> heavens.

DIRECTIONS: As you read, use the following chart to record Columbus's favorable descriptions and events. Then, explain his purpose for describing them in that way.

Descriptions	Columbus's Purpose

from *Journal of the First Voyage to America* by Christopher Columbus

Literary Analysis: Journals

A **journal** is an individual's day-by-day account of events. Although a journal provides valuable details that can be supplied only by a participant or an eyewitness, it is not necessarily an accurate record of facts. The writer's impressions may color the telling of events. Furthermore, a journal written for publication—such as the journal of Columbus, which was written for his investors, the king and queen of Spain—is less likely to be objective. Nevertheless, journals can provide insights into the writer's personality and character.

DIRECTIONS: Read each of the following excerpts from *Journal of the First Voyage to America.* Write what each excerpt reveals about Christopher Columbus.

1. I went ashore, and found no habitation save a single house, and that without an occupant; we had no doubt that the people had fled in terror at our approach, as the house was completely furnished. I suffered nothing to be touched, and went with my captains and some of the crew to view the country.

   _____

   _____

2. This island even exceeds the others in beauty and fertility. Groves of lofty and flourishing trees are abundant, as also large lakes, surrounded and overhung by the foliage, in a most enchanting manner. . . . The melody of birds was so exquisite that one was never willing to part from the spot, and the flocks of parrots obscured the heavens.

   _____

   _____

3. I discovered also the aloe tree, and am determined to take on board the ship tomorrow, ten quintals of it, as I am told it is valuable.

   _____

   _____

4. Presently we saw several of the natives advancing towards our party, and one of them came up to us, to whom we gave some hawk's bells and glass beads, with which he was delighted. We asked him in return, for water, and after I had gone on board the ship, the natives came down to the shore with their calabashes full, and showed great pleasure in presenting us with it. I ordered more glass beads to be given them, and they promised to return the next day.

   _____

   _____

5. . . . I shall depart immediately, if the weather serve, and sail round the island, till I succeed in meeting with the king, in order to see if I can acquire any of the gold, which I hear he possesses.

   _____

   _____

from *The General History of Virginia* by John Smith
from *Of Plymouth Plantation* by William Bradford

Build Vocabulary

Spelling Strategy When adding the ending *-ed* to words that end in *-ify*, change *y* to *i*: *mollify* + *ed* = *mollified*.

Using Related Words

A. DIRECTIONS: Many words have related forms with similar meanings. For example, the noun *peril* means "danger"; a related form is the adjective *perilous*, which means "dangerous." Using your understanding of the Word Bank words, circle the letter of the best answer to the following questions about related forms of those words.

1. Which word most likely means "to make up for; to repay"?

    a. imperil   b. compensate   c. pilferer

2. Which word probably means "to place in danger"?

    a. imperil   b. compensate   c. pilferer

3. Which word could refer to someone who takes things that don't belong to him or her?

    a. imperil   b. compensate   c. pilferer

Using the Word Bank

pilfer	mollified	sundry	palisades
peril	recompense	conceits	loath

B. DIRECTIONS: On the line provided, write the word from the Word Bank that best completes each of the following sentences. Use each word only once.

1. They locked the grainhouse to make sure no one would _____ any grain.

2. Of the _____ routes to the Americas, the Pilgrims chose a northerly one.

3. The soldiers generously donated their time, serving with no _____.

4. Strongly built _____ helped to keep the colony secure.

5. In the starving time of winter, the Pilgrims faced great _____.

6. Most Europeans were _____ to risk the hazards of the dangerous voyage.

7. Sometimes the settlers _____ hostile natives with gifts.

8. Smith's exaggerated reports fed European _____ about the New World.

from *The General History of Virginia* by John Smith
from *Of Plymouth Plantation* by William Bradford

Grammar and Style: Plural and Possessive Nouns

The **possessive case** of nouns shows possession or ownership. Add an apostrophe (') and *s* to form the possessive of singular nouns:

the *leader's* decision   the *colony's* inhabitants   *Columbus's* voyage

Add just an apostrophe to show the possessive of plural nouns ending in *s*:

the *leaders'* decisions   the *colonists'* houses   the *Pilgrims'* landing

Add an apostrophe and *s* to show the possessive of plural nouns not ending in *s*:

the *men's* quarters   the *geese's* cries   the ten *sheep's* fleeces

A. Practice: For each sentence, circle the correct form—singular possessive, plural, or plural possessive—of the words in parentheses.

1. Pocahontas was the (king's, kings, kings') dearest daughter.

2. (Pocahontas, Pocahontas's, Pocahontas') kindness helped the settlers survive.

3. The twelve (guide's, guides, guides') quarters were in the forest.

4. The settlers gave (children's, childrens, childrens') toys to the native.

B. Writing Application: For each noun listed, write one sentence using the singular possessive form and another using the plural possessive form.

1. passenger

Singular Possessive: _____

Plural Possessive: _____

2. compass

Singular Possessive: _____

Plural Possessive: _____

3. woman

Singular Possessive: _____

Plural Possessive: _____

4. child

Singular Possessive: _____

Plural Possessive: _____

from *The General History of Virginia* by John Smith

from *Of Plymouth Plantation* by William Bradford

Reading Strategy: Break Down Sentences

One way to understand complex passages in a selection is to break down sentences to help unlock their meaning. This strategy is especially useful for reading the work of writers from centuries past, who tend to write in long, complicated sentences. In the following passage from *The General History of Virginia*, notice how the vital information telling who and what has been underlined, while all the unessential material has been bracketed. Breaking down material in this way helps you analyze clarity of meaning.

[Two days after,] Powhatan, [having disguised himself in the most fearfulest manner he could,] caused Captain Smith to be brought forth to a great house in the woods [and there upon a mat by the fire to be left alone]. [Not long after, from behind a mat that divided the house, was made the most dolefulest noise he ever heard; then] Powhatan [more like a devil than a man, with some two hundred more as black as himself,] came unto him and told him now they were friends, [and presently he should go to Jamestown].

DIRECTIONS: Break down the following passages by bracketing unessential material and underlining the essential information that tells who and what.

1. But now was all our provision spent, the sturgeon gone, all helps abandoned, each hour expecting the fury of the savages; when God, the patron of all good endeavors, in that desperate extremity so changed the hearts of the savages that they brought such plenty of their fruits and provision as no man wanted.

2. And of these, in the time of most distress, there was but six or seven sound persons who to their great commendations, be it spoken, spared no pains night or day, but with abundance of toil and hazard of their own health, fetched them wood, made them fires, dressed them meat, made their beds, washed their loathsome clothes, clothed and unclothed them. In a word, did all the homely and necessary offices for them which dainty and queasy stomachs cannot endure to hear named; and all this willingly and cheerfully, without any grudging in the least, showing herein their true love unto their friends and brethren; a rare example and worthy to be remembered.

from *The General History of Virginia* by John Smith
from *Of Plymouth Plantation* by William Bradford

Literary Analysis: Narrative Accounts

Smith's **account** of the Virginia colony and Bradford's **narrative account** of Plymouth Plantation are both **historical narratives**, writing that provided a factual, chronological account of significant historical events. Historical narratives can be **firsthand accounts** written by people who lived through the events, or **secondhand accounts** by people who research the events later. Either way, they may include analysis and explanation, in addition to factual information. A firsthand historical narrative, having been written by a participant, is likely to be subjective and possibly inaccurate, but it may also effectively capture the flavor of the time in which it was written.

DIRECTIONS: On the lines that follow the passages, list examples and details that show that the passages are firsthand historical narratives.

1. While the ships stayed, our allowance was somewhat bettered by a daily proportion of biscuit which the sailors would pilfer to sell, give, or exchange with us for money, sassafras, or furs. But when they departed, there remained neither tavern, beer house, nor place of relief but the common kettle. Had we been as free from all sins as gluttony and drunkenness we might have been canonized for saints, but our President would never have been admitted for engrossing to his private, oatmeal, sack, oil, aqua vitae, beef, eggs, or what not but the kettle; that indeed he allowed equally to be distributed.

   _____
   _____
   _____
   _____
   _____
   _____

2. . . . after long beating at sea they fell with that land which is called Cape Cod; the which being made and certainly known to be it, they were not a little joyful. After some deliberation had amongst themselves and with the master of the ship, they tacked about and resolved to stand for the southward (the wind and weather being fair) to find some place about Hudson's River for their habitation. But after they had sailed that course about half the day, they fell amongst dangerous shoals and roaring breakers, and they were so far entangled therewith as they conceived themselves in great danger; and the wind shrinking upon them withal, they resolved to bear up again for the Cape and thought themselves happy to get out of those dangers before night overtook them, as by God's good providence they did.

   _____
   _____
   _____
   _____
   _____
   _____

from *The Right Stuff* by Tom Wolfe

Build Vocabulary

Using Space-Age Vocabulary

A. DIRECTIONS: Many words in *The Right Stuff* are related to the exploration of outer space in the second half of the twentieth century. To show your mastery of such terms, use the numbered clues to complete the following crossword puzzle.

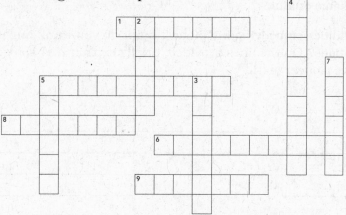

Across

1. pilot's space
5. machine that pulls things outward around a center
6. it "pumps" through your system when you're excited
8. detachable compartment
9. liftoff

Down

2. path around a heavenly body
3. units measuring inertial pressure during rapid acceleration
4. range of speed from subsonic to supersonic
5. person speaking directly to an astronaut
7. spacecraft

Using the Word Bank

malevolent	trajectory	jettisoned	obliterated

B. DIRECTIONS: For each item, choose the word in the box that best completes the meaning of the sentence as a whole.

1. The dark cloud looked _____, as if it would surely harm us if it could.

2. The astronauts _____ the burning fuel tank, sending it into space.

3. The _____ of the craft will bring it down in the South Pacific.

4. Such tiny meteors never reach Earth, for they are _____ by the atmosphere.

C. DIRECTIONS: Circle the letter of word that is closest in meaning to the word in capital letters.

1. MALEVOLENT: a. mean   b. evil   c. unhappy   d. stormy

2. OBLITERATED: a. jammed   b. melted   c. crashed   d. destroyed

3. TRAJECTORY: a. path   b. rocket   c. journey   d. plan

4. JETTISONED: a. leaped   b. flew   c. ejected   d. slowed

from *The Right Stuff* by Tom Wolfe

Thematic Connection: The Pioneer Spirit

When he uses the phrase "the right stuff," Tom Wolfe is describing a certain set of personal characteristics exhibited by the early astronauts that might also be described as the pioneer spirit. You're familiar with a number of pioneers, from the early explorers of the Americas, to the pioneers who settled the American west, to the astronauts who lifted off during the American space program. How would you describe the pioneer spirit? What occupations in today's world require those same qualities?

DIRECTIONS: What qualities embodying the pioneer spirit do you think might apply to each of the following occupations? On the lines provided, briefly explain how someone in each occupation might display the pioneer spirit.

1. archaeologist

_____

_____

_____

_____

2. social worker

_____

_____

_____

_____

3. architect

_____

_____

_____

_____

4. astronomer

_____

_____

_____

_____

Name _____ Date _____

"To My Dear and Loving Husband" by Anne Bradstreet
"Huswifery" by Edward Taylor

Build Vocabulary

Spelling Strategy In general, use just *th* at the end of a word for the unvoiced sound: *cloth, breath, myth*. Include a final *e* for the voiced sound: *clothe, breathe, soothe*.

Using the Suffix *-fold*

A. DIRECTIONS: The suffix *-fold*, which means "a specific number of times or ways," can be used to form both adjectives and adverbs. On the lines provided, write a sentence using each word below as the part of speech indicated.

1. tenfold (use as an adverb) _____

_____

2. multifold (use as an adjective) _____

_____

Using the Word Bank

recompense	manifold	persevere

B. DIRECTIONS: On the line provided, write the word from the Word Bank that best completes each sentence.

1. I expected no _____ from my friend for the help I gave him.

2. There are _____ reasons for studying the literature of the Puritans.

3. I will not quit; I will _____ in my efforts to learn about the Puritans.

C. DIRECTIONS: On the line, write the letter of the pair of words that expresses a relationship most like the relationship of the words in capital letters.

____ 1. RECOMPENSE : MONEY ::
   a. spend : save
   b. contest : win
   c. avenge : vengeance
   d. goods : barter

____ 2. ONCE : MANIFOLD ::
   a. usually : abnormally
   b. single : multitude
   c. briskly : quickly
   d. hundredfold : tenfold

____ 3. PERSEVERE : PROCRASTINATE ::
   a. try : attempt
   b. attempt : fail
   c. continue : dawdle
   d. dawdle : delay

"To My Dear and Loving Husband" by Anne Bradstreet
"Huswifery" by Edward Taylor

Grammar and Style: Direct Address

A term of direct address is a name, title, or phrase used in speaking directly to someone or something. In the following line from Edward Taylor's poem, the words *O Lord* are an example of direct address. Note that the term of direct address is set off by commas.

Make me, O Lord, Thy spinning wheel complete.

A. Practice: In each sentence, underline the term or terms of direct address.

1. I told the farmer, a young man, "Please, my friend, join us for evening meal."

2. Frankly, I would like to know what troubles you, my dear.

3. In the square, brother John, you will find the fruit vendor, I think.

4. I wonder, Sally, what would have happened if I, an unworthy man, had not met you.

5. Come, please, sit with me by the spinning wheel, cousin.

B. Writing Application: Rewrite each sentence that follows, adding a term of direct address. Be sure to punctuate the new sentence correctly.

1. Would you please read that poem again?

   _____

   _____

2. Your report on the Puritans was fascinating, especially the part about their experiences before coming to America.

   _____

   _____

   _____

3. In what ways do the poems reflect the world view of the Puritans?

   _____

   _____

4. Did you finish your attempt to write a poem modeled on Bradstreet's?

   _____

   _____

5. You know, the Puritans have had a great effect on later generations of Americans.

   _____

   _____

"To My Dear and Loving Husband" by Anne Bradstreet

"Huswifery" by Edward Taylor

Reading Strategy: Paraphrasing

The old-fashioned language and sophisticated imagery of Bradstreet's and Taylor's poems can make them difficult to understand. When confronted with a challenging poem or piece of prose, you will often understand it better if you **paraphrase**, or restate ideas in your own words.

Bradstreet's version:
If ever wife was happy in a man,
Compare with me ye women if you can.

Paraphrased:
No woman could be happier with her husband than I am.

DIRECTIONS: On the lines provided, paraphrase the following excerpts from Bradstreet's and Taylor's poems.

1. If ever two were one, then surely we.

   _____

   _____

   _____

2. I prize thy love more than whole mines of gold,
   Or all the riches that the East doth hold.

   _____

   _____

   _____

   _____

3. Then clothe therewith mine understanding, will,
   Affections, judgment, conscience, memory
   My words, and actions, that their shine may fill
   My ways with glory and Thee glorify.

   _____

   _____

   _____

   _____

   _____

   _____

"To My Dear and Loving Husband" by Anne Bradstreet
"Huswifery" by Edward Taylor

Literary Analysis: Puritan Plain Style

Just as the Puritans' style of life was spare, simple, and straightforward, so too was their writing style. The Puritan Plain Style, as it is called, is characterized by short words, direct statements, and references to ordinary, everyday objects.

DIRECTIONS: On the following lines, indicate which aspects of the **Puritan Plain Style** are displayed by each poetry excerpt.

1. If ever two were one, then surely we.
   If ever man were lov'd by wife, then thee:

   _____

   _____

   _____

2. I prize thy love more than whole mines of gold,
   Or all the riches that the East doth hold.

   _____

   _____

   _____

3. Make me, O Lord, Thy spinning wheel complete.
   Thy holy word my distaff make for me.

   _____

   _____

   _____

4. Make me Thy loom, then, knit therein this twine:
   And make Thy holy spirit, Lord, wind quills:
   Then weave the web Thyself. The yarn is fine.

   _____

   _____

   _____

5. Then dye the same in heavenly colors choice.
   All pinked with varnished flowers of paradise.

   _____

   _____

   _____

from *Sinners in the Hands of an Angry God* by Jonathan Edwards

Build Vocabulary

Spelling Strategy To decide how to spell the unstressed vowel sound represented by a schwa (∂), think of another form of the word in which the vowel is stressed so that you can hear it. Then use the same vowel. For example, think of *morality* and you'll know it's *moral*; think of *potent* and you'll know it's *omnipotent*.

Using the Prefix *omni-*

A. Directions: The prefix *omni-* means "all" or "everywhere." Bearing that in mind, circle the letter of the best answer to the following questions.

1. If laughter is *omnipresent*, where is it found?

   a. here   b. there   c. everywhere   d. nowhere

2. Giraffes are *herbivorous*, eating only plants; cats are *carnivorous*, eating only meat. If monkeys are *omnivorous*, what do you think they eat?

   a. only plants   b. only meat   c. only bananas   d. plants and meat

3. *Science* is from a root meaning "to know." What kind of narrator is an *omniscient* narrator?

   a. a character in the story who knows only his or her own thoughts

   b. someone outside the story who knows all the characters' thoughts

   c. someone outside the story who knows just one character's thoughts

   d. someone outside the story who knows no characters' thoughts

Using the Word Bank

omnipotent	ineffable	dolorous

B. Directions: On the line, write the letter of the definition next to the word it defines.

_____ 1. dolorous   a. inexpressible

_____ 2. omnipotent   b. sad; mournful

_____ 3. ineffable   c. all-powerful

C. Directions: For each pair of sentences, circle the letter of the sentence in which the italicized word is used correctly.

1. a. The athlete's *ineffable* muscles were visible even under his thick robe.

   b. The *ineffable* sadness of the bereaved parents covered them like a cloak.

2. a. Startled by the bat, she let out a *dolorous* shriek of terror.

   b. The *dolorous* tones of the great violinist moved the audience to tears.

3. a. The *omnipotent* ruler declared that he would pardon the six prisoners.

   b. Sorry for insulting his friend, the boy walked for miles on the *omnipotent* sand.

Name _____ Date _____

from *Sinners in the Hands of an Angry God* by Jonathan Edwards

Grammar and Style: Forms of Adjectives and Adverbs

The **basic** or **positive form** of an adjective or adverb is used when no comparison is being made. The **comparative form** is used to compare two things. The **superlative form** is used to compare more than two, or one out of many, things.

Positive: Edwards was a **famous** eighteenth-century minister.

Comparative: His sermons are **more famous** than his other writings.

Superlative: *Sinners in the Hands of an Angry God* is his **most famous** sermon.

One-syllable words and many two-syllable words form the comparative by adding *-er* and the superlative by adding *-est*. Other adjectives and adverbs form the comparative by adding *more* and the superlative by adding *most*.

Positive: high, holy, famous, mercifully

Comparative: higher, holier, more famous, more mercifully

Superlative: highest, holiest, most famous, most mercifully

A. Practice: Circle the correct form of the adjective in parentheses.

1. Edwards spoke of a power (mightier, more mightier) than ours.

2. He compared the wrath of God to great waters forever rising (higher, highest).

3. Were we ten thousand times (stronger, more stronger) than the (stouter, stoutest), (sturdier, sturdiest) devil in Hell, God's wrath would be (stronger, strongest).

4. Clearly, of Heaven and Hell, he found Heaven (more powerful, most powerful).

5. Still, he seems to have found Hell (colorfuller, more colorful) to describe.

B. Writing Application: Rewrite each sentence using either a comparative or a superlative form of the adjective or adverb in *italics*.

1. Edwards speaks of the *dreadful* pit in the world.

   _____

2. He feels that while we now may not be fully convinced of the truth, eventually we will be *fully* convinced.

   _____

3. Compared to physical danger, he considers the sinner's danger *fearful.*

   _____

4. Of all the world's sufferings, sinners will suffer a *horrible* misery.

   _____

5. However, the door of mercy has opened *wide* to let the poor sinners in.

   _____

Name _____ Date _____

from *Sinners in the Hands of an Angry God* by Jonathan Edwards

Reading Strategy: Context Clues

When you come across an unfamiliar word in your reading, you can often determine its meaning from its **context**—the words, phrases, and sentences which surround it. For example, notice how the context provides clues to the meaning of *avail* in the sentence that follows:

But indeed these things are nothing; if God should withdraw his hand, they would *avail* no more to keep you from falling than the thin air to hold up a person that is suspended in it.

Since we know that "these things are nothing" and that "they would avail no more" than "thin air" to keep a person from falling, we can figure out that *avail* must mean "help."

DIRECTIONS: As you read these sentences from *Sinners in the Hands of an Angry God*, use context clues to determine the meaning of each italicized word. Write your definition on the lines provided, along with an explanation of how you used context clues to help determine the word's meaning.

1. It is only the power and mere pleasure of God that holds you up. You are probably not *sensible* of this; you find you are kept out of Hell, but do not see the hand of God in it.

   _____

   _____

2. It is a great furnace of wrath, a wide and bottomless pit, full of the fire of wrath, that you are held over in the hand of that God, whose wrath is provoked and *incensed* as much against you, as against many of the damned in Hell.

   _____

   _____

3. You hang by a slender thread, with the flames of divine wrath flashing about it, and ready every moment to *singe* it, and burn it asunder.

   _____

   _____

4. He will not *forbear* the executions of his wrath, or in the least lighten his hand: there shall be no moderation or mercy.

   _____

   _____

5. There will be no end to this exquisite horrible misery. When you look forward, you shall see a long forever, a *boundless* duration before you, which will swallow up your thoughts and amaze your soul.

   _____

   _____

6. To see so many *rejoicing* and singing for joy of heart, while you have cause to mourn for sorrow of heart.

   _____

   _____

   _____

from *Sinners in the Hands of an Angry God* by Jonathan Edwards

Literary Analysis: Sermon

A **sermon** is a speech given from a pulpit in a house of worship, usually as part of a religious service. Jonathan Edwards delivered many sermons that dealt with "fire and brimstone," or the torments of hell. Although he delivered his words in a level and calm voice, his message often caused listeners to shriek with fright. Edwards achieved such results by appealing to the emotions of his congregation and by using such literary devices as vivid imagery, striking similies and metaphors, and repetition of key ideas.

A. DIRECTIONS: Answer each of the following questions.

1. To what emotion does the following passage appeal? Explain your answer.

   It would be dreadful to suffer this fierceness and wrath of Almighty God one moment; but you must suffer it to all eternity. There will be no end to this exquisite horrible misery. When you look forward, you shall see a long forever, a boundless duration before you, which will swallow up your thoughts and amaze your soul; and you will absolutely despair of ever having any deliverance, any end, any mitigation, any rest at all.

   _____

2. What is the message of this passage from the sermon?

   And now you have an extraordinary opportunity, a day wherein Christ has thrown the door of mercy wide open, and stands in calling and crying with a loud voice to poor sinners; a day wherein many are flocking to him, and pressing into the kingdom of God . . . many that were very lately in the same miserable condition that your are in, are now in a happy state, with their hearts filled with love to him who has loved them, and washed them from their sins in his own blood, and rejoicing in hope of the glory of God.

   _____

B. DIRECTIONS: Below each of the passages from *Sinners in the Hands of an Angry God*, list the type of literary device(s) employed and explain how the passage exemplifies the device(s).

   Imagery: the descriptive or figurative language used to create word pictures
   Metaphor: a figure of speech in which one thing is spoken of as if it were something else
   Simile: a figure of speech that makes a comparison between two subjects using either *like* or *as*
   Repetition: the repeated use of any element of language

1. Were it not for the sovereign pleasure of God, the earth would not bear you one moment . . . There are black clouds of God's wrath now hanging directly over your heads, full of the dreadful storm, and big with thunder; and were it not for the restraining hand of God, it would immediately burst forth upon you.

   _____

2. The wrath of God is like great waters that are damned for the present.

   _____

3. Now they see, that those things on which they depended for peace and safety, were nothing but thin air and empty shadows.

   _____

from *The Autobiography* and from *Poor Richard's Almanack* by Benjamin Franklin

Build Vocabulary

Spelling Strategy When you add a suffix beginning with a vowel to a one-syllable word ending in a consonant, double the consonant: *fop + -ery = foppery*.

Using the Root *-vigil*

A. DIRECTIONS: The word root *-vigil-* can mean "remaining awake to watch or observe." The suffix *-ance* means "the state of"; *-ant* means "being in the state of." The prefix *hyper-* means "excessively; overly; too." Write a probable definition for each term.

1. vigilant _____

2. hypervigilance _____

Using the Word Bank

arduous	avarice	fasting
disposition	squander	felicity

B. DIRECTIONS: Match each word on the left with its definition on the right. Write the letter of the definition in the blank next to the word it defines.

___ 1. arduous   a. happiness

___ 2. avarice   b. management

___ 3. fasting   c. difficult

___ 4. disposition   d. waste

___ 5. squander   e. greed

___ 6. felicity   f. not eating

C. DIRECTIONS: Circle the letter of the word that best completes each sentence.

1. Her felicity was short-lived, however, and _____ once again reigned.

   a. joyousness   b. sadness   c. tidiness   d. carelessness

2. His avarice was apparent, for he always _____ more money.

   a. lent   b. borrowed   c. wanted   d. ignored

3. It was an arduous but _____ task.

   a. laborious   b. strenuous   c. exhausting   d. rewarding

4. To squander each opportunity is to treat life as a _____.

   a. waste   b. pleasure   c. duty   d. sign

from *The Autobiography* and from *Poor Richard's Almanack* by Benjamin Franklin

Grammar and Style: Pronoun Case

Pronoun case refers to the different forms a pronoun takes to show its function in a sentence. Use **subjective case pronouns** (such as *I, we, you, he, she, it,* and *they*) when the pronoun is the subject of the sentence or renames the subject after a linking verb. Use **objective case pronouns** (such as *me, us, you, him, her, it,* and *them*) when the pronoun receives the action of the verb or is the object of a preposition.

A. Practice: These sentences are adapted from *The Autobiography*. Underline the subjective case pronouns and circle the objective case pronouns.

1. The smith ground it bright for him.

2. In exchange, he only had to turn the wheel.

3. He turned, while the smith pressed the broad face of the ax hard and heavily on the stone, which made the turning of it very fatiguing.

4. "We shall have it bright by and by," said the smith.

5. "I like it best speckled," the man replied.

B. Writing Application: Complete each sentence by writing the correct pronoun on the line.

1. My classmates and _____ (I, me) read about Ben Franklin's list of virtues.

2. His attempts to better himself impressed my friend Jim and _____ (I, me).

3. Some other students and _____ (we, us) are investigating further.

4. Jim and _____ (they, them) are reading more of Franklin's autobiography.

5. Janis and _____ (he, him) are reading portions of *Poor Richard's Almanack.*

6. Jim and _____ (she, her) are also trying to follow Franklin's example.

7. For Janis and _____ (he, him), living up to Franklin's list of virtues may prove a difficult task.

8. The rest of the class is keeping an eye on Jim and _____ (she, her).

9. Even though Franklin lived centuries ago, his advice strikes the others and _____ (I, me) as very relevant to modern life.

10. In fact, the wisest founding father could have been _____ (he, him).

from *The Autobiography* **and from** *Poor Richard's Almanack* by Benjamin Franklin

Reading Strategy: Draw Conclusions

Reading involves more than understanding the definition of each word in a sentence. The overall meaning may come from what an author *doesn't* tell you explicitly. To understand what an author is saying, **draw conclusions** based on supporting details and reasons in the text. For example, you may conclude that Benjamin Franklin does not like gossips, based on his value of the virtue of silence: "Speak not but what may benefit others or yourself; avoid trifling conversation."

Remember to draw conclusions based only on solid details and reasons. Unsupported conclusions may lead you away from the real meaning of a selection.

DIRECTIONS: As you read the selections from Franklin's *The Autobiography* and *Poor Richard's Almanack*, identify several conclusions about Franklin, and record the supporting details and reasons in the following chart.

Conclusion	Supporting Details and Reasons

Unit 2: A Nation Is Born (1750–1800)

Name _____ Date _____

from *The Autobiography* and from *Poor Richard's Almanack* by Benjamin Franklin

Literary Analysis: Autobiography

An **autobiography** is a person's written account of his or her own life. Though by its nature subjective, it nevertheless offers valuable insight into the author's personality, thoughts, and feelings.

DIRECTIONS: Read these passages from *The Autobiography*. Then, on the lines provided, sum up what they reveal about Franklin's attitudes and personality.

1. "As I knew, or thought I knew, what was right or wrong, I did not see why I might not always do the one and avoid the other."

   _____
   _____
   _____

2. "While my care was employed in guarding against one fault, I was often surprised by another."

   _____
   _____
   _____

3. "I determined to give a week's strict attention to each of the virtues successively."

   _____
   _____
   _____

4. "I was surprised to find myself so much fuller of faults than I imagined."

   _____
   _____
   _____

5. "The man came every now and then from the wheel to see how the work went on, and at length would take his ax as it was, without further grinding. 'No,' said the smith, 'turn on, turn on; we shall have it bright by and by; as yet, it is only speckled.' 'Yes,' said the man, 'but I think I like a speckled ax best.'"

   _____
   _____
   _____

6. ". . . a perfect character might be attended with the inconvenience of being envied and hated; and that a benevolent man should allow a few faults in himself, to keep his friends in countenance."

   _____
   _____
   _____

The Declaration of Independence by Thomas Jefferson
from *The Crisis, Number 1*, by Thomas Paine

Build Vocabulary

Spelling Strategy In words that join the prefix *ac-* to a root beginning with *q* or *k*, remember to retain the *c*: *acquiesce, acquaint, acquire, acquit, acknowledge.*

Using the Root -*fid*-

A. Directions: The Latin root -*fid*- means "faith" or "trust." For each sentence that follows, use the context plus your understanding of the root -*fid*- to determine the meaning of the word in italics. Write the meaning on the lines after the sentence.

1. Tamara raised her hand because she was *confident* she knew the answer.

   _____

   _____

2. In the wedding ceremony, the bride and groom vow *fidelity* to one another.

   _____

   _____

3. The information you give your doctor is *confidential* and will not be revealed to others.

   _____

   _____

4. The guardian kept his ward's bank savings in a *fiduciary* fund.

   _____

   _____

Using the Word Bank

unalienable	perfidy	magnanimity	acquiesce	infidel
usurpations	redress	consanguinity	impious	

B. Directions: Circle the letter of the pair of words that expresses a relationship most similar to the relationship of the pair in CAPITAL LETTERS.

1. BULLY : MAGNANIMITY ::
   a. hero : courage
   b. soldier : march
   c. relative : consanguinity
   d. miser : generosity

2. LOYALTY : PERFIDY ::
   a. anger : fury
   b. kindness : cruelty
   c. soldier : march
   d. courtesy : manners

3. INFIDEL : RELIGION ::
   a. orphan : parents
   b. librarian : data
   c. priest : prayers
   d. tyrant : usurpations

4. ACQUIESCE : NOD ::
   a. delight : frown
   b. shiver : freeze
   c. approve : applaud
   d. refuse : gesture

The Declaration of Independence by Thomas Jefferson
from *The Crisis, Number 1,* by Thomas Paine

Grammar and Style: Parallelism

Parallelism is the repeated use of words, phrases, or clauses with similar grammatical structures or meanings. Like all forms of repetition, it helps emphasize ideas and make them more memorable. In each example, notice how the parallel use of words, phrases, or clauses sets up a balance and rhythm that makes the sentence more emphatic and memorable.

Parallel words (adjectives): He has called together legislative bodies at places *unusual, uncomfortable,* and *distant* from the depository of their public records.

Parallel phrases: He has constrained our fellow citizens taken captive on the high seas *to bear arms against their country, to become the executioners of their friends and brethren, or to fall themselves by their hands.*

Parallel clauses: *The harder the conflict [is], the more glorious the triumph [is].* [In both clauses, the verb *is* is understood.]

A. Practice: Each of the following sentences contains at least one example of parallelism. Use a single underscore to identify the first example in a sentence, double underscores to identify a second example in the same sentence, and triple underscores to identify a third example, if any.

1. We hold these truths to be self-evident: that all men are created equal; that they are endowed by their creator with certain inalienable rights; that among these are life, liberty and the pursuit of happiness.

2. It is the right of the people to alter or to abolish it, and to institute new government, laying its foundation on such principles and organizing its power in such form, as to them shall seem most likely to affect their safety and happiness.

3. As free and independent states, they have full power to levy war, conclude peace, contract alliances, establish commerce, and to do all other acts and things which independent states may of right do.

B. Writing Application: Rewrite the following sentences so that all elements are parallel.

1. The delegates pledge their lives, the fortunes they have made, and their honor, a sacred thing.

   _____

   _____

2. Jefferson criticizes the king for taking away colonial charters, the abolishment of colonial laws, and altering the colonial government.

   _____

   _____

3. Jefferson had a wide knowledge of political philosophy; fine writing talent was something he also displayed.

   _____

   _____

The Declaration of Independence by Thomas Jefferson
from *The Crisis, Number 1*, by Thomas Paine

Reading Strategy: Recognizing Charged Words

Charged words evoke an emotional response that can make writing more memorable. Charged words are especially useful in making persuasive writing more forceful. In *The Crisis*, for example, Thomas Paine uses many negatively charged words to attack the British monarchy:

> I cannot see on what grounds the king of Britain can look up to heaven for help against us: a *common murderer*, a *highwayman*, or a *housebreaker*, has as good a pretense as he.

A. DIRECTIONS: Underline the charged words in these sentences. Then, on the lines provided, briefly explain the emotional response each word evokes.

1. "But when a long train of abuses and usurpations, pursuing invariably the same object, evinces a design to reduce them under absolute despotism. . . . "

   _____
   _____
   _____
   _____

2. "He has refused his assent to laws the most wholesome and necessary for the public good."

   _____
   _____
   _____
   _____

3. "In every stage of these oppressions we have petitioned for redress in the most humble terms."

   _____
   _____
   _____
   _____

4. "Tyranny, like hell, is not easily conquered."

   _____
   _____
   _____
   _____

5. "I turn with the warm ardor of a friend to those who had nobly stood, and are yet determined to stand the matter out."

   _____
   _____
   _____
   _____

Unit 2: A Nation Is Born (1750–1800)

Name _____ Date _____

The Declaration of Independence by Thomas Jefferson
from *The Crisis, Number 1,* by Thomas Paine

Literary Analysis: Persuasion

Persuasion is writing that attempts to convince readers to accept a specific viewpoint about an issue and to take a particular action. A good persuasive writer generally uses a combination of logical and emotional appeals, involving the audience both intellectually and emotionally in order to persuade them thoroughly.

A **logical appeal** uses a chain of reasoning to establish the validity of a proposed argument. Whether reasoning from particular examples to a general conclusion, or from the general to the specific, writers use evidence to persuade their audiences intellectually. Notice how Paine moves from specific evidence to more general remarks in the chain of reasoning he presents here.

> Britain, with an army to enforce her tyranny, has declared that she has a right (*not only to* TAX) but "*to* BIND *us in* ALL CASES WHATSOEVER," and if being *bound in that manner*, is not slavery, then is there not such a thing as slavery upon earth.

An **emotional appeal** seeks to stir the reader's feelings. It relies not so much on reasoned arguments as on charged words and symbols that evoke sympathy or distaste. Among the strongest emotional appeals are anecdotes or examples that dramatize a situation. For instance, Paine's story of the Tory tavernkeeper and his nine-year-old child makes a strong appeal to the human desire to ensure a good future for one's children.

A. DIRECTIONS: For each of these passages, clarify the the type or types of appeal that Paine uses and the effect he hopes to have on the audience.

1. Tyranny, like hell, is not easily conquered; yet we have this consolation with us, that the harder the conflict, the more glorious the triumph. What we obtain too cheap, we esteem too lightly; 'tis dearness only that gives everything its value.

_____

_____

_____

2. I turn with the warm ardor of a friend to those who have nobly stood, and are yet determined to stand the matter out: I call not upon a few, but upon all; not on *this* state or *that* state, but on *every* state.

_____

_____

3. Not all the treasurers of the world, so far as I believe, could have induced me to support an offensive war, for I think it murder; but if a thief breaks into my house, burns and destroys my property, and kills or threatens to kill me, or those that are in it, and to "*bind me in all cases whatsoever,*" to his absolute will, am I to suffer it? . . . If we reason to the root of things we shall find no difference; neither can any just cause be assigned why we should punish in the one case and pardon in the other.

_____

_____

_____

"To His Excellency, General Washington" and **"An Hymn to the Evening"**
by Phillis Wheatley

Build Vocabulary

Spelling Strategy The -re ending in British words is usually spelled -er in American English: British *sceptre*, American *scepter*; British *centre*, American *center*.

Using the Prefix *re-*

A. DIRECTIONS: The prefix *re-* can mean "again" or "back." For each sentence that follows, use the context plus your understanding of the prefix *re-* to determine the meaning of the word in italics. Write the meaning on the lines after the sentence.

1. The government began an environmental cleanup to *reclaim* the land.

   _____

   _____

2. She quickly *rebounded* from the illness and came back to work.

   _____

   _____

Using the Word Bank

celestial	propitious	pensive	scepter
refulgent	refluent	placid	

B. DIRECTIONS: After each line from the poem, two possible definitions are given in parentheses for the word in italics. Underline the correct definition.

1. *Celestial* choir! enthroned in realms of light. (heavenly, off-key)

2. She flashes dreadful in *refulgent* arms. (bad smelling, shining)

3. Muse! bow *propitious* while my pen relates. (rude, favorable)

4. The *refluent* surges beat the pounding shore. (flowing back, stagnant)

5. Anon Britannia droops the *pensive* head. (lighthearted, thoughtful)

6. Let *placid* slumbers soothe each weary mind. (mysterious, calm)

7. Night's leaden *scepter* seals my drowsy eyes. (rod or staff, cynic)

C. DIRECTIONS: Circle the letter of the word that best completes each sentence.

1. She studied the sky at night to observe ____ bodies.

   a. celestial   b. propitious   c. refluent   d. pensive

2. A scepter would most likely be seen in a king's or queen's ____.

   a. boot   b. fur-lined cape   c. last will and testament   d. hand

Unit 2: A Nation Is Born (1750–1800)

Name _____ Date _____

"To His Excellency, General Washington" and **"An Hymn to the Evening"**
by Phillis Wheatley

Grammar and Style: Subject and Verb Agreement

Verb forms should agree with their subjects in number. Singular subjects take singular verb forms: *She runs.* Plural subjects take plural verb forms: *They run.*

A. Practice: In each of the following lines from Wheatley's poems, underline the subject once and the verb twice. Then circle *singular* or *plural* to indicate the number of the subject and verb.

1. She flashes dreadful in refulgent arms. SINGULAR PLURAL

2. And nations gaze at scenes before unknown. SINGULAR PLURAL

3. Unnumbered charms and recent graces rise. SINGULAR PLURAL

4. The refluent surges beat the sounding shore. SINGULAR PLURAL

5. In bright array they seek the work of war. SINGULAR PLURAL

6. Anon Britannia droops the pensive head. SINGULAR PLURAL

7. From the zephyr's wing exhales the incense of the blooming spring.

    SINGULAR PLURAL

8. Beauteous dyes are spread. SINGULAR PLURAL

9. The west glories in the deepest red. SINGULAR PLURAL

10. Night's leaden scepter seals my drowsy eyes. SINGULAR PLURAL

B. Writing Application: Complete these sentences by writing in the correct form of the verb in parentheses.

1. From Christopher Columbus _____ names like Columbia. (come)

2. There _____ no goddesses called Columbia in Greek or Roman mythology. (be)

3. This creation of American neoclassical writers in the era of the Revolution

    _____ often depicted on coins and monuments. (be)

4. Like the bald eagle, she _____ America. (represent)

5. In Wheatley's poems there often _____ the goddess Columbia. (appear)

6. One of these poems vividly _____ the goddess. (describe)

7. Several lines in this poem _____ George Washington. (praise)

"To His Excellency, General Washington" and **"An Hymn to the Evening"**
by Phillis Wheatley

Reading Strategy: Clarify Meaning

All writing is easier to understand if you check the definitions of unfamiliar words. In addition, poetry is often clearer if you rearrange the words into more normal grammatical structures. For example, instead of using regular subject-verb order, poetry sometimes inverts the order, placing the subject after the verb: *Wherever shines this native of the skies*. Rearranging the words into a more usual order can help you understand the poem's meaning: *Wherever this native of the skies shines*.

A. DIRECTIONS: Clarify the meaning of these lines from the poems by rewriting them in more normal word order. Also substitute a simpler or more modern word or phrase for each word in italics. Use the context or a dictionary to help you define the italicized words.

1. Columbia's scenes of glorious *toils* I write.

   _____

2. While freedom's cause her anxious breast *alarms*

   _____

   _____

3. As when *Eolus* heaven's fair face *deforms*

   _____

4. Where high *unfurl'd* the *ensign* waves in air

   _____

5. Shall I to Washington their praise *recite*?

   _____

6. Hear every tongue *thy guardian* aid *implore*!

   _____

   _____

7. From the *zephyr's* wing *exhales* the *incense* of the blooming spring.

   _____

   _____

8. Soft *purl* the streams

   _____

9. And through the air their *mingled* music floats.

   _____

   _____

10. So may our breasts with *ev'ry* virtue glow.

    _____

Unit 2: A Nation Is Born (1750–1800)

"To His Excellency, General Washington" and **"An Hymn to the Evening"**
by Phillis Wheatley)

Literary Analysis: Personification

Personification attributes human powers and characteristics to something that is not human, such as an object, an aspect of nature, or an abstract idea. For example, in the sentence "The room waited patiently for laughter to return," the human characteristic of patience is attributed to the room.

DIRECTIONS: On the lines after each quotation from "To His Excellency, General Washington," explain what is being personified and what human characteristic or characteristics it is being given.

1. "See mother earth her offspring's fate bemoan."

   _____

   _____

   _____

   _____

2. "And nations gaze at scenes before unknown."

   _____

   _____

   _____

   _____

3. "Muse! bow propitious while my pen relates. . . . "

   _____

   _____

   _____

   _____

4. "Or thick as leaves in Autumn's golden reign."

   _____

   _____

   _____

   _____

5. "One century scarce perform'd its destined round."

   _____

   _____

   _____

   _____

Name _____ Date _____

from *Letter From Birmingham City Jail* by Martin Luther King, Jr.

Build Vocabulary

Using Language of Protest and Hope

Martin Luther King, Jr., makes use of a language of protest—and hope—that is vivid, bold, and impassioned.

A. Directions: Read the following passage advocating voting rights for all citizens. Edit the paragraph, adding words and phrases that make the writing more vivid and impassioned. As you revise the passage, consider how Martin Luther King, Jr., sometimes paired opposite ideas in order to get his point across.

I stand before you today with a message. Our democracy will not function if all are not allowed to participate in the democratic process. In parts of our country, barriers have been erected to prevent the exercise of the voting franchise. These barriers have been erected around the poor, those in minority groups, those who are against the powers that be. We shouldn't allow such a situation to exist in this land of ours.

Using the Word Bank

motives	vitality	impelled	flagrant
profundity	monotony	scintillating	

B. Directions: For each item, circle the word that is most nearly opposite in meaning to the Word Bank word.

1. vitality
   a. liveliness   b. apathy   c. enthusiasm   d. boredom

2. flagrant
   a. apparent   b. frivolous   c. subtle   d. colorful

3. impelled
   a. suggested   b. persuaded   c. stabbed   d. forced

C. Directions: For each item, choose a Word Bank word that best completes the meaning of the sentence as a whole.

1. The _____ of the presentations almost put the entire class to sleep.

2. Her performance was so _____ that it sent chills up my spine.

3. His _____ in seeking the help of the authorities could not be questioned.

4. The _____ of the professor's presentation deepened our understanding of democracy.

from _Letter From Birmingham City Jail_ by Martin Luther King, Jr.

Thematic Connection: Voices for Freedom

What causes do people champion today in the name of freedom? How are people going about meeting their goals? Who are today's champions? What memorable "battle cries" resound in today's world?

DIRECTIONS: Work together with a number of your classmates to research a struggle that men and women are currently engaged in. The struggle could involve preserving the environment, securing political rights, or any other topic spurring people to action. As you do your research, fill out the items below. If there are no memorable "battle cries" associated with the struggle you explore, offer one or two of your own devising.

Cause: _____

_____

_____

_____

_____

Activists: _____

_____

_____

_____

_____

Organizations: _____

_____

_____

_____

_____

_____

"Battle Cry": _____

_____

_____

_____

_____

_____

"Speech in the Virginia Convention" by Patrick Henry
"Speech in the Convention" by Benjamin Franklin

Build Vocabulary

Spelling Strategy When you add the suffix -ity to a word that ends in
-able or -ible, drop the final e and insert an i between the b and l: able + -ity = ability;
infallible + -ity = infallibility.

Using the Suffix -ity

A. DIRECTIONS: The suffix -ity, meaning 'the state of,' is generally used to turn adjectives into nouns. Complete each of these sentences using the -ity noun form of one of the following adjectives:

complex   believable   flexible   creative   infallible

1. The realistic setting gave the story an aura of _____.

2. The _____ of the puzzle made it difficult to solve.

3. You can achieve _____ by doing stretching exercises.

4. Because of Jim's mistake, we questioned his _____.

5. The game the child invented showed imagination and _____.

Using the Word Bank

arduous	subjugation	infallibility	salutary	posterity
insidious	vigilant	despotism	unanimity	manifest

B. DIRECTIONS: Using Synonyms and Antonyms On the line after each pair of words, indicate whether the two words are synonyms or antonyms.

1. devious, insidious _____

2. unwholesome, salutary _____

3. obvious, manifest _____

4. oblivious, vigilant _____

5. easy, arduous _____

6. enslavement, subjugation _____

7. dictatorship, despotism _____

8. discord, unanimity _____

9. ancestry, posterity _____

10. mistakenness, infallibility _____

"Speech in the Virginia Convention" by Patrick Henry
"Speech in the Convention" by Benjamin Franklin

Grammar and Style: Double Negatives

It takes only one negative word or contraction to communicate a negative idea. If you use two negatives, they logically cancel each other out, resulting in a positive statement.

Double Negative: I wo**n't never** approve it.
              logically means
              I may at some time approve it.

If your intention is to make a *negative* statement, you should not use a double negative. Instead, use only one negative word or contraction.

Correct Negative Form: I will **never** approve it.
                  or
                  I wo**n't ever** approve it.

Most negative words start with *n—no*, *not* (often contracted to **n't**), *never*, *none*, *no one*, *nothing*, *nobody*, and *nowhere*, for example. A few other words, such as *hardly*, *barely*, and *scarcely*, are also negatives.

A. Practice: Read the following conversation. Underline any double negatives.

1. I'll never go to no Badgers games again.

2. Why won't you go to none of those Badgers games?

3. The Badgers don't know nothing about football!

4. They play as if they haven't got no sense.

5. No one even tried to block that field goal.

6. Well, maybe it just wouldn't have done no good.

7. That star player allows hardly no one to get in his way.

B. Writing Application: On the lines below, Rewrite the sentences in part A that contain double negatives. Correct all the double negatives to make them acceptable usage. If a sentence is correct, write correct.

1. _____

2. _____

3. _____

4. _____

5. _____

6. _____

7. _____

"Speech in the Virginia Convention" by Patrick Henry
"Speech in the Convention" by Benjamin Franklin

Reading Strategy: Evaluating Persuasive Appeals

Unit 2:
A Nation Is Born
(1750–1800)

Orators often rely on **persuasive appeals** to convince an audience of their ideas. An appeal to reason calls upon the audience to think logically about an issue. An emotional appeal attempts to stir listeners by tapping into their hopes, fears, likes, and dislikes. An effective persuasive speech usually blends the two types of appeals. For example, consider Patrick Henry's famous final remark:

I know not what course others may take; but as for me, give me liberty or give me death.

Though Henry's willingness to die for the liberty he cherishes clearly makes a strong emotional appeal, the statement also makes an appeal to reason with its logical either/or structure.

DIRECTIONS: On the lines provided, indicate whether each passage appeals to reason, emotion, or both, and explain how the passage makes each appeal.

1. "I know of no way of judging of the future but by the past."

   _____

   _____

   _____

2. "I ask gentlemen, sir, what means this martial array, if its purpose be not to force us to submission? Can gentlemen assign any other possible motive for it?"

   _____

   _____

   _____

3. "Our petitions have been slighted; our remonstrances have produced additional violence and insult; our supplications have been disregarded; and we have been spurned with contempt from the foot of the throne! In vain, after these things, may we indulge the fond hope of peace and reconciliation."

   _____

   _____

   _____

4. "There is a just God who presides over the destinies of nations and who will raise up friends to fight our battles for us."

   _____

   _____

   _____

5. "Gentlemen may cry, 'Peace, peace,'—but there is no peace. The war is actually begun! The next gale that sweeps from the north will bring to our ears the clash of resounding arms!"

   _____

   _____

   _____

Name _____ Date _____

Literary Analysis: Speeches

Effective speeches often make use of these techniques to emphasize key ideas and make them more memorable: (1) **repetition** of an idea in the same words; (2) **restatement** of a key idea in different words; (3) **parallelism**, or repeated use of the same grammatical structures; and (4) **rhetorical questions**, or questions with obvious answers that are asked not because answers are expected but to involve the audience emotionally in the speech.

DIRECTIONS: Reread Patrick Henry's speech, and look for examples of each technique. Record the examples on the chart below.

Restatement

Repetition

Parallelism

Rhetorical Questions

"Inaugural Speech" by John F. Kennedy

Build Vocabulary

Using Emotional Appeal

John F. Kennedy's inaugural speech is effective because many of the words he uses in his speech appeal to the emotions. Using vocabulary with emotional appeal can make your writing more compelling and persuasive.

A. DIRECTIONS: Use each pair of words below in a persuasive sentence of your own.

1. victory/celebration

_____

_____

2. sworn/solemn

_____

_____

3. burden/hardship

_____

_____

Using the Word Bank

heirs	tyranny	alliance	invective
adversary	invoke	eradicate	

B. DIRECTIONS: Circle the word that is most similar in meaning to the Word Bank word.

1. invoke
   a. repeal   b. correct   c. summon   d. radiate

2. alliance
   a. axis   b. union   c. formulation   d. reliance

3. eradicate
   a. erase   b. alleviate   c. combat   d. increase

4. heirs
   a. friends   b. relatives   c. inheritors   d. lawyers

C. DIRECTIONS: Circle the word or phrase that is most nearly opposite in meaning to the Word Bank word.

1. adversary
   a. friend   b. partner   c. stranger   d. enemy

2. invective
   a. invasion   b. comment   c. praise   d. criticism

3. tyranny
   a. meanness   b. freedom   c. oppression   d. discipline

"Inaugural Speech" by John F. Kennedy

Thematic Connection: American Speechmaking

Public speaking has been an important American tradition for hundreds of years. Speeches have inspired, taught, enraged, thrilled—and sometimes bored—Americans through the years, shaping and reflecting the history of our country. What speeches have you heard? Have you ever given a speech? How would you go about writing a speech?

DIRECTIONS: You are a speechwriter preparing a major address for a politician. Complete the items below to prepare your work.

Topic: Challenges Facing Americans Today

Basic Point of Speech: _____

_____

_____

_____

_____

References in Speech: _____

_____

_____

_____

_____

Quotations to Use: _____

_____

_____

_____

_____

Outline of Speech: _____

_____

_____

_____

_____

_____

_____

"Letter to Her Daughter from the New White House" by Abigail Adams
from ***Letters from an American Farmer*** by Michel-Guillaume Jean de Crèvecoeur

Build Vocabulary

Spelling Strategy To remember that *subsistence ends* in *-ence*, not *-ance*, remember that we all need subsist**e**nce to **e**xist.

Using Etymologies

A. DIRECTIONS: A word's *etymology*, or history, can help you determine the meaning of the word today. Circle the letter of the correct meaning of each word below based on the etymology provided in brackets. In the etymologies, the symbol < means "derived from."

1. **cot** [Middle English < Old English *cot*, "cottage"]

   a. hut   b. mansion   c. castle   d. monument

2. **parlor** [Middle English parlour < Old French *parleor* < *parler*, "to speak"]

   a. bedroom   b. bathroom   c. living room   d. attic

3. **haunch** [Middle English *haunche* < Old French *hanche*, "hip"]

   a. ear   b. hoof   c. loin   d. wing

4. **frolicsome** [Dutch *vrolijk* < Middle Dutch *vrolijc*, "merry"]

   a. playful   b. forceful   c. beautiful   d. gloomy

Using the Word Bank

extricate	asylum	despotic
agues	penury	subsistence

B. DIRECTIONS: Choose the word from the word bank that best completes the meaning of each sentence, and write the word on the line provided. Use each word only once.

1. Many people, fleeing _____ treatment in other lands, have found a freer life in the United States.

2. Often they came to escape a life of _____ in which they often found it difficult to put food on the table.

3. Their poverty left them subject to _____ and other types of illness.

4. They sought to _____ themselves from their impoverished lives.

5. For such immigrants, America offered _____ from political oppression.

6. In America they could own and farm land or find other means of _____ .

"Letter to Her Daughter from the New White House" by Abigail Adams
from *Letters from an American Farmer* by Michel-Guillaume Jean de Crèvecoeur

Grammar and Style: Semicolons

The semicolon is often used to join closely related independent clauses. Sometimes the second clause explains or elaborates on the first. For example:

Six chambers are made comfortable; two are occupied by the President and Mr. Shaw.

Sometimes the second clause presents a contrasting idea. For example:

Formerly they were not numbered in any civil lists of their country, except in those of the poor; here they rank as citizens.

A. Practice: Read each sentence. If the semicolon connects contrasting independent clauses, write *C* on the line provided. If the semicolon connects two clauses in which the second explains or elaborates on the first, write *E*.

_____ 1. Crèvecoeur saw America as a melting pot of different nationalities; one family he described had an English grandfather, a Dutch wife, and a French daughter-in-law.

_____ 2. Abigail Adams wrote her letter only to her daughter; Crèvecoeur addressed his epistle to the public at large.

_____ 3. Adams did not want others to learn of her criticisms of the new capital; she told her daughter to report only positive things.

_____ 4. In Europe, said Crèvecoeur, poor people were held down by "want, hunger, and war"; in America, they could become citizens and property owners.

B. Writing Application: On the lines provided, rewrite each pair of sentences as a single sentence in which a semicolon joins related independent clauses.

1. The White House seems superbly designed.
   Its excellent situation offers a fine view of the Potomac River.

   _____

   _____

2. The oval drawing room will be beautiful when it is completed.
   Even unfinished, it is handsome.

   _____

   _____

3. There are forests all around, but no one will cut wood.
   There is coal, but no grates to burn it in.

   _____

   _____

4. America offers asylum to the poor of Europe.
   Here, people can farm their own land.

   _____

   _____

"Letter to Her Daughter from the New White House" by Abigail Adams
from ***Letters from an American Farmer*** by Michel-Guillaume Jean de Crèvecoeur

Reading Strategy: Distinguish Between Fact and Opinion

Opinions state personal beliefs or preference and cannot be proven. **Facts**, in contrast, can be proven. Here are examples from Adams's letter.

> **Fact:** The river, which runs up to Alexandria, is in full view of my window.

> **Opinion:** The house is upon a grand and superb scale.

Opinions can make writing lively and provocative, but good writers support their opinions with facts. Good readers distinguish facts from opinions and make sure they are not too easily influenced by unsupported opinions.

DIRECTIONS: In the left column of the chart below, list the opinions the following paragraph contains. In the right column, list the facts used to support each opinion.

> Abigail Smith married John Adams, a young Boston lawyer, in 1764. During the ten years that began in 1774, Abigail's life was extraordinarily difficult. She spent most of those years apart from her husband, who was engaged in government matters in Philadelphia. In addition to raising four young children, she had to manage the family farm in her husband's absence. Meanwhile, John had become one of the infant American nation's most influential political figures, first as a member of the Continental Congress and later as second President of the United States. Abigail herself, though she had no formal education, had a voice of some importance in the new nation. An early American advocate of women's rights, she once admonished her husband to "Remember the ladies. Do not put unlimited power in the hands of husbands." She also said, "If particular care and attention is not paid to the ladies, we are determined to foment rebellion, and will not be bound by any laws in which we have no voice or representation."

OPINION	FACTS THAT SUPPORT IT

"Letter to Her Daughter from the New White House" by Abigail Adams
from *Letters from an American Farmer* by Michel-Guillaume Jean de Crèvecoeur

Literary Analysis: Private and Public Letters (Epistles)

While Abigail Adams penned a **private letter** that she intended only for her daughter, Crèvecoeur's letter qualifies as an **epistle**, a letter intended for public readership. Epistles are usually written in a style more formal than that of a personal letter. The letter form, however, allows the author to present personal ideas and opinions as if he or she were actually writing a private letter.

DIRECTIONS: In each blank, write *E* if the sentence seems more likely to be found in an epistle. Write *PL* if the sentence seems more likely to be found in a private letter.

_____ 1. Future generations who read this missive must recognize the dreams of our era.

_____ 2. You must visit us soon; we are all eager to see you again.

_____ 3. What a glorious sensation of self-worth overcomes them as they establish homes upon a land that is their *own*!

_____ 4. Please tell no one this secret I am about to confess.

_____ 5. Guess what? We met your sister while we were visiting the White House.

_____ 6. We must all recognize the sense of purposefulness that gives people the strength to persevere.

_____ 7. Perhaps the greatest question that each of us faces, now and in the future, is how to define and renew the American dream.

from *Roots* by Alex Haley

Build Vocabulary

Using Descriptive Vocabulary to Set a Scene

In *Roots*, Alex Haley uses vocabulary that brings the scenes he describes to vivid life, whether in present-day Africa or some time in the past.

A. DIRECTIONS: Review the meanings of the words or phrases listed below. Then, on the lines next to each word or phrase, write a sentence of your own that uses the given vocabulary to paint a vivid word picture.

1. jet-black

_____

2. back-country road

_____

3. tortuous

_____

4. reddish puffs of dust

_____

5. buoyant

_____

Using the Word Bank

congealed	crux	cacophony

B. DIRECTIONS: For each item, choose the Word Bank word that best completes the meaning of the sentence as a whole.

1. The _____ of the matter was that escape was impossible.

2. He couldn't hear himself think because of the _____ in the confined space.

3. The muddy pond had _____ into a hard, black mass.

C. DIRECTIONS: For each three-word grouping, circle the letter of the word whose meaning does not match the other two.

1. a. cacophony   b. noise   c. confusion

2. a. point   b. crux   c. horizon

3. a. congealed   b. melted   c. solidified

Name _____ Date _____

from *Roots* by Alex Haley

Thematic Connection: The Emerging American Identity—Defining an American

What is an American? This has been perhaps the central question in the history of the United States. The definition of an American is constantly developing and expanding. A number of different factors contribute to a definition of what it means to be an American. How would you answer the question? What are the most important elements to being an American?

DIRECTIONS: Use the items below to help you organize your thoughts on the American identity. Use your responses to write your own definition of an American.

Elements Contributing to the American Identity

1. Family Ties:

   _____
   _____
   _____
   _____
   _____
   _____

2. Historical Perspectives:

   _____
   _____
   _____
   _____
   _____
   _____

3. Traditional Values and Beliefs:

   _____
   _____
   _____
   _____
   _____
   _____

4. Contemporary Challenges:

   _____
   _____
   _____
   _____
   _____
   _____

"The Devil and Tom Walker" by Washington Irving

Build Vocabulary

Spelling Strategy When the prefix ex- means "out," do not use a hyphen after it: *extort*, *export*, *extract*. When it means "former," use a hyphen: *ex-president*, *ex-wife*.

Using the Prefix *ex-*

A. DIRECTIONS: The prefix *ex-* often means "out." On the line provided, write the word from the box that best completes each sentence.

exhale	extract	export	extrovert	exoskeleton	extricate

1. If you ship a product out of the country, you _____ it.

2. An _____ is an outgoing person.

3. When you breathe out, you _____.

4. A hard, protective covering on the outside of the body, like the shells on insects, is called an _____.

5. When you pull out a tooth, you _____ it.

6. If you get out of trouble, you _____ yourself from a tricky situation.

Using the Word Bank

avarice	usurers	extort	ostentation	parsimony

B. DIRECTIONS: The following sentences are missing two words. On the line before each number, write the letter of the pair of terms that best completes each sentence. For each pair, assume that the first term goes in the first blank and the second term goes in the second blank.

_____ 1. He was a _____ who tried to _____ money.
      a. criminal—extort   c. avarice—treasure
      b. usurer—give   d. extortionist—donate

_____ 2. Her _____ was awakened when she heard about the _____.
      a. husband—ostentation   c. avarice—treasure
      b. dog—usurer   d. parsimony—earthquake

_____ 3. The house was _____, a monument to _____.
      a. loving—avarice   c. extorted—love
      b. bright—parsimony   d. lavish—ostentation

_____ 4. The _____ was evidence of her _____.
      a. mouse—avarice   c. small portion—parsimony
      b. usurer—intelligence   d. tasteful decor—ostentation

_____ 5. The _____ collected the _____ that was due.
      a. extortionist—video   c. child—avarice
      b. teacher—parsimony   d. usurer—fee

Unit 3: A Growing Nation (1800–1870)

Name _____ Date _____

Grammar and Style: Adjective Clauses

A subordinate clause is one that cannot stand alone as a sentence. An **adjective clause**, also called a relative clause, is a subordinate clause that adds information about a noun or pronoun. It is generally introduced by a relative pronoun: *who, whom, whose, which, that.*

Tom, *who had been picking his way through the forest,* met a stranger.

The stranger *that he met* was the devil.

A. Practice: Underline the adjective clause in each sentence.

1. Many and fierce were the conflicts that took place.

2. The swamp was thickly grown with great gloomy pines and hemlocks, which made it dark at noonday.

3. Tom had long been picking his way cautiously through this treacherous forest; stepping from tuft to tuft of rushes and roots, which afforded precarious footholds among deep sloughs.

4. Here they had thrown up a kind of fort, which they had looked upon as almost impregnable, and had used as a place of refuge for their squaws and children.

5. On the bark of the tree was scored the name of Deacon Peabody, an eminent man, who had waxed wealthy by driving shrewd bargains with the Indians.

B. Writing Application: Complete each sentence so that it contains an adjective clause. In some sentences, the relative pronoun is already provided.

1. She greatly admired her teacher, who _____
_____

2. The man felt compassion for the stranger, whose _____
_____

3. They were astounded by the action, which _____
_____

4. He was captivated by the child, whose _____
_____

5. She pointed at the statue that _____
_____

6. We were impressed with the architecture, which _____
_____

7. The mountains, _____
_____

8. The singer, _____
_____

"The Devil and Tom Walker" by Washington Irving

Reading Strategy: Infer Cultural Attitudes

The characters in "The Devil and Tom Walker" are American colonists living in New England in the late 1720s and early 1730s. The dialogue, the narrator's comments about the characters, and the events that the characters experience help the reader **to infer cultural attitudes** of the period. Of course, some of these influences and attitudes are often exaggerated in Irving's satirical story. Nevertheless, readers do get a picture of colonial life in the New England of Tom Walker's day.

DIRECTIONS: On the basis of each passage that follows, draw an inference about the ethical, social, and cultural influences and attitudes of New Englanders, or American colonists in general, in the 1720s and 1730s. Write the inference on the lines provided.

1. Tom Walker . . . had a wife as miserly as himself: they were so miserly that they even conspired to cheat each other . . . many and fierce were the conflicts that took place about what ought to have been common property.

   _____

   _____

   _____

   _____

2. "I [the Devil] amuse myself by presiding at the persecutions of Quakers and Anabaptists; I am the great patron and prompter of slave dealers, and the grandmaster of the Salem witches."

   _____

   _____

   _____

   _____

3. About the year 1727, just at the time that earthquakes were prevalent in New England, and shook many tall sinners down upon their knees. . . .

   _____

   _____

   _____

   _____

4. Such was the end of Tom Walker and his ill-gotten wealth. Let all griping money brokers lay this story to heart.

   _____

   _____

   _____

   _____

"The Devil and Tom Walker" by Washington Irving

Literary Analysis: Omniscient Narrator

The narrator who stands outside the action and relates many characters' thoughts and feelings is called the **omniscient narrator**. *Omniscient* means "all-knowing."

DIRECTIONS: On the lines provided, identify what the omniscient narrator tells the reader about a character's thoughts and feelings in each passage.

1. What these conditions were may easily be surmised, though Tom never disclosed them publicly. They must have been very hard, for he required time to think of them, and he was not a man to stick at trifles where money was in view.

   _____

   _____

2. He [Tom] was not prone to let his wife into his confidence; but as this was an uneasy secret, he willingly shared it with her.

   _____

   _____

3. All her [Tom's wife's] avarice was awakened at the mention of hidden gold, and she urged her husband to comply with the black man's [Devil's] terms and secure what would make them wealthy for life.

   _____

   _____

4. However Tom might have felt disposed to sell himself to the Devil, he was determined not to do so to oblige his wife; so he flatly refused, out of the mere spirit of contradiction.

   _____

   _____

5. At length she [Tom's wife] determined to drive the bargain on her own account, and if she succeeded, to keep all the gain to herself.

   _____

   _____

6. The old blacklegs [the Devil] played shy, for whatever people may think, he is not always to be had for calling for: he knows how to play his cards when pretty sure of his game.

   _____

   _____

7. Still, in spite of all this strenuous attention to forms, Tom had a lurking dread that the Devil, after all, would have his due.

   _____

   _____

Build Vocabulary

Spelling Strategy Several English words that come from Greek open with a silent *p* before the *s*—for example: *psalm, pseudonym, psychology.*

Using the Root *-face-*

A. DIRECTIONS: The root *-face-* means "appearance or outward aspect." Study the meanings of the following prefixes. Then write a word containing one of these prefixes and the root *-face-* on the line before the word's definition.

de-: reverse, remove, reduce	**re-:** again	**inter-:** between or among
sur-: above, upon	**pre-:** before	

1. _____: the top or outer part of something

2. _____: the section before the main section of a book

2. _____: to put on a new front

4. _____: to mar or spoil the appearance of

5. _____: the point or plane forming a boundary between two areas

Using the Word Bank

bivouac	efface	sublime

B. DIRECTIONS: On the lines provided, rewrite each sentence, substituting a synonym or description for each italicized word.

1. In the *bivouac* of Life, / Be not like dumb, driven cattle! _____

_____

2. Lives of great men all remind us / We can make our lives *sublime.* _____

_____

3. The little waves, with their soft, white hands, / *Efface* the footprints in the sands.

_____

C. DIRECTIONS: On the line before each number, write the letter of the pair of words that expresses a relationship most like the relationship of the pair in capital letters.

____ 1. BIVOUAC : HOUSE ::
   a. colossal : tiny b. costly : expensive c. primary : secondary d. temporary : permanent

____ 2. NOBLE : SUBLIME ::
   a. aristocratic : lowborn b. angry : enraged c. depressed : ecstatic d. sad : tired

____ 3. ERASER : EFFACE ::
   a. nail : hammer b. staple : unhinge c. scissors : cut d. pen : paint

Unit 3: A Growing Nation (1800–1870)

"A Psalm of Life" and **"The Tide Rises, The Tide Falls"**
by Henry Wadsworth Longfellow

Grammar and Style: Inverted Word Order

In a typical English sentence, the subject comes before the verb. In a sentence using **inverted word order**, the subject follows the verb. For example:

Regular: The traveler hastens toward the town.

Inverted: Hastens the traveler toward the town.

Poets often use inverted word order to achieve rhyme, maintain rhythm, and/or emphasize a key word or idea.

A. Practice: On the line before each sentence, write *R* if the sentence uses regular word order and *I* if it uses inverted word order. Put one line under the subject and two lines under the verb.

_____ 1. Life is but an empty dream!

_____ 2. Not enjoyment, and not sorrow, is our destined end or way.

_____ 3. We can make our lives sublime and, departing, leave behind us footprints on the sands of time.

_____ 4. Along the sea sands damp and brown the traveler hastens toward the town.

_____ 5. Nevermore returns the traveler to the shore.

B. Writing Application: Rewrite the following sentences on the lines provided. If the sentence uses regular word order, rewrite it using inverted order. If the sentence uses inverted order, rewrite it using regular word order.

1. The waves rolled over the pier.

_____

_____

2. The stars gleamed brightly in the dark night sky.

_____

_____

3. A child played alone in the tall, waving grass.

_____

_____

4. Through the dappled dawn flew an orange butterfly.

_____

_____

5. There was silence all round except for the calls of birds.

_____

_____

"A Psalm of Life" and **"The Tide Rises, The Tide Falls"**
by Henry Wadsworth Longfellow

Reading Strategy: Associate Images With Life

You will often find greater meaning in the poetry you read if you consider its images as symbols of larger themes or principles. **Associate the images with life** by thinking about how the theme or meaning represents a comment on broader life themes. For example, if a poem describes the first bloom on a rose, the image might more broadly symbolize the theme of youth, innocence, or beauty. If a poem describes how the petals of a rose slowly drop, the image might represent how a person's youth, innocence, or beauty fades over time.

DIRECTIONS: Complete the chart below by identifying a possible broader life theme for each image on the left. Be sure to consider the image in the context of the poem in which it appears.

Image	How It Might Relate to Broader Life Themes
1. Footprints on the sands of time	
2. Sailing o'er life's solemn main	
3. A forlorn and shipwrecked brother	
4. the sea sands damp and brown	
5. the sea in the darkness calls	
6. nevermore returns the traveler to the shore	

Unit 3: A Growing Nation
(1800–1870)

Name _____ Date _____

"A Psalm of Life" and **"The Tide Rises, The Tide Falls"**
by Henry Wadsworth Longfellow

Literary Analysis: Stanza Forms

Just as prose writers organize their ideas into paragraphs, poets frequently organize their verse into stanzas, groups of two or more lines of poetry that share a common pattern of rhythm (or meter) and rhyme. Each stanza often presents a single main idea or explores a particular subject, viewpoint, or image. Stanzas are named according to the number of lines they contain—for example, a **couplet** is a two-line stanza, a **quatrain** is a four-line stanza, and a **cinquain** is a five-line stanza.

DIRECTIONS: Reread "The Tide Rises, The Tide Falls." Then, on the lines provided, answer the following questions.

1. What type of stanza is used in this poem? _____

2. Describe the pattern of end rhymes in the first stanza. _____
_____
_____

3. Is the rhyme pattern the same in each stanza?_____

4. How many stressed syllables does each line of the first stanza contain?_____
_____

5. Is the pattern of stressed syllables the same in each stanza? _____

6. How is the rhythmic pattern of the stanzas appropriate to the central image of the poem?
_____
_____

7. Briefly explain what ideas or events are described in each stanza.

   a. _____
   _____
   _____

   b. _____
   _____
   _____

   c. _____
   _____
   _____

8. Each stanza ends with the same line. How does the repetition relate to the poem's meaning?_____
_____
_____
_____

"Thanatopsis" by William Cullen Bryant
"Old Ironsides" by Oliver Wendell Holmes
"The First Snowfall" by James Russell Lowell
from *Snowbound* by John Greenleaf Whittier

Build Vocabulary

Spelling Strategy When torn between *-able* and *-ible*, keep in mind that nearly 1,200 adjectives (including *venerable*) end in *-able* but only about 200 end in *-ible*. In addition, *-able* is a "living suffix," still used to form new adjectives: *biodegradable, customizable*.

Using the Root *-patr-*

A. DIRECTIONS: The word root *-patr-* or *-pater-* means "father" or, by extension, "fatherland." Keeping that in mind, write on the line the letter of the choice that best completes each item.

____ 1. If a social system is a *patriarchy*, who most likely heads a household?
a. a male parent   b. a bachelor   c. an unwed mother   d. a wise grandmother

____ 2. A *patrician* is a person of high social status. What do you think determined status in the society in which this word originated?
a. elections   b. academic achievement   c. salary   d. family background

____ 3. Which word means "to return someone to the homeland after an extended absence"?
a. expatriate   b. repatriate   c. patronize   d. patriciate

Using the Word Bank

sepulcher	venerable	ominous	patriarch
pensive	gloaming	querulous	

B. DIRECTIONS: On the lines provided, rewrite each sentence below, substituting the correct word from the Word Bank in place of its italicized definition.

1. The darkness that morning was a very *menacing* prophecy of the snow to come.

_____

2. The valleys were blanketed in a *thoughtful* quietness.

_____

3. The rooster looked indignant, and his call seemed almost *cranky.*

_____

4. The wise, the good, and everyone else are buried now in one mighty *tomb*.

_____

5. The ram ruled the flock of sheep like a biblical *father figure.*

_____

6. The snow had begun in the *twilight.*

_____

7. The woods are old and *deserving of respect.*

_____

Thanatopsis/Old Ironsides/First Snowfall/Snowbound   **67**

Unit 3: A Growing Nation (1800–1870)

"Thanatopsis" by William Cullen Bryant
"Old Ironsides" by Oliver Wendell Holmes
"The First Snowfall" by James Russell Lowell
from *Snowbound* by John Greenleaf Whittier

Grammar and Style: Participles as Adjectives

A **participle** is a verb form that can act as an adjective. When it does, it generally answers the question *what kind?* or *which one?* about the noun or pronoun it modifies. **Present participles** are formed by adding *-ing* to a verb. In this sentence, the present participle *moaning* modifies the noun *boughs*:

The *moaning* boughs swayed.

Past participles are usually formed by adding *-ed* to a verb. If the verb already ends in silent *e*, you drop the *e* before adding *-ed*. In the following sentences, the past participle *sharpened* modifies the noun *face*, and the past participle *baffled* modifies the noun *wind*. Note that *baffled* is a predicate adjective following a linking verb, *seemed*.

I turned a *sharpened* face to the cold.   The north wind seemed *baffled*.

Some past participles are formed irregularly. These irregular forms often end in *n* or *t*. In the following sentence, the irregular past participles *blown* and *burnt* both modify the noun *leaves*.

The leaves, *burnt* and *blown*, covered the ground.

A. Practice: For each sentence below, underline the participle being used as an adjective, and circle the noun or pronoun that it modifies. If it is a present participle, write *present* on the line before the number. If it is a past participle, write *past*. If the sentence contains no participles used as adjectives, write *none* on the line before the sentence.

_____ 1. It seemed to tell of Pisa's leaning miracle.

_____ 2. The cock his lusty greeting said, and forth his speckled harem led.

_____ 3. We minded that the sharpest ear the buried brooklet could not hear.

_____ 4. Our own warm hearth seemed blazing free.

_____ 5. The hill range stood transfigured in the silver flood.

_____ 6. Its blown snows flashed cold and keen.

B. Writing Application: For the first four items below, describe each noun with a past or present participle. For the next four items, turn each verb into a past or present participle and use it to describe a noun of your choice.

Nouns

1. _____ book   3. _____ sky

2. _____ rain   4. _____ child

Verbs

5. to soothe _____   7. to burn _____

6. to conquer _____   8. to drape _____

"Thanatopsis" by William Cullen Bryant
"Old Ironsides" by Oliver Wendell Holmes
"The First Snowfall" by James Russell Lowell
from _Snowbound_ by John Greenleaf Whittier

Reading Strategy: Summarize

Summarizing is a valuable way to check your reading comprehension. When you **summarize** something, you briefly state its main points and key details in your own words.

DIRECTIONS: Summarize each stanza below on the lines provided.

1. "Thanatopsis": Yet not to thine eternal resting place
   Shalt thou retire alone, nor couldst thou wish
   Couch more magnificent. Thou shalt lie down
   With patriarchs of the infant world—with kings,
   The powerful of the earth—the wise, the good,
   Fair forms, and hoary seers of ages past,
   All in one mighty sepulcher.

   _____
   _____
   _____

2. "Old Ironsides": Oh, better that her shattered hulk
   Should sink beneath the wave;
   Her thunders shook the mighty deep,
   And there should be her grave;
   Nail to the mast her holy flag.
   Set every threadbare sail,
   And give her to the god of storms,
   The lightning and the gale!

   _____
   _____
   _____

3. from _Snowbound_:
   A prompt, decisive man, no breath   A tunnel walled and overlaid
   Our father wasted: "Boys, a path!"   With dazzling crystal: we had read
   Well pleased (for when did farmer boy   Of rare Aladdin's wondrous cave,
   Count such a summons less than joy?)   And to our own his name we gave,
   Our buskins on our feet we drew;   With many a wish the luck were ours
   With mittened hands, and caps drawn low,   To test his lamp's supernal powers.
   To guard our necks and ears from snow,   We reached the barn with merry din,
   We cut the solid whiteness through.   And roused the prisoned brutes within . . .
   And where the drift was deepest, made

   _____
   _____
   _____
   _____
   _____

"Thanatopsis" by William Cullen Bryant
"Old Ironsides" by Oliver Wendell Holmes
"The First Snowfall" by James Russell Lowell
from *Snowbound* by John Greenleaf Whittier

Literary Analysis: Meter

The **meter** of a poem is the rhythmic pattern created by the arrangement of stressed and un-stressed syllables. The basic unit of meter is the **foot**, which usually consists of one stressed syllable and one or more unstressed syllables. The most common foot in English-language po-etry is the **iamb**, an unstressed syllable followed by a stressed syllable, as in the word *today'*.

The type and number of feet per line determine the poem's meter. For example, a pattern of three iambs per line is called **iambic trimeter**; four iambs per line, **iambic tetrameter**; five iambs per line, **iambic pentameter**. The process of analyzing a poem's meter is called **scan-sion**, or **scanning** the poem. Here are examples of scanned lines.

    Iambic tetrameter: Beneath it rung the battle shout
    Iambic pentameter: Let each new temple, nobler than the last

DIRECTIONS: Scan the following stanza of "Old Ironsides" by marking the stressed and un-stressed syllables. Then describe the metrical pattern of the poem on these lines:

_____

_____

Oh, better that her shattered hulk

    Should sink beneath the wave;

Her thunders shook the mighty deep,

    And there should be her grave;

Nail to the mast her holy flag.

    Set every threadbare sail,

And give her to the god of storms,

    The lightning and the gale

"Crossing the Great Divide" by Meriwether Lewis
"The Most Sublime Spectacle on Earth" by John Wesley Powell

Build Vocabulary

Spelling Strategy In general, use *-tion* when the syllable begins with the sound of *sh* (*demarcation, foundation*) and *-sion* when it begins with the sound of *zh* (*version, vision*).

Using the Prefix *multi-*

A. DIRECTIONS: The prefix *multi-* means "much" or "many." Use the prefix in the words you write to complete the following items.

1. *Bi-* means "two." If a person who speaks two languages is *bilingual*, then a person who speaks many languages must be _____.

2. _____ wool is wool that combines many colors.

3. A one-dimensional character has only one personality trait, but a _____ character has quite a few personality traits.

4. *Uni-* means "one." If an amoeba is a *unicellular* creature, a human being must be a _____ creature.

5. If a military force has members from many nations, you might describe it as a _____ force.

Using the Word Bank

conspicuous	excavated	multifarious	sublime
demarcation	multitudinous	labyrinth	

B. DIRECTIONS: On the lines provided, write a synonym for each italicized word.

1. We took care to make them a *conspicuous* object of our own good wishes and the care of our government. _____

2. Yet all these canyons unite to form one grand canyon, the most *sublime* spectacle on the earth.
_____

3. The vast *labyrinth* of canyon by which the plateau region drained by the Colorado is dissected is also the work of waters. _____

4. Every river has *excavated* its own gorge. _____

5. No plane of *demarcation* between wall and blue firmament can be seen._____

6. The elements that unite to make the Grand Canyon the most sublime spectacle in nature are *multifarious.* _____

7. The forms are wrought into endless details, to describe which would be a task equal in magnitude to that of describing the stars of the heavens or the *multitudinous* beauties of the forest._____
_____

Great Divide/Sublime Spectacle **71**

"Crossing the Great Divide" by Meriwether Lewis
"The Most Sublime Spectacle on Earth" by John Wesley Powell

Grammar and Style: Participial Phrase

A **participial phrase** consists of a present or past participle and its modifiers and complements. The entire phrase serves as an adjective, modifying a noun or pronoun. In the first sentence below, for example, the participial phrase consists of a present participle, *carrying*, plus its complement, the direct object *sand*. The entire participial phrase works as an adjective, modifying the noun *creeks*. In the second sentence below, the participial phrase *drained by the Colorado* consists of a past participle, *drained*, plus a modifier, the prepositional phrase *by the Colorado*. The entire participial phrase modifies the noun *region*.

Carrying sand, the many creeks join the Colorado River.

The plateau region *drained by the Colorado* is dissected by canyons.

A. Practice: Underline the participial phrases in the following sentences, and circle the nouns or pronouns that they modify.

1. Each is a composite structure, a wall composed of many walls.

2. The erosion represented in the canyons, although vast, is but a small part of the great erosion of the region.

3. The heavens mount into a vast dome spanning the Grand Canyon with empyrean blue.

4. Following the multiplied courses of these gorges, the heavens seem to be alive.

B. Writing Application: For each item below, write a sentence with a participial phrase that modifies the noun provided.

1. river _____

_____

2. canoes _____

_____

3. canyon _____

_____

4. gorge _____

_____

5. rocks _____

_____

6. clouds _____

_____

"Crossing the Great Divide" by Meriwether Lewis
"The Most Sublime Spectacle on Earth" by John Wesley Powell

Reading Strategy: Noting Spatial Relationships

Keeping track of physical dimensions and relative positions of things—and comparing them with those of other objects—can help you envision what the writer is describing. Be alert for words and phrases that indicate spatial relationships, such as *behind, next to, in front of, at the bottom, on the left, in the north, inside, outside, above, below,* and *between.*

DIRECTIONS: For each passage from the selections, underline the words or phrases that denote spatial relationships and answer the question or questions on the lines provided.

1. Drewyer had been gone about 2 hours when an Indian who had straggled some little distance down the river returned and reported that the white men were coming, that he had seen them just below.

    In comparison with the speaker, where was the Indian when he saw the white men?

    _____

    Where were the white men?

    _____

2. The erosion represented in the canyons, although vast, is but a small part of the great erosion of the region, for between the cliffs blocks have been carried away far superior in magnitude to those necessary to fill the canyons.

    In relation to the cliffs, where were the blocks originally?

    _____

    Where are they now?

    _____

3. The black gneiss below, the variegated quartzite, and the green or alcove sandstone form the foundation for the mighty red wall. The banded sandstone entablature is crowned by the tower limestone.

    Where is the black gneiss relative to the other layers of rock?

    _____

    Where is the limestone relative to the other layers of rock?

    _____

4. In the imagination the clouds belong to the sky, and when they are in the canyon the skies come down into the gorges and cling to the cliffs and lift them up to immeasurable heights, for the sky must still be far away.

    In this description, where are the clouds?

    _____

    Where do the skies seem to be in relation to the gorges and the cliffs?

    _____

    When the skies seem to be in this position, where do they seem to take the cliffs?

    _____

© Prentice-Hall, Inc.

Unit 3: A Growing Nation (1800–1870)

"**Crossing the Great Divide**" by Meriwether Lewis
"**The Most Sublime Spectacle on Earth**" by John Wesley Powell

Literary Analysis: Description

Description is writing that captures sights, sounds, smells, tastes, and physical feelings or sensations. Through description, writers bring scenes and objects to life.

DIRECTIONS: On the line after each passage, indicate whether the passage appeals to the sense of *sight, sound, taste, smell,* or *touch.* Some passages may appeal to more than one of the senses.

1. We now formed our camp just below the junction of the forks on the Lard. [larboard] side in a level smooth bottom covered with a fine turf of greensward. Here we unloaded our canoes and arranged our baggage on shore; formed a canopy of one of our large sails and planted some willow brush in the ground to form a shade for the Indians to sit under while we spoke to them.

   _____

2. Consider a rock 200,000 square miles in extent and a mile in thickness, against which the clouds have hurled their storms and beat in into sands and the rills have carried the sands into the creeks and the creeks have carried them into the rivers and the Colorado has carried them into the sea.

   _____

3. The black gneiss below, the variegated quartzite, and the green or alcove sandstone form the foundation for the mighty red wall. The banded sandstone entablature is crowned by the tower limestone.

   _____

4. The river thunders in perpetual roar, swelling in floors of music when the storm gods play upon the rocks and fading away in soft and low murmurs when the infinite blue of heaven is unveiled.

   _____

5. Mountains of music swell in the rivers, hills of music billow in the creeks, and meadows of music murmur in the rills that ripple over the rocks. Altogether it is a symphony of multitudinous melodies. All this is the music of waters. The adamant foundations of the earth have been wrought into a sublime harp, upon which the clouds of the heavens play with mighty tempests or with gentle showers.

   _____

"Seeing" from *Pilgrim at Tinker Creek* by Annie Dillard

Build Vocabulary

Using Scientific Vocabulary

Although this selection is not a scientific essay, author Annie Dillard makes use of a number of scientific terms. Readers must be prepared for specialized vocabulary even in nonscientific pieces of writing.

ganglia	herpetologist	mount

A. Directions: Use the correct word from the box to complete each sentence below.

1. The scientist will _____ the specimen on a slide.

2. The _____ explained the way the reptiles take in water.

3. No control room transmits information faster than the _____ in the human body.

Using the Word Bank

tremulous	rueful	minutiae

B. Directions: Choose the word from the box that best completes each sentence below.

1. I was _____, thinking of all the natural wonders I had missed in my haste.

2. The frightened, _____ pup shivered in my hand.

3. The endless _____ of the natural world are what I find most fascinating.

C. Directions: For each item, write on the line the letter of the pair of words that best expresses a similar relationship.

____ 1. TREMULOUS : NERVOUS ::
   a. cranky : mournful
   b. shaking : fearful
   c. anxious : calm
   d. soothing : abrasive

____ 2. RUEFUL : REGRETFUL ::
   a. suggestion : command
   b. relieved : glad
   c. calmly : giddily
   d. thin : slender

____ 3. MINUTIAE : ENTIRETY ::
   a. atoms : universe
   b. puzzle : solve
   c. game : outcome
   d. bird : fly

Unit 3: A Growing Nation (1800–1870)

Name _____ Date _____

Thematic Connection: Views of Nature

Annie Dillard and the other authors whose work you have read in this section make careful observations about nature. Scientists and naturalists record in nature logs the observations they make during their studies. You can borrow this scientific device to help you organize your thoughts and observations about nature as well as your interpretations of various authors.

DIRECTIONS: Fill in the entries in the nature log below to help you interpret the phenomena you encounter during a visit to a natural setting and to relate your observations to the authors you have read.

Date/Time:_____ Location: _____

Conditions: _____
_____

Observations: _____
_____
_____

Interpretations: _____
_____
_____
_____

What the authors might say:

Longfellow:_____
_____
_____
_____

Bryant: _____
_____
_____
_____

Lowell: _____
_____
_____
_____

Dillard: _____
_____
_____
_____

"The Fall of the House of Usher" and **"The Raven"** by Edgar Allan Poe

Build Vocabulary

Spelling Strategy The sound of *sh* is sometimes spelled *ci*, as in *specious*, or *ti*, as in *sentience*.

Using the Root -*voc*-

A. DIRECTIONS: The root -*voc*- comes from the Latin *vox*, meaning "voice." On the lines provided, explain how the root -*voc*- influences the meaning of each of the italicized words.

1. The environmental board in our town *advocates* passage of a strong law against dumping waste in Lake Jasper.

    _____

2. Studying the works of Poe will probably improve your *vocabulary*.

    _____

3. The cottage was *evocative* of happy childhood memories.

    _____

Using the Word Bank

importunate	appellation	sentience	munificent	specious
obeisance	equivocal	anomalous	craven	

B. DIRECTIONS: For each item, write on the line the letter of the pair of words that expresses a relationship most like the pair in capital letters.

_____ 1. JESSICA : APPELLATION ::
    a. light : sun   b. magenta : color   c. government : nation   d. mammal : horse

_____ 2. FALSE : SPECIOUS ::
    a. beautiful : ugly   b. violent : wicked   c. plentiful : abundant   d. fat : hungry

_____ 3. NORMAL : ANOMALOUS ::
    a. valuable : worthless   b. blue : color   c. sleepy : tired   d. loving : living

_____ 4. EQUIVOCAL : SURE ::
    a. physician : disease   b. vocal : talkative   c. vague : clear   d. disappear : vanish

_____ 5. SENTIENCE : FEELING ::
    a. capable: skill   b. visible : darkness   c. worth : value   d. sentence : verb

_____ 6. BENEFACTOR : MUNIFICENT ::
    a. donor : charity   b. philanthropist : generous   c. giver : taker   d. charitable : kind

_____ 7. IMPORTUNATE : INSIST ::
    a. unlucky : luck   b. proportionate : equal   c. create : thought   d. talkative : chat

_____ 8. HERO : CRAVEN ::
    a. villain : evil   b. flatterer : complimentary   c. diplomat : tactless   d. raven : black

_____ 9. BOW : OBEISANCE ::
    a. salute : hand   b. smile : happiness   c. frown : joy   d. yawn : silence

Name _____ Date _____

Grammar and Style: Coordinate Adjectives

Coordinate adjectives are adjectives of equal rank that separately modify a noun. They should be separated by commas or coordinating conjunctions (such as *and* or *or*).

> that *abrupt, weighty, unhurried, and hollow-sounding* enunciation

> a *pestilent and mystic* vapor

Adjectives that do not separately modify their noun are not coordinate and do not need commas or a conjunction between them. In the following example, *certain* and *boyish* do not separately modify the noun *traits*; instead, *certain* modifies the entire phrase *boyish traits*.

> reminiscences of *certain boyish traits*

Usually, if the order of the adjectives can be reversed with no change in meaning, they are coordinate.

A. Practice: On the line before each phrase below, label the adjectives *C* for *coordinate* or *NC* for *not coordinate*. Add commas in the phrases where necessary.

_____ 1. a black and lurid tarn

_____ 2. acute bodily illness

_____ 3. an eye large liquid and luminous

_____ 4. his peculiar physical conformation

_____ 5. stern deep and irredeemable gloom

_____ 6. the consequent undeviating transmission

_____ 7. a quaint and curious volume

_____ 8. the silken sad uncertain rustling

_____ 9. a grim ungainly ghastly gaunt and ominous bird

_____ 10. the rare and radiant maiden

B. Writing Application: On the lines provided, write a phrase that describes each noun with two or more coordinate adjectives, and then another phrase that describes it with two or more adjectives that are not coordinate. Be sure to punctuate your phrases correctly.

1. coordinate: _____ raven

   not coordinate: _____ raven

2. coordinate: _____ tarn

   not coordinate: _____ tarn

3. coordinate: _____ mansion

   not coordinate: _____ mansion

4. coordinate: _____ friend

   not coordinate: _____ friend

Name _____ Date _____

"The Fall of the House of Usher" and "The Raven" by Edgar Allan Poe

Reading Strategy: Break Down Long Sentences

When an author writes a long, complicated sentence, you can clarify the meaning by breaking it down into its logical parts. Look especially for the subject and predicate at its core. After you have identified them, state the core in your own words.

Poe's sentence: A cadaverousness of complexion; an eye large, liquid, and luminous beyond comparison; lips somewhat thin and very pallid, but of a surpassingly beautiful curve; a nose of a delicate Hebrew model, but with a breadth of nostril unusual in similar formations; a finely molded chin, speaking, in its want of prominence, of a want of moral energy; hair of a more than weblike softness and tenuity—these features, with an inordinate expansion above the region of the temple, made up altogether a countenance not easily to be forgotten.

Core sentence: These features made up a countenance not easily forgotten.

Own words: He had a memorable face.

DIRECTIONS: Underline the core of the following sentences from "The Fall of the House of Usher." Then restate the core in your own words.

1. During the whole of a dull, dark, and soundless day in the autumn of that year, when the clouds hung oppressively low in the heavens, I had been passing alone, on horseback, through a singularly dreary tract of country, and at length found myself, as the shades of evening drew on, within view of the melancholy House of Usher.

   _____

2. I reined my horse to the precipitous brink of a black and lurid tarn that lay in unruffled luster by the dwelling, and gazed down—but with a shudder even more thrilling than before—upon the remodeled and inverted images of the gray sedge, and the ghastly tree stems, and the vacant and eyelike windows.

   _____

3. He admitted, however, although with hesitation, that much of the peculiar gloom which thus afflicted him could be traced to a more natural and far more palpable origin—to the severe and long-continued illness—indeed to the evidently approaching dissolution of a tenderly beloved sister, his sole companion for long years, his last and only relative on earth.

   _____

4. Our books—the books which, for years, had formed no small portion of the mental existence of the invalid—were, as might be supposed, in strict keeping with this character of phantasm.

   _____

5. Having deposited our mournful burden upon trestles within this region of horror, we partially turned aside the yet unscrewed lid of the coffin, and looked upon the face of the tenant.

   _____

6. No sooner had these syllables passed my lips, than—as if a shield of brass had indeed, at the moment, fallen heavily upon a floor of silver—I became aware of a distinct, hollow, metallic, and clangorous, yet apparently muffled, reverberation.

   _____

"The Fall of the House of Usher" and **"The Raven"** by Edgar Allan Poe

Literary Analysis: Single Effect

Edgar Allan Poe said that a short story should be written to create a **single effect**. Every character, detail, and incident, from the first sentence on, should contribute to this effect. Certainly the effect of "The Fall of the House of Usher" is one of eerie terror, with mounting dread in every scene.

DIRECTIONS: Following are settings and characters described in "The Fall of the House of Usher." On the lines below each setting or character, list three specific details about that setting or character that you feel contribute to the single effect.

1. *Setting:* The room in which Usher spends his days

   a. _____

   b. _____

   c. _____

2. *Setting:* Madeline's tomb

   a. _____

   b. _____

   c. _____

3. *Setting:* The house at the end of the story

   a. _____

   b. _____

   c. _____

4. *Character:* Roderick Usher

   a. _____

   b. _____

   c. _____

5. *Character:* Madeline Usher

   a. _____

   b. _____

   c. _____

"The Minister's Black Veil" by Nathaniel Hawthorne

Build Vocabulary

Spelling Strategy The prefix *in-* meaning "not" (*iniquity, indecorous*) changes to *im-* before many words beginning with *p*: *impersonal, impertinent* or *m*: *immature, immoderate.*

Using the Root -equi-

A. DIRECTIONS: The word root *-equi-* means "equal." Keep that in mind as you answer the following questions on the lines provided.

1. What would you guess about the sides of an *equilateral* triangle?

   _____

2. Why might the imaginary line around the middle of the earth be called the *equator*?

   _____

3. To what do you think *equity* in the legal system might refer?

   _____

4. What would you guess about the length of day and night on the spring or autumn day called the *equinox*?

   _____

5. What circus performer do you think might be called an *equilibrist*? Why?

   _____

Using the Word Bank

venerable	sagacious	waggery	iniquity	vagary
impertinent	indecorous	tremulous	obstinacy	ostentatious

B. DIRECTIONS: On the line before each word in the left column, write the letter of its definition in the right column.

____	1. venerable	a. characterized by trembling
____	2. iniquity	b. not showing proper respect
____	3. indecorous	c. wise
____	4. ostentatious	d. mischievous humor
____	5. sagacious	e. commanding respect
____	6. vagary	f. improper
____	7. tremulous	g. intended to attract notice
____	8. waggery	h. stubbornness
____	9. impertinent	i. an unpredictable occurrence
____	10. obstinacy	j. sin

Unit 3: A Growing Nation (1800–1870)

"The Minister's Black Veil" by Nathaniel Hawthorne

Grammar and Style: Varying Sentence Openers

To make writing lively and interesting, it helps to vary sentence openings. Notice how Hawthorne varies his sentence openers in the following passage.

> **1** The cause of so much amazement may appear sufficiently slight. **2** Mr. Hooper, a gentle-manly person, about thirty, though still a bachelor, was dressed with due clerical neatness, as if a careful wife had starched his band, and brushed the weekly dust from his Sunday's garb. **3** There was but one thing remarkable in his appearance. **4** Swathed about his forehead, and hanging down over his face, so low as to be shaken by his breath, Mr. Hooper had on a black veil. **5** On a nearer view it seemed to consist of two folds of crape, which entirely concealed his features, except the mouth and chin.

Sentences 1 and 2 both open in the most common way, with their subjects (preceded in sentence 1 by the article *The*). Sentence 3, on the other hand, uses inverted order, placing the subject (*thing*) after the verb (*was*). Sentence 4 adds more variety by opening with a participial phrase (*Swathed about his forehead*). Sentence 5 opens in yet another way, with a prepositional phrase (*On a nearer view*).

A. Practice: On the lines provided, explain how Hawthorne varies his sentence openers in this passage.

> After a brief interval, forth came good Mr. Hooper also, in the rear of his flock. Turning his veiled face from one group to another, he paid due reverence to the hoary heads, saluted the middle-aged with kind dignity as their friend and spiritual guide, greeted the young with mingled authority and love, and laid his hands on the little children's heads to bless them. Such was always his custom on the Sabbath day.

_____

_____

_____

_____

B. Writing Application: On the lines provided, rewrite the following paragraph so that the sentence openers are more varied.

> The clergyman stepped into the room where the corpse was laid. He bent over the coffin to take a last farewell of his deceased parishioner. His veil hung straight down from his forehead as he stooped. The dead maiden's eyes were closed forever, otherwise she might have seen his face. Mr. Hooper nevertheless seemed fearful of her glance, for he hastily caught back the black veil.

_____

_____

_____

_____

_____

Name _____ Date _____

Reading Strategy: Drawing Inferences About Meaning

When you **draw an inference** in reading a story, you use the surrounding details to make a reasonable guess about what parts of the story mean. To draw thoughtful inferences, look carefully at the writer's description of events and characters and use of literary devices. For example, note Hawthorne's detail as he describes Mr. Hooper's black veil on the Sunday he appears in church.

> Swathed about his forehead, and hanging down over his face, so low as to be shaken by his breath, Mr. Hooper had on a black veil. On a nearer view it seemed to consist of two folds of crape . . . With this gloomy shade before him, good Mr. Hooper walked onward, at a slow and quiet pace, stooping somewhat, and looking on the ground . . .

Based on Hawthorne's description, you might infer that something bad has happened to someone close to Hooper.

DIRECTIONS: Read the details from "The Minister's Black Veil" in the following chart. Write down what you know from the story and from your own life. Write what you think the author means.

Details	What I Know	Inference
1. That mysterious emblem was never once withdrawn. It shook with his measured breath . . . it threw its obscurity between him and the holy page . . . and while he prayed, the veil lay heavily upon his uplifted countenance.		
2. It was remarkable that of all the busybodies and impertinent people in the parish, not one ventured to put the plain question to Mr. Hooper . . . Hitherto whenever there appeared the slightest call for such interference, he had never lacked advisers . . .		
3. "When the friend shows his inmost heart to his friend; the lover to his best beloved; when man does not vainly shrink from the eye of his Creator, loathsomely treasuring up the secret of his sin; then deem me a monster, for the symbol beneath which I have lived and die! I look around me, and lo! on every visage a Black Veil."		

"The Minister's Black Veil" by Nathaniel Hawthorne

Literary Analysis: Parable

A **parable** teaches a moral lesson through a simple story about humans. Often a parable leaves out specific details about characters or about the location of the story. This technique makes the story more applicable to all readers. For example, in "The Minister's Black Veil," Hawthorne does not reveal the reason Parson Hooper is wearing the veil because the people's reaction to the veil is the critical part of the parable.

Hawthorne calls "The Minister's Black Veil" a parable because he feels strongly about the moral lesson of the story.

DIRECTIONS: Look at each of the following excerpts. Then, in the space provided, write how you think the language reinforces the message of the parable for all readers.

Excerpt	How the Language Conveys the Parable
1. Children, with bright faces, tripped merrily beside their parents, or mimicked a graver gait, in the conscious dignity of their Sunday clothes. Spruce bachelors looked sidelong at the pretty maidens, and fancied that the Sabbath sunshine made them prettier than on weekdays.	
2. At its conclusion, the bell tolled for the funeral of a young lady. The relatives and friends were assembled in the house, and the more distant acquaintances stood about the door, speaking of the good qualities of the deceased . . .	
3. When Mr. Hooper came, the first thing that their eyes rested on was the same horrible black veil, which had added deeper gloom to the funeral, and could portend nothing but evil to the wedding.	
4. The next day, the whole village of Milford talked of little else than Parson Hooper's black veil. That, and the mystery concealed behind it, supplied a topic for discussion between acquaintances meeting in the street, and good women gossiping at their open windows.	

from *Moby-Dick* by Herman Melville

Build Vocabulary

Spelling Strategy The letters *sc* usually have the sound of *sk* (*scout, describe*). Sometimes, however, they have the sound of *sh* (*prescient, omniscient*) or just *s* (*science, muscle*).

Using the Prefix *mal-*

A. Directions: The root *mal-* means "bad." Keep that in mind as you write on the line the letter of the choice that best completes each of these sentences.

1. _____ is often described as *malodorous*.
   a. Cinnamon   b. A rose   c. A squirrel   d. A skunk

2. A *malnourished* child most likely eats _____ meals.
   a. well-balanced   b. skimpy   c. hearty   d. tasty

3. A *malcontent* probably _____ his or her job.
   a. loves   b. hates   c. is puzzled by   d. never complains about

4. A man with a *malady* has _____.
   a. a disease   b. great wealth   c. happiness   d. an aristocratic wife

5. A woman might be called a *malefactor* if she _____.
   a. gives to charity   b. teaches math   c. commits a crime   d. loves her husband

Using the Word Bank

inscrutable	prescient	pertinaciously	maledictions

B. Directions: On the line before each word in the left column, write the letter of its definition in the right column.

____ 1. inscrutable   a. having foreknowledge

____ 2. maledictions   b. holding firmly to some purpose

____ 3. prescient   c. curses

____ 4. pertinaciously   d. not able to be easily understood

C. Directions: For each item, write on the line the letter of the pair of words that expresses a relationship most like the relationship of the pair in capital letters.

____ 1. PERTINACIOUSLY : STRONG-WILLED ::
      a. slowly : driving   b. hungrily : food   c. happily : depressed   d. reverently : religious

____ 2. BLESSINGS : MALEDICTIONS ::
      a. engines : machines   b. courtesy : rudeness   c. wisdom : intelligence   d. clouds : rain

____ 3. PRESCIENT : PROPHET ::
      a. operation : surgeon   b. airplane : pilot   c. nimble : gymnast   d. uneducated : professor

____ 4. INSCRUTABLE : MYSTERIOUS ::
      a. incredible : believable   b. flammable : fireproof   c. indelible : permanent
      d. independent : freedom

Grammar and Style: Agreement With Collective Nouns

A **collective noun** names a group of people, places, things, or ideas. It may be singular or plural. If the collective noun refers to the whole group as a single unit, it is singular. If it refers to individual group members, it is plural.

Singular: The *crew has* finished *its* work on the ship.

Plural: The *crew were* beginning to straggle back from *their* time on shore.

A. Practice: In each of the following sentences, underline the collective nouns. Also circle the correct word from each pair in parentheses.

1. The *Pequod's* company (is, are) drawn from many different regions of the world and stations in life.

2. The crew (performs, perform) (its, their) various duties to keep the ship running smoothly.

3. When Ahab waves his hand, the entire crew (disperses, disperse).

4. The team of harpooners selected by the captain (was, were) the best available.

5. At one point a school of dolphins (breaks, break) the surface of the ocean.

6. A flock of birds (flies, fly) overhead, (its, their) appearance taken as an omen.

7. A host of troubles (plagues, plague) the *Pequod* at different times.

8. The population of 19th-century New England (is, are) well aware of the dangers of whaling.

9. Whenever there is news of a whaling ship, a crowd (fills, fill) the town square.

10. The group (wonders, wonder) if the news (it, they) will hear will be good or bad.

B. Writing Application: For each collective noun supplied below, write two sentences using the noun as the subject with a verb in the present tense. In one sentence, have the noun refer to a single unit. In the other, have it refer to individual group members.

1. herd

_____

_____

_____

2. committee

_____

_____

_____

3. jury

_____

_____

_____

from *Moby-Dick* by Herman Melville

Reading Strategy: Recognize Symbols

To recognize symbols, take note of any connections an author makes between a person, place, event, or object and an abstract idea or concept. Consider, for example, the following passage:

> "Give way!" cried Ahab to the oarsmen, and the boats darted forward to the attack; but maddened by yesterday's fresh irons that corroded in him, Moby-Dick seemed combinedly possessed by all the angels that fell from heaven.

Here Melville connects Moby-Dick to a larger idea by comparing him to "all the angels that fell from heaven," or devils. The connection suggests that Moby-Dick might be a symbol of evil or of the darker side of human nature.

DIRECTIONS: Read the following passage, which opens your textbook selection from *Moby-Dick.* Then, on the lines provided, answer the questions about the passage.

> One morning shortly after breakfast, Ahab, as was his wont, ascended the cabin gangway to the deck. There most sea captains usually walk at that hour, as country gentlemen, after the same meal, take a few turns in the garden.
>
> Soon his steady, ivory stride was heard, as to and fro he paced his old rounds, upon planks so familiar to his tread, that they were all over dented, like geological stones, with the peculiar mark of his walk. Did you fixedly gaze, too, upon that ribbed and dented brow; there also, you would see still stranger footprints—the footprints of his one unsleeping, ever-pacing thought.
>
> But on the occasion in question, those dents looked deeper, even as his nervous step that morning left a deeper mark. And, so full of his thought was Ahab, that at every uniform turn that he made, now at the mainmast and now at the binnacle, you could almost see that thought turn in him as he turned, and pace in him as he paced; so completely possessing him, indeed, that it all but seemed the inward mold of every outer movement.

1. Which details suggest that Ahab is a symbol?

   _____

   _____

2. With what abstract idea or ideas does Melville seem to connect him here?

   _____

   _____

3. Identify one more thing in the passage that might have symbolic significance.

   _____

4. Which details suggest that it is a symbol?

   _____

   _____

5. What abstract idea or ideas does it seem to symbolize?

   _____

   _____

© Prentice-Hall, Inc.

Unit 3: A Growing Nation (1800–1870)

from *Moby-Dick* by Herman Melville

Literary Analysis: Symbol

In *Moby-Dick*, many elements take on symbolic meanings as the novel progresses. A **symbol** is a person, place, action, or thing that also represents an abstract meaning beyond itself. In the following passage, for example, the sharks may be symbols of Ahab's destructive behavior or the destructive response of nature to Ahab's mad pursuit of the whale.

> And still as Ahab glided over the waves the unpitying sharks accompanied him; and so pertinaciously struck to the boat; and so continually bit at the plying oars, that the blades became jagged and crunched, and left small splinters in the sea, at almost every dip.

DIRECTIONS: Read the following passages from *Moby-Dick*. On the lines provided after each passage, identify one symbol that the passage contains and explain what the symbol might represent.

1. "I came here to hunt whales, not my commander's vengeance. How many barrels will thy vengeance yield thee even if thou gettest it, Captain Ahab? it will not fetch thee much in our Nantucket market."

   "Nantucket market! hoot! But come closer, Starbuck. . . . "

   "Vengeance on a dumb brute!" cried Starbuck, "that simply smote thee from blindest instinct! Madness! Madness! To be enraged with a dumb thing, Captain Ahab, seems blasphemous."

   _____
   _____
   _____
   _____
   _____

2. "The ship? Great God, where is the ship?". . . Concentric circles seized the lone boat itself, and all its crew, and each floating oar, and every lance pole, and spinning, animate and inanimate, all round and round in one vortex, carried the smallest chip of the *Pequod* out of sight.

   _____
   _____
   _____
   _____
   _____

3. A sky hawk that tauntingly had followed the main-truck downwards from its natural home among the stars, . . . this bird now chanced to intercept its broad fluttering wing between the hammer and the wood: and simultaneously feeling that ethereal thrill, the submerged savage beneath, in his deathgrasp, kept his hammer frozen there: and so the bird of heaven, with archangelic shrieks, and his imperial beak thrust upwards, and his whole captive form folded in the flag of Ahab, went down with his ship, which like Satan, would not sink to hell till she had dragged a living part of heaven along with her.

   _____
   _____
   _____
   _____
   _____

"Where *Is* Here?" by Joyce Carol Oates

Build Vocabulary

Using Vocabulary to Set a Mood

Joyce Carol Oates skillfully uses vocabulary to set certain moods. Choosing the right words—whether they are adjectives, adverbs, or verbs—can be crucial in imparting a specific tone or mood.

A. DIRECTIONS: For each item below, write a sentence that sets the mood listed. Make sure to use vocabulary that helps set the particular mood.

1. terror: _____

_____

2. happiness: _____

_____

3. desperation: _____

_____

4. mystery:_____

_____

Using the Word Bank

| genial | gregarious | galvanic |
| covertly | avuncular | |

B. DIRECTIONS: On each line, write the letter of the word that doesn't belong in that grouping.

____ 1. a. genial   b. avuncular   c. distant

____ 2. a. covertly   b. secretly   c. overtly

____ 3. a. gregarious   b. shy   c. introspective

C. DIRECTIONS: On each line, write the letter of the word that is most similar in meaning to the numbered word.

____ 1. galvanic
    a. rocky
    b. energizing
    c. subtle
    d. complicated

____ 2. gregarious
    a. sociable
    b. related
    c. difficult
    d. hilarious

____ 3. genial
    a. prophetic
    b. humorous
    c. smooth
    d. friendly

Name _____ Date _____

*"Where **Is** Here?"* by Joyce Carol Oates

Thematic Connection: Shadows of the Imagination

In this story, Joyce Carol Oates continues a shadowy literary tradition that includes a number of the other authors you've read in this section. Oates, like Edgar Allan Poe, Nathaniel Hawthorne, and Herman Melville, often portrays disturbed characters who act in chilling, sometimes extraordinary ways, their motivations often ambiguous, malevolent, or macabre. How might each of these others portray a situation set in your town?

DIRECTIONS: In the first space below, write a plot summary of a story that takes place in your town or in another setting with which you are familiar. Try to think of an ordinary situation with ordinary characters. Then, use your imagination and what you're learned to speculate on what fictional treatment each of the authors listed might have come up with using the plot summary you created. Write a short description of each author's work on the lines.

Basic Plot Summary: _____

_____

_____

_____

_____

Oates: _____

_____

_____

_____

_____

Poe: _____

_____

_____

_____

_____

Hawthorne: _____

_____

_____

_____

_____

Melville: _____

_____

_____

_____

_____

from *Nature*, from *Self-Reliance*, "The Snowstorm," and "Concord Hymn"
by Ralph Waldo Emerson

Build Vocabulary

Spelling Strategy A final silent *e* often helps create the sound of a long vowel followed by a voiced *th*: *blithe, breathe, clothe, lithe.*

Using the Root *-radi-*

A. Directions: The root *-radi-* means "spoke" or "ray." On the line after each sentence below, explain how the italicized word reflects the meaning of the root *-radi-*.

1. The bride's happiness seemed to *radiate* from her very soul.

   _____

2. The *radius* of a circle extends from the center to the outer edge.

   _____

3. The *radiator* emitted enough heat to warm the entire room.

   _____

4. Professor Diaz transmitted the message across the air waves via *radio*.

   _____

5. *Radioactive* elements emit energy as a result of nuclear decay.

   _____

Using the Word Bank

blithe	chaos	suffrage	radiant	bastions
connate	aversion	divines	tumultuous	

B. Directions: On the line, write the letter of the word that is most nearly the same in meaning as the word in capitals.

____ 1. BLITHE: a. lighthearted   b. sorrowful   c. well-lit   d. gloomy

____ 2. CONNATE: a. imply   b. denote   c. dishonest   d. inborn

____ 3. CHAOS: a. joy   b. pain   c. confusion   d. silence

____ 4. AVERSION: a. attraction   b. distaste   c. discrepancy   d. revision

____ 5. SUFFRAGE: a. vote   b. anxiety   c. legality   d. femininity

____ 6. DIVINES: a. politicians   b. clerics   c. performers   d. inventors

____ 7. RADIANT: a. cool   b. eager   c. glowing   d. moist

____ 8. TUMULTUOUS: a. simple   b. persuasive   c. momentous   d. stormy

____ 9. BASTIONS: a. villains   b. soldiers   c. fortresses   d. dungeons

from *Nature*, from *Self-Reliance*, "The Snowstorm," and "Concord Hymn"
by Ralph Waldo Emerson

Grammar and Style: Vary Sentence Length

Nothing is more monotonous than a series of similarly structured sentences of about the same length. Good writers vary sentence length to establish an interesting rhythm that captures the reader's attention. Often they follow a long sentence with a short one:

> The greatest delight which the fields and woods minister is the suggestion of an occult relation between man and the vegetable. I am not alone and unacknowledged.

A. Practice: For each item, circle the letter of the sentence that would *sound* better after the sentence in italics.

1. *Within these plantations of God, a decorum and sanctity reign, a perennial festival is dressed, and the guest sees not how he should tire of them in a thousand years.*

   a. In the woods, we return to reason and faith.

   b. Within the woods where God himself dwells, I as a human being return to reason of the most elemental kind, and I also return also to faith.

2. *Trust thyself.*

   a. Accept your place. Don't fight divine providence. Acknowledge your contemporaries. Join society. Accept the connection of events.

   b. Accept the place the divine providence has found for you: the society of your contemporaries, the connection of events.

B. Writing Application: On the lines below, rewrite this paragraph to create more sentence variety. Feel free to add new words and leave out insignificant ones, but do not omit any of the facts presented.

> On April 19, 1775, a group of American farmers serving as Minute Men began the American Revolution when they fired at the British at Lexington and Concord, Massachusetts. Some decades later, Ralph Waldo Emerson called the first shot of the Revolution "the shot heard round the world." Emerson used the phrase in his "Concord Hymn," which was sung on April 19, 1836, at the unveiling of a monument honoring the Minute Men's stand.

_____

_____

_____

_____

_____

_____

_____

_____

_____

from *Nature*, from *Self-Reliance*, "The Snowstorm," and "Concord Hymn"
by Ralph Waldo Emerson

Reading Strategy: Challenging the Text

One way to gain more understanding of a work is to **challenge the text**, or question the author's assertions. Here are some guidelines.

- Identify the author's opinions and restate them in your own words.

- Evaluate the examples, reasons, or other evidence the author provides to support his or her opinions.

- Consider other evidence that supports or refutes the author's opinions.

- On the basis of the evidence, decide if you agree or disagree with the author.

DIRECTIONS: Read the following passage from *Self-Reliance*. Then challenge the text by performing the numbered activities below. Write your responses on the lines provided.

> Society everywhere is in conspiracy against the manhood of every one of its members. Society is a joint-stock company in which the members agree for the better securing of his bread to each shareholder, to surrender the liberty and culture of the eater. The virtue in most request is conformity. Self-reliance is its aversion. It loves not realities and creators, but names and customs.

1. Restate Emerson's basic opinion about society.

   _____

   _____

2. Identify and evaluate the evidence Emerson uses to support that opinion.

   _____

   _____

   _____

3. Provide examples from everyday life to support and refute Emerson's opinion of society.

   Support:_____

   _____

   _____

   Refute: _____

   _____

   _____

4. Indicate whether you agree or disagree with Emerson's opinion of society, and briefly explain how the evidence led you to your position.

   _____

   _____

   _____

from *Nature*, from *Self-Reliance*, "The Snowstorm," and "Concord Hymn"
by Ralph Waldo Emerson

Literary Analysis: Transcendentalism

Transcendentalism was an offshoot of romanticism that became the philosophy of Ralph Waldo Emerson and several other American intellectuals of his day. Emerson's writings embody the following important principles of Transcendentalism.

A. The human spirit can intuitively comprehend the fundamental truths of the universe.

B. The human spirit is reflected in nature.

C. All forms of being are spiritually united.

DIRECTIONS: Read these passages from Emerson's essays. Then, on the line provided, write the letter of the principle of Transcendentalism (from the list above) that each passage best illustrates.

_____ 1. Nature is a setting that fits equally well a comic or a mourning piece. In good health, the air is a cordial of incredible virtue.

_____ 2. The currents of the Universal Being circulate through me; I am part or parcel of God.

_____ 3. The greatest delight which the fields and woods minister is the suggestion of an occult relation between man and the vegetable.

_____ 4. Nature always wears the colors of the spirit.

_____ 5. The power which resides in him is new in nature, and none but he knows what it is which he can do.

_____ 6. Trust thyself: every heart vibrates to that iron string.

_____ 7. Nothing is at last sacred but the integrity of our own mind.

from *Walden* and from *Civil Disobedience* by Henry David Thoreau

Build Vocabulary

Spelling Strategy If a word ends in -ent (*expedient*, for example) its parallel forms end in -ence or -ency (*expedience, expediency*).

Using the Root *-flu-*

A. DIRECTIONS: The root *-flu-* means "flow." Using that information, write on the line the letter of the choice that best completes each sentence.

____ 1. If Laura shows *fluency* in Russian,
    a. she has little knowledge of Russian.
    b. she has studied Russian but cannot master it.
    c. she speaks it easily.

____ 2. In an *affluent* society,
    a. many people have and spend money.
    b. most people are very poor.
    c. most people earn good money but refuse to spend it.

____ 3. The root *-mell-* means "honey." If you have a *mellifluous* voice,
    a. you speak in sweet tones.
    b. you need to lower your voice.
    c. your words stick in your throat.

Using the Word Bank

dilapidated	superfluous	magnanimity	posterity
sublime	evitable	expedient	alacrity

B. DIRECTIONS: Circle the letter of the choice that best completes each sentence.

1. The building was so dilapidated that the city wanted to have it
    a. demolished. b. publicized. c. photographed. d. landscaped.

2. Anna saved all of her war memorabilia for posterity, hoping to show it eventually to her
    a. neighbors. b. parents. c. grandchildren. d. aunts.

3. Her novels include a fair amount of superfluous information, making them rather
    a. easy to read. b. time consuming. c. melancholy. d. desirable.

4. The city's architecture was absolutely sublime, so viewing it usually inspired
    a. disgust. b. boredom. c. awe. d. indifference.

5. When Jill accepted with alacrity the difficult task he gave her, her boss was
    a. annoyed. b. impressed. c. furious. d. displeased.

6. When Thoreau calls government an expedient, he means it is a
    a. tool. b. monstrosity. c. bureaucracy. d. useless enterprise.

7. People display magnanimity when they
    a. hold a grudge. b. seek revenge. c. perform tasks efficiently. d. give to charity.

8. Capture was evitable if the fugitive remained
    a. unknown. b. hidden. c. calm. d. conspicuous.

Name _____ Date _____

from **Walden** and from **Civil Disobedience** by Henry David Thoreau

Grammar and Style: Infinitives and Infinitive Phrases

An **infinitive** usually consists of the basic form of a verb preceded by the word *to*. It can function as a noun, an adjective, or an adverb.

Thoreau liked *to read*. [noun; object of verb *liked*]

Jo had several chapters *to read*. [adjective; modifies noun *chapters*]

Some people live *to read*. [adverb; modifies verb *live*]

An **infinitive phrase** consists of an infinitive and its complement and/or modifiers. The entire phrase serves as a noun, adjective, or adverb.

Thoreau liked *to read philosophy*. [noun; object of verb *liked*]

Jo had several chapters *to read quickly*. [adjective; modifies noun *chapters*]

Some people live *to read novels*. [adverb; modifies verb *live*]

A. Practice: For each sentence, underline the infinitive or infinitive phrase and indicate how it is functioning by writing *n* for noun, *adj* for adjective, or *adv* for adverb. Place the abbreviation on the line before the sentence.

_____ 1. I wished to live deliberately.

_____ 2. I wanted to ponder only the essential facts of life.

_____ 3. Perhaps it seemed to me that I had several more lives to live.

_____ 4. Do not trouble yourself much to get new things.

B. Writing Application: Rewrite the following pairs of wordy sentences by turning one sentence into an infinitive phrase. You will need to change or delete some words.

1. Thoreau wanted a certain kind of life. He was interested in living simply.

_____

_____

2. He follows the Transcendentalist teaching. That teaching stresses making a friend of nature.

_____

_____

3. Thoreau tells individuals some advice. He advises that they heed the sound of a different drummer.

_____

_____

4. Thoreau uses many similes and metaphors. He employs them as devices that teach important principles.

_____

_____

from *Walden* and from *Civil Disobedience* by Henry David Thoreau

Reading Strategy: Evaluate the Writer's Statement of Philosophy

In both *Walden* and *Civil Disobedience*, Thoreau expresses his **philosophy**, the system of beliefs and values that guided his life and actions. As you read, you should decide whether you agree with Thoreau's philosophy. To evaluate Thoreau's philosophy, note his main ideas and the evidence he uses to support those ideas. Then evaluate his ideas and evidence by comparing them with your own life experiences. Organize your evaluation in the following chart.

Thoreau's Main Ideas	
Thoreau's Evidence	
My Experiences	
Evaluation	

Unit 3: A Growing Nation (1800–1870)

from _Walden_ and **from _Civil Disobedience_** by Henry David Thoreau

Literary Analysis: Style

Readers should look not only at what a writer has to say but also at how the writer says it. The way a writer puts thoughts into words is called **style**. Following are some important elements of style and some questions useful in analyzing a writer's style.

- **Choice of words:** Does the writer choose simple and direct words or words that are more complex and formal?

- **Length of sentences:** Does the writer make frequent use of long or short sentences? Does the sentence length vary?

- **Type and structure of sentences:** Does the writer use a fair amount of questions or commands? Many simple sentences, or compound-complex sentences? Does the writer always open with the subject of a sentence or vary sentence beginnings?

- **Rhythm:** Does the writer create an internal rhythm by repeating words or ideas from sentence to sentence?

- **Use of literary devices:** Does the writer use vivid imagery and strong similes, metaphors, and other figures of speech?

DIRECTIONS: Read this passage from _Walden_. Then, on the lines below the passage, analyze the different elements of Thoreau's style.

To my imagination it retained throughout the day more or less of this auroral character, reminding me of a certain house on a mountain which I had visited the year before. This was an airy and unplastered cabin, fit to entertain a traveling god, and where a goddess might trail her garments. The winds which passed over my dwelling were such as sweep over the ridges of mountains, bearing the broken strains, or celestial parts only, of terrestrial music.

1. Word choice:_____

_____

2. Sentence length: _____

_____

3. Sentence type/structure:_____

_____

_____

_____

4. Rhythm:_____

_____

5. Literary devices: _____

_____

_____

_____

Emily Dickinson's Poetry

Build Vocabulary

Spelling Strategy *Carriage* and *marriage* both have an *i* and an *a* before the *ge*.

Using the Root -finis-

A. DIRECTIONS: The root -*finis*-, often shortened to -*fin*-, means "end" or "limit." On the lines provided, explain how the meaning of the word is conveyed in each of the following words.

1. define_____

   _____

2. refinish_____

   _____

3. finale_____

   _____

Using the Word Bank

cornice	surmised	oppresses	finite	infinity

B. DIRECTIONS: On the line provided, write the word from the Word Bank that best completes each sentence.

1. From her expression, I _____ that she was not happy to see me.

2. There had to be an end to the tunnel, but it seemed to stretch into
   _____.

3. Whenever a sad thought _____ me, I get a headache.

4. Only a _____ number of ways existed to solve the problem.

5. The skyscraper's northwest _____ was too high to see from the ground.

C. DIRECTIONS: On the line, write the letter of the pair of words that expresses a relationship most like the pair in capital letters.

____ 1. FINITE : INFINITY ::
    a. fatal : fate
    b. endless : eternity
    c. mortal : immortality
    d. significant : importance

____ 2. CORNICE : HOUSE ::
    a. pizza : pepperoni
    b. sweep : broom
    c. flue : chimney
    d. hat : head

____ 3. SURMISED : SPECULATION ::
    a. anticipated : compliment
    b. forewarned : prediction
    c. flattered : insult
    d. pampered : aid

____ 4. OPPRESSED : CAREFREE ::
    a. thoughtful : serious
    b. grumpy : cheerful
    c. ancient : old
    d. depressed : sad

Unit 3: A Growing Nation (1800–1870)

Name _____ Date _____

Grammar and Style: Gerunds

Gerunds are verb forms that end in -*ing* but are used as nouns, functioning as subjects, direct objects, predicate nominatives, or objects of prepositions.

Gerund as subject: *Socializing* was difficult for Dickinson.

Gerund as direct object: She avoided *socializing*.

Gerund as predicate nominative: Perhaps her least favorite task was *socializing*.

Gerund as object of a preposition: She disliked the small talk of *socializing*.

A. Practice: Circle the gerunds in the following sentences. On the line before each sentence, write *S* if the gerund is used as a subject, *DO* if it is used as the direct object of a verb, *PA* if it is used as a predicate nominative, or *OP* if it is used as the object of a preposition.

_____ 1. Talking about politics always made Mario's grandmother angry.

_____ 2. Alex dreamed about dancing with the Joffrey Ballet.

_____ 3. When it comes to sports, Germaine prefers swimming.

_____ 4. My favorite sport is running.

_____ 5. Grandfather is famous for his cooking.

B. Writing Application: On the lines provided, write a sentence using each word as a gerund. In the eight sentences you write in total, try to illustrate all four gerund uses: subject, direct object, predicate nominative, and object of a preposition.

1. jumping _____

_____

2. asking _____

_____

3. participating _____

_____

4. debating _____

_____

5. signaling _____

_____

6. driving _____

_____

7. motivating _____

_____

8. running _____

_____

© Prentice-Hall, Inc.

Emily Dickinson's Poetry

Reading Strategy: Analyze Images

Good poets use language efficiently to create images that appeal to one or more of the five senses: sight, touch, hearing, taste, and smell. Often these concrete images help a poet convey abstract ideas. Consider the images in this stanza, which appeal to the senses of sight and touch:

> The Brain is deeper than the sea—
> For—hold them—Blue to Blue—
> The one the other will absorb—
> As Sponges—Buckets—do—

The brain, says Dickinson, is like a wide blue sea, only deeper—so deep, in fact, that it absorbs the sea as easily as a sponge absorbs a bucketful of water. The image of the wide blue sea helps us visualize the brain. The image of the sponge absorbing the bucketful of water helps us visualize the brain's activity and appreciate its capacity.

DIRECTIONS: On the lines after each stanza from "The Soul selects her own Society—," explain how the image or images that the stanza contains help to convey abstract ideas.

1. The Soul selects her own Society—
   Then—shuts the door—
   To her divine Majority—
   Present no more—

   _____
   _____
   _____
   _____
   _____

2. Unmoved—she notes the Chariots—pausing—
   At her low Gate—
   Unmoved—an Emperor be kneeling
   Upon her Mat—

   _____
   _____
   _____
   _____
   _____

3. I've known her—from an ample nation—
   Choose One—
   Then—close the Valves of her attention—
   Like Stone—

   _____
   _____
   _____
   _____
   _____

Name _____ Date _____

Emily Dickinson's Poetry

Literary Analysis: Slant Rhyme

In **exact rhyme**, two or more words have the identical vowel and final consonant sounds in their last stressed syllables. For example, *pound* and *sound* rhyme exactly, as do *brain* and *contain*. In **slant rhyme**, the final sounds are similar but not identical. For example, *pond* and *sound* are slant rhymes, as are *brain* and *frame*.

DIRECTIONS: On the lines after each passage from Dickinson's poetry, identify the words that rhyme, and indicate whether the rhymes are exact or slant.

1. My life closed twice before its close—
    It yet remains to see
    If Immortality unveil
    A third event to me.

    _____

    _____

2. Or rather—He passed Us—
    The Dews drew quivering and chill—
    For only Gossamer, my Gown—
    My Tippet—only Tulle—

    _____

    _____

3. None may teach it—Any—
    'Tis the Seal Despair—
    An imperial affliction
    Sent us of the Air—

    _____

    _____

4. Compared with that profounder site
    That polar privacy
    A soul admitted to itself—
    Finite Infinity.

    _____

    _____

5. Water, is taught by thirst.
    Land—by the Oceans passed.
    Transport—by throe—
    Peace—by its battles told—
    Love, by Memorial Mold—
    Birds, by the Snow.

    _____

    _____

    _____

    _____

Walt Whitman's Poetry

Build Vocabulary

Spelling Strategy The sound of *y* followed by long *u* is sometimes created by the letter *u* alone: *effuse, puny*. Other spellings of this sound include *ew*, as in *few*; *ue*, as in *hue*; *yu*, as in *yule*; and *you*, as in *youth*.

Using the Root *-fus-*

A. DIRECTIONS The root *-fus-* means "pour." Keep that in mind as you write on the line the letter of the choice that best completes the following sentences.

1. If Stella is perspiring *profusely*, she is probably sweating _____.
   a. a bit   b. a lot   c. due to illness   d. during sleep

2. During a blood *transfusion*, blood _____.
   a. congeals   b. turns blue   c. cannot reach the heart   d. goes from one person to another

3. If the sky at sunset is *suffused* with red, it _____.
   a. is filled with red   c. clashes with red
   b. contains very little red   d. has no red in it whatsoever

4. _____ might cause two pieces of metal to *fuse* together.
   a. High heat   b. High cost   c. Thickness   d. Moisture

Using the Word Bank

abeyance	effuse

B. DIRECTIONS: On the lines provided, rewrite each sentence by replacing the italicized word with a simpler word that means the same thing.

1. I depart as air, I shake my white locks at the runaway sun, I *effuse* my flesh in eddies, and drift it in lacy jags.

   _____

2. Creeds and school in *abeyance*, retiring back a while sufficed at what they are, but never forgotten.

   _____

C. DIRECTIONS: On the line, write the letter of the word that is most nearly *opposite* in meaning to the word in capital letters.

____ 1. ABEYANCE :   ____ 2. EFFUSE :
         a. suspension   a. pour
         b. continuation   b. appear
         c. vacation   c. contract
         d. legality   d. boil

Unit 3: A Growing Nation
(1800–1870)

Walt Whitman's Poetry

Grammar and Style: Pronoun-Antecedent Agreement

A pronoun must agree in number and gender with its **antecedent,** the word to which it refers.

Singular masculine pronoun and antecedent: The *boatman* sings as *he* sails *his* boat.
Singular feminine pronoun and antecedent: The young *wife* sings as *she* does *her* work.
Singular neuter pronoun and antecedent: The *spider* reached a high promontory where *it* made *its* web.
Plural pronoun and antecedent: I heard many *astronomers,* and *they* all brought *their* charts with *them.*

A. Practice: Circle the pronoun in parentheses that correctly completes each sentence, and underline the antecedent to which the pronoun refers.

1. Mrs. Pell likes poetry, and (his, her, its) favorite poet is Walt Whitman.

2. Mrs. Pell's volume of Whitman's poems has (its, her, their) cover damaged.

3. Two pictures of Whitman in (his, her, their) hat appear on the cover.

4. The book is published by a company in Boston; (it, he, they) also published Whitman's original volumes of verse in the late nineteenth century.

5. Mrs. Pell bought her edition when (he, she, it) was in college fifty years ago.

6. Several poems in the book have (her, its, their) words underlined.

B. Writing Application: On the lines provided, rewrite these sentences by replacing each italicized term with a pronoun that agrees with its antecedent in number and gender.

1. Whitman leans and loafs at *Whitman's* ease, observing a spear of summer grass.

_____

2. Whitman notes that *Whitman's* ancestors include *Whitman's* parents and *Whitman's parents'* parents.

_____

3. When Whitman listened to the lecture, *Whitman* became tired and sick from looking at the charts and diagrams and measuring *the charts and diagrams*.

_____

4. Whitman's noiseless, patient spider explores a large area, and *the spider* spins filaments out of *the spider's* body, tirelessly unreeling *the filaments*.

_____

5. In "I Hear America Singing," the mother sings what belongs to *the mother* and no one else.

_____

6. As Whitman lifted *Whitman's* eyes to look at the shrubs and trees, *Whitman* thought that *the shrubs and trees* were watching *Whitman*.

_____

Walt Whitman's Poetry

Reading Strategy: Infer the Poet's Attitude

By examining a writer's choice of words and details, you can make inferences about the writer's attitude and gain insight into his or her feelings and beliefs. For example, in "When I Heard the Learn'd Astronomer," the words "tired" and "sick" suggest that Whitman has a negative attitude toward the astronomer and toward science in general, while the phrase "mystical, moist night air" and the detail about looking up "in perfect silence" at the stars suggest that Whitman has a positive attitude toward the nighttime sky and a more poetic approach toward viewing it.

DIRECTIONS: Read each of these passages from "Song of Myself." Then circle the letter of the statement that comes closest to the attitude or world view that Whitman expresses in the passage.

1. I loaf and invite my soul,
    I lean and loaf at my ease observing a spear of summer grass.

    a. People should not interfere with nature.
    b. Observation of nature is a valuable activity.
    c. Only lazy people have time to enjoy nature.

2. I, now thirty-seven years old in perfect health begin,
    Hoping to cease not till death.

    a. Life is an active business, not a passive one.
    b. Good health is essential to leading a good life.
    c. As one grows older, one naturally slows down.

3. The wild gander leads his flock through the cool night,
    Ya-honk he says, and sounds it down to me like an invitation.

    a. Wild creatures can inspire a sense of adventure in people.
    b. People are essentially followers, looking for a strong leader.
    c. Birds are unpleasant creatures that send secret messages few
       humans understand.

4. These are really the thoughts of all men in all ages and lands, they are not original with me, / If they are not yours as much they are mine they are nothing, or next to nothing.

    a. Any individual's voice is a humble voice, prone to error.
    b. The human soul is essentially the same in every time and place.
    c. If poetry does not express new ideas and feelings, it is worthless.

5. Do I contradict myself? / Very well then I contradict myself, /
    (I am large, I contain multitudes.)

    a. People who contradict themselves are phony hypocrites.
    b. To feel shame for being overweight is a foolish contradiction.
    c. The human spirit is capable of contradiction, which is no bad thing.

6. I too am not a bit tamed, I too am untranslatable, / I sound my barbaric yawp over the roofs of the world.

    a. Good poets should never use slang, which is untranslatable.
    b. People need to be tame if they wish to be understood.
    c. A wild lifestyle and informal speech are both admirable.

Name _____   Date _____

Walt Whitman's Poetry

Literary Analysis: Free Verse

Free verse is poetry with no fixed pattern of rhythm or line length. Instead, its rhythm captures the sound of natural speech, and its line lengths are determined solely by the content of the lines, with the poet breaking a line where there is a natural pause or where he or she wants a particular word or image emphasized. Whitman was a nineteenth-century pioneer of free verse, which he used in part to reflect his belief in individuality, democracy, and freedom.

DIRECTIONS: The following stanza from "A Noiseless Patient Spider" has been rewritten using a fixed rhythmic pattern, or meter. On the lines below the two versions, comment on the differences between them.

Whitman's version:

> A noiseless patient spider,
> I'd mark'd where on a little promontory it stood isolated,
> Mark'd how to explore the vacant vast surrounding,
> It launch'd forth filament, filament, filament, out of itself,
> Ever unreeling them, ever tirelessly speeding them.

Metrical version:

> A noiseless patient spider;
> I marked the spot it stood on.
> Alone on a high mountain,
> It launched its silk lines forward,
> Exploring its surroundings.

_____

_____

_____

_____

_____

_____

_____

_____

_____

_____

_____

_____

_____

_____

"I, Too" by Langston Hughes
"To Walt Whitman" by Angela de Hoyos

Thematic Connection: The Emergence of an American Voice

Both Langston Hughes and Angela de Hoyos use Walt Whitman as a point of reference in their poems, which take the definition of the American voice as a theme. While both Hughes and de Hoyos pose a challenge to Whitman's conception of America, their work undoubtedly is built on that of the author of "Song of Myself." In a similar way, can you build on all three poets' work to formulate your own ideas on the emergence of an American voice? Use the worksheet below to plan a poem of your own on America and the American voice.

DIRECTIONS: Fill in the following chart to help plan a poem that celebrates the American voice, discusses how it is changing, poses a challenge to the ideas in the poems you have read, or touches on the idea in some other way. Begin by listing the images in the poems you have read; then brainstorm images that you might include in your poem.

Poetic Images

Whitman:_____

_____

_____

_____

_____

Hughes: _____

_____

_____

_____

_____

de Hoyos: _____

_____

_____

_____

_____

My images: _____

_____

_____

_____

_____

_____

Unit 3: A Growing Nation (1800–1870)

"An Episode of War" by Stephen Crane

"Willie Has Gone to the War," words by George Cooper, music by Stephen Foster

Build Vocabulary

Spelling Strategy The long a sound can be spelled a-consonant-e, as in *glade* or the verb forms of *precipitate*, and *aggregate*. It can also be spelled *ai*, as in *disdain*.

Using the Root -greg-

A. DIRECTIONS: The word root *-greg-* means "herd or flock." On the line, write a word from the list that is suggested by the bracketed word or phrase.

gregarious	egregious	aggregate	congregation

1. Marc is so _____ [sociable] _____ that he always has a crowd of friends around him.
2. His mistake was so _____ [conspicuously bad] _____ , Eli asked if he could begin his audition again.
3. Lourdes' family has belonged to the same _____ [church group] _____ for generations.
4. The students at Hoffman School are a(n) _____ [collection] _____ of the city's diverse population.

Using the Word Bank

aggregation	glade	precipitate	disdainfully	inscrutable

B. DIRECTIONS: On the line, write the letter of the word or phrase that has the same meaning as the word in CAPITAL letters.

____ 1. GLADE: a. jungle b. open space in a wood c. alcove d. covered bridge

____ 2. PRECIPITATE: a. prevent b. dissuade c. cause d. expect

____ 3. DISDAINFULLY: a. loudly b. contemptuously c. gladly d. beautifully

____ 4. INSCRUTABLE: a. visible b. immediate c. different d. obscure

____ 5. AGGREGATION: a. irritant b. group c. object d. elimination

C. DIRECTIONS: On the line, write the letter of the word or phrase that best completes each sentence.

1. Laurel looked upon her brother disdainfully when he _____.
   a. spilled syrup on her skirt   c. helped her fix her car
   b. won the race   d. gave her the CD she'd wanted

2. Amelie was afraid that her grandmother's pneumonia might precipitate her _____.
   a. recovery   b. cough   c. death   d. lungs

3. The moving van was stuffed with an _____ of furniture, tools, and automobile parts.
   a. extravaganza   b. aggregation   c. imbalance   d. offload

4. Kim's face is easy to read, but Fiona's is _____.
   a. inscrutable   b. large   c. important   d. immovable

5. After they walked through the forest, they came to the cabin set in a lovely open _____.
   a. mountain   b. trail   c. corral   d. glade

"An Episode of War" by Stephen Crane
"Willie Has Gone to the War," words by George Cooper, music by Stephen Foster

Grammar and Style: Correct Use of *Like* and *As*

Although they are often used interchangeably, the words *as*, *as if*, *as though*, and *like* serve different functions. *As*, *as if*, and *as though* are subordinate conjunctions that are used to introduce a subordinate clause. *Like* is a preposition that takes a noun or a pronoun as its object and is used to introduce a prepositional phrase, rather than a clause. Look at these examples:

... this aggregation of wheels, levers, motors had a beautiful unity, *as if* it were a missile. [introduces subordinate clause]

This wounded officer . . . breathed *like* a wrestler. [introduces a prepositional phrase]

A. Practice: In the following passages from "An Episode of War," circle the word from the pair in *italics* that best fits.

1. . . . contemplated the distant forest (*as if/like*) their minds were fixed upon the mystery. . . .

2. He looked at it in a kind of stupefaction, (*as if/like*) he had been endowed with a trident. . . .

3. . . . It is (*as if/like*) the wounded man's hand is upon the curtain. . . .

4. It was, for a wonder, precisely (*as/like*) a historical painting.

5. . . . where the shooting sometimes crackled (*as/like*) bush-fires. . . .

B. Writing Application: *Like* and *as* are often used in descriptions to compare one thing to another. Write a paragraph in which you describe an event. In your paragraph, use the preposition *like* at least twice. Include at least two examples of the subordinating conjunctions *as*, *as if*, and *as though*. Be sure to distinguish correctly between the uses of *like* and *as*.

_____
_____
_____
_____
_____
_____
_____
_____
_____
_____
_____
_____
_____

Unit 4: Division, Reconciliation, and Expansion (1850–1914)

"An Episode of War" by Stephen Crane
"Willie Has Gone to the War" words by George Cooper, music by Stephen Foster

Reading Strategy: Recognize Historical Details

Your knowledge of the historical time period of a selection can help you make the most of a reading experience. Consider the historical, social, and political climate surrounding a piece of writing as part of its setting and context. For example, in "An Episode of War," the author writes, "His lips pursed as he drew with his sword various crevices in the heap . . ." The detail about the sword helps you to realize that the story did not happen recently—it happened in a time when swords were weapons of war.

Pay careful attention to **historical details** that make the story more vivid and meaningful.

DIRECTIONS: Record some of your historical knowledge about the following issues during the American Civil War. Then write how the details affect your reading of the selections.

Issues	Historical Knowledge	Affect on Reading
1. War tactics		
2. Medicine		
3. Communication		
4. Transportation		

"An Episode of War" by Stephen Crane

"Willie Has Gone to the War," words by George Cooper, music by Stephen Foster

Literary Analysis: Realism and Naturalism

Realism is a type of literature that tries to show people and their lives as realistically as possible. Authors who write material within this literary movement focus on ordinary people rather than on exaggerated models of idealistic behavior. Often such writers emphasize the harsh realities of ordinary daily life, even though their characters are fictional.

Naturalism expands on the base begun by realism. Writers who create naturalistic literature follow the traits of realism, but they add the ideas that people and their lives are often deeply affected by natural forces such as heredity, environment, or even chance. People cannot control such forces, yet they must carry on the best way they can.

The main difference between the two movements is that naturalism emphasizes the lack of control its realistic characters have over the changes taking place in their lives. The influence of both literary movements can often be seen in the same piece of literature, such as "An Episode of War" by Stephen Crane.

DIRECTIONS: Read the following passages from "An Episode of War." Tell whether you think each one reflects realism, naturalism, or both. Explain your answer.

1. He was on the verge of a great triumph in mathematics, and the corporals were thronging forward, each to reap a little square [of coffee], when suddenly the lieutenant cried out and looked quickly at a man near him as if he suspected it was a case of personal assault. The others cried out also when they saw blood upon the lieutenant's sleeve.

   Realism, Naturalism, or both: _____

   Explain: _____

   _____

   _____

2. One, seeing his arm, began to scold. "Why, man, that's no way to do. You want to fix that thing." He appropriated the lieutenant and the lieutenant's wound. He cut the sleeve and laid bare the arm, every nerve of which softly fluttered under his touch. He bound his handkerchief over the wound, scolding away in the meantime.

   Realism, Naturalism, or both: _____

   Explain: _____

   _____

   _____

3. When he reached home, his sisters, his mother, his wife, sobbed for a long time at the sight of the flat sleeve. "Oh, well," he said, standing shamefaced amid these tears. "I don't suppose it matters so much as all that."

   Realism, Naturalism, or both: _____

   Explain: _____

   _____

Unit 4: Division, Reconciliation, and Expansion (1850–1914)

Name _____ Date _____

Build Vocabulary

Spelling Strategy When adding -ed to a word ending in a double consonant, keep both consonants, as in oppress + ed = oppressed.

Using the Root -press-

A. DIRECTIONS: The root -press- means "push." In addition to being a complete word itself in English, press is also combined with many different prefixes and suffixes to form other words. Choose one of the words in the box to complete each sentence.

express	suppress	pressurize
depression	press	impression

1. Barry tried hard to control himself, but he could not _____ his laughter.

2. In order to communicate with others, you must _____ your ideas clearly.

3. It is necessary to _____ an airplane's cabin so people can breathe at higher altitudes.

4. The dry cleaners will _____ the suit so it looks neat.

5. Anyone going on a job interview wants to make a good _____.

6. A person who feels sad all the time may be suffering from _____.

Using the Word Bank

oppressed	smite

B. DIRECTIONS: Match each word in the left column with its definition in the right column. Write the letter of the definition on the line next to the word it defines.

____ 1. oppressed   a. kill with a powerful blow

____ 2. smite   b. kept down by a cruel power or authority

C. DIRECTIONS: On the line, write the letter of the pair of words that best expresses a relationship similar to that expressed in the pair in CAPITAL LETTERS.

____ 1. SMITE: SLAP ::
     a. language: French
     b. seek: discover
     c. costume: clothing
     d. happy: miserable
     e. laugh: smile

____ 2. OPPRESSED : FREE ::
     a. myth : legend
     b. waiter : restaurant
     c. temporary : permanent
     d. computer : monitor
     e. scuff : scrape

"Swing Low, Sweet Chariot" and **"Go Down, Moses"** Spirituals

Grammar and Style: Direct Address

Direct address is the addressing of something or someone by name. In written works, the name of the person or thing being addressed directly is set off by one or more commas, depending on the element's location in the sentence.

Anne, sing this spiritual. [comma follows]

Sing the words more clearly, **Anne**. [comma precedes]

One goal of a spiritual, **Anne**, is to arouse strong emotion. [commas precede and follow]

A. Practice: In each sentence that contains an example of direct address, add one or more commas where necessary. If there is no direct address in a sentence, write *N* next to the number.

____ 1. Boys you should sing only the refrain.

____ 2. Listen carefully Stephanie and you'll hear the rhythm.

____ 3. Hand in the sheet music to Mr. Taylor after class.

____ 4. Spirituals often referred to biblical people and places such as Moses and Jordan.

____ 5. You can be the next soloist Troy.

____ 6. Let Caitlin improvise new lyrics.

____ 7. My dear child you must not be nervous about singing.

____ 8. Once again Ms. Lipton you've done an excellent job of preparing the chorus.

B. Writing Application: Direct address is often used in dialogue. Imagine a conversation among three or more characters on a subject of your own choosing. Write several lines of dialogue. Use three examples of direct address in your dialogue: one at the beginning of a sentence, one in the middle of a sentence, and one at the end of a sentence. Punctuate each example correctly.

_____

_____

_____

_____

_____

_____

_____

_____

_____

_____

_____

Unit 4: Division, Reconciliation, and Expansion (1850–1914)

"Swing Low, Sweet Chariot" and **"Go Down, Moses"** Spirituals

Reading Strategy: Listen

DIRECTIONS: Listen carefully to the sounds and rhythms of "Swing Low, Sweet Chariot" and "Go Down, Moses" as the two spirituals are read aloud. Pay particular attention to the rhymes and the sounds or phrases that are repeated. Often rhythm and repetition suggest a certain mood or attitude and contribute to the intensity of feeling generated by the song and its message. Fill in the two charts below to help you focus on your listening skills and identify the message presented in each spiritual.

"Swing Low, Sweet Chariot"
Words that rhyme
Words or phrases that are repeated
Mood or attitude suggested by rhyme and repetition
Overall message of spiritual
"Go Down, Moses"
Words that rhyme
Words or phrases that are repeated
Mood or attitude suggested by rhyme and repetition
Overall message of spiritual

"Swing Low, Sweet Chariot" and **"Go Down, Moses"** Spirituals

Literary Analysis: Refrain

A **refrain** is a word, phrase, line, or group of lines repeated at regular intervals. In spirituals, one of the main things a refrain does is emphasize the most important ideas. In "Go Down, Moses," for example, the refrain "Let my people go" is repeated seven times. The constant repetition serves to turn the cry for freedom into a demand for freedom.

DIRECTIONS: Answering the following questions will help you understand how the refrains in "Go Down, Moses" and "Swing Low, Sweet Chariot" function to enrich the spirituals' meanings.

1. Identify a refrain in "Swing Low, Sweet Chariot." _____
   _____
   _____

2. In "Go Down, Moses," are the words "Tell old Pharaoh" a refrain? Why or why not?
   _____
   _____

3. In "Swing Low, Sweet Chariot," are the words "a band of angels coming after me" a refrain? Why or why not?_____
   _____
   _____

4. In "Go Down, Moses" what emotional effect does the continual repetition of the refrains have? _____
   _____
   _____

5. Compare the refrains of "Go Down, Moses" and "Swing Low, Sweet Chariot." How are they alike and different? In your answer, consider what the refrains ask for or hope for and how those desires are conveyed in the two spirituals. _____
   _____
   _____
   _____
   _____
   _____
   _____
   _____
   _____
   _____
   _____
   _____

Unit 4: Division, Reconciliation, and Expansion (1850–1914)

from *My Bondage and My Freedom* by Frederick Douglass

Build Vocabulary

Spelling Strategy When creating the noun form of adjectives that end in *-ent* , replace the *t* with *-ce* or *-cy*. For example, the words *benevolent* and *stringent* become *benevolence* and *stringency.*

Using the Root *-bene-*

A. DIRECTIONS: The root *-bene-* means "well" or "good" and is part of many words relating to good-ness. Complete each sentence with one of these words: *beneficent, beneficial, beneficiary, benign.*

1. As a _____, my mother received some money and jewelry after her aunt's death.

2. The petitioners were fortunate to have a judge with a _____ temperament.

3. Her work with the sick in Calcutta made Mother Teresa one of the most _____ people of our time.

4. The labor reforms of the nineteenth century were _____ to factory workers struggling for better working conditions.

Using the Word Bank

congenial	benevolent	stringency
depravity	consternation	redolent

B. DIRECTIONS: Match each word in the left column with its definition in the right column. Write the letter of the definition on the line next to the word it defines.

____ 1. benevolent   a. agreeable

____ 2. congenial   b. strictness; severity

____ 3. consternation   c. kindly; charitable

____ 4. depravity   d. dismay; alarm

____ 5. redolent   e. corruption; wickedness

____ 6. stringency   f. suggestive

C. DIRECTIONS: For each item, choose the lettered word that is closest in meaning to the num-bered word. Circle the letter of your choice.

1. CONGENIAL:
   a. contagious b. advantageous c. contrasting d. friendly

2. BENEVOLENT:
   a. impartial b. generous c. sporadic d. impatient

3. STRINGENCY:
   a. indifference b. tightness c. dullness d. dishonesty

4. DEPRAVITY:
   a. viciousness b. indulgence c. abstinence d. deprivation

Name _____ Date _____

Grammar and Style: Correlative Conjunctions

Correlative conjunctions are pairs of connectors that link words and phrases that are grammatically similar. Common correlative conjunctions include *either . . . or; neither . . . nor; whether . . . or; not only . . . but also;* and *just as . . . so.* The following sentence from *My Bondage and My Freedom* illustrates the use of the correlative conjunctions *either . . . or.*

> She **either** thought it unnecessary, **or** she lacked the depravity indispensable to shutting me up in mental darkness.

A. Practice: In the following sentences, underline the correlative conjunctions. Write *N* next to the number if the sentence has none.

____ 1. Not only was he speeding, but he also ran a stop sign.

____ 2. The superintendent was concerned with whether the board would pass or vote down the resolution for a new gymnasium.

____ 3. Neither the ice cream parlor nor the supermarket had butter pecan ice cream.

____ 4. She collected money for the coaches' gifts just as she said she would.

____ 5. Did you read either of the books I gave you?

B. Writing Application: Complete each sentence so that the final version contains a pair of correlative conjunctions.

1. Just as soldiers must obey their superiors, _____

_____.

2. Neither the general _____

_____.

3. We didn't know whether we should visit the battlefield _____

_____.

4. Not only did soldiers fight each other, _____

_____.

5. The armies must either march through the forest_____

_____.

from *My Bondage and My Freedom* by Frederick Douglass

Reading Strategy: Establish a Purpose

Establishing a purpose for reading helps you get more out of what you read. In reading the excerpt from *My Bondage and My Freedom*, one possible purpose is to find out what slavery was like from the point of view of an enslaved person. As you read the selection, use this chart to list things that Frederick's intimate view of that experience can tell you.

Thoughts	
Feelings	
Events	

from *My Bondage and My Freedom* by Frederick Douglass

Literary Analysis: Autobiography

In his autobiography, Frederick Douglass provides his readers with a unique view of what it was like to be a slave. Douglass could have chosen to write a fictional work instead of an autobiography, but using an autobiographical form adds the power of real experiences to Douglass's story.

DIRECTIONS: Read the following passages from the selection. Describe the effect of each passage and suggest how the use of autobiography strengthens that effect.

> It was no easy matter to induce her to think and to feel that the curly-headed boy, . . . who was loved by little Tommy, and who loved little Tommy in turn; sustained to her only the relation of a chattel. I was *more* than that, and she felt me to be more than that. I could talk and sing; I could laugh and weep; I could reason and remember; I could love and hate.

_____

_____

_____

_____

> I was no longer the light-hearted, gleesome boy, full of mirth and play, as when I landed first at Baltimore. Knowledge had come . . . This knowledge opened my eyes to the horrible pit, and revealed the teeth of the frightful dragon that was ready to pounce upon me, but it opened no way for my escape.

_____

_____

_____

_____

> It was slavery—not its mere *incidents*—that I hated. I had been cheated. I saw through the attempt to keep me in ignorance . . . The feeding and clothing me well, could not atone for taking my liberty from me. The smiles of my mistress could not remove the deep sorrow that dwelt in my young bosom. Indeed, these, in time, came only to deepen my sorrow. She had changed; and the reader will see that I had changed, too. We were both victims to the same overshadowing evil—*she* as mistress, *I* as slave.

_____

_____

_____

_____

© Prentice-Hall, Inc.

Unit 4: Division, Reconciliation, and Expansion (1850–1914)

"An Occurrence at Owl Creek Bridge" by Ambrose Bierce

Build Vocabulary

Spelling Strategy When following the vowel *i*, the cluster *gn* at the end of a word or syllable makes that vowel long without adding a final *e*, as in *sign* and *assign*.

Using the Root *-sum-*

A. DIRECTIONS: The word root *-sum-* is Latin in origin and means "the highest." Some Latin phrases including this root are common in English. Given the meaning of the other words in these phrases, write a probable definition for each one.

1. *summum bonum;*   *bonum* means "good" _____

2. *summa cum laude;*   *cum laude* means "with praise" _____

Using the Word Bank

etiquette	deference	imperious	dictum	summarily
effaced	oscillation	apprised	malign	ineffable

B. DIRECTIONS: Replace the underlined word or phrase with a synonym from the Word Bank.

1. Any citizen caught ... will be <u>immediately</u> hanged.

_____

2. The intellectual part of his nature was already <u>erased</u>.

_____

3. circumstances of an <u>urgent</u> nature

_____

4. in the code of military <u>behavior</u>

_____

5. which had a secret and <u>very harmful</u> significance

_____

6. He swung through unthinkable arcs of <u>regular back-and-forth movement</u>.

_____

7. silence and fixity are forms of <u>courtesy</u>

_____

8. A sharp pain in his wrist <u>informed</u> him.

_____

9. with a smile of <u>inexpressible</u> joy

_____

10. a part of the frankly villainous <u>statement</u>

_____

"An Occurrence at Owl Creek Bridge" by Ambrose Bierce

Grammar and Style: Semicolons in Compound Sentences

Compound sentences can be formed by linking independent clauses with a **semicolon** instead of a conjunction. A semicolon emphasizes a very close connection between the ideas in the clauses; it can be a powerful stylistic writing tool.

No; I will not be shot; that is not fair.

A. Practice: Use a semicolon to combine each pair of sentences into a compound sentence.

1. It did not appear to be the duty of these two men to know what was occurring at the center of the bridge. They merely blockaded the two ends of the foot planking that traversed it.

   _____

   _____

2. He wore a mustache and pointed beard, but no whiskers. His eyes were large and dark gray, and had a kindly expression which one would hardly have expected in one whose neck was in the hemp.

   _____

   _____

3. The intervals of silence grew progressively longer. The delays became maddening.

   _____

   _____

4. The power of thought was restored. He knew that the rope had broken and he had fallen into the stream.

   _____

   _____

5. The captain had drawn his pistol, but did not fire. The others were unarmed.

   _____

B. Writing Application: Write a pair of compound sentences about what Peyton Farquhar thinks is happening and what is actually happening. In the first version, link the two clauses with a conjunction. In the second pair, link the two clauses with a semicolon. Both versions should contain the same information.

1. compound sentence with conjunctions:

   _____

   _____

   _____

2. compound sentence with semicolon:

   _____

   _____

   _____

Unit 4: Division, Reconciliation, and Expansion (1850–1914)

Name _____ Date _____

Reading Strategy: Chronological Order

To make their stories interesting, writers often begin with an especially dramatic event and then flash backward in time to supply the reader with necessary information. In "An Occurrence at Owl Creek Bridge," the author begins with Peyton Farquhar standing on the railroad bridge about to be hanged. Then he follows with a flashback to tell how Peyton Farquhar got into that situation. In addition, Bierce flashes forward to show events leaping forward in time.

As you read stories like this one, it is a good strategy to keep the **chronological order** clear in your mind.

DIRECTIONS: In the "mental" flashforward, Ambrose Bierce gives the reader many clues that the events are taking place in an imaginary future rather than in an actual present. Below are excerpts from the story. In the space provided, explain how each excerpt provides a clue to the nature of the flashforward.

1. He was now in full possession of his physical senses. They were, indeed, preternaturally keen and alert. Something in the awful disturbance of his organic system had so exalted and refined them that they made record of things never before perceived. He felt the ripples upon his face and heard their separate sounds as they struck.

   _____
   _____
   _____
   _____
   _____

2. Suddenly he felt himself whirled around and round—spinning like a top. The water, the banks, the forests, the now distant bridge, fort and men—all were commingled and blurred.

   _____
   _____
   _____
   _____

3. At last he found a road which led him in what he knew to be the right direction. It was as wide and straight as a city street, yet it seemed untraveled. No fields bordered it, no dwelling anywhere. Not so much as the barking of a dog suggested human habitation.

   _____
   _____
   _____
   _____
   _____

"An Occurrence at Owl Creek Bridge" by Ambrose Bierce

Literary Analysis: Point of View

A writer's purpose helps to determine the **point of view** from which a story is told. In "An Occurrence at Owl Creek Bridge," for example, Ambrose Bierce reveals the tragically ironic nature of war through the events surrounding one person—Peyton Farquhar. Limited third-person narration allows Bierce to explore Farquhar's thoughts and feelings while preserving the objective distance needed for the story's ironic ending.

DIRECTIONS: Rewrite the following passages of "An Occurrence at Owl Creek Bridge" from the point of view indicated. Be prepared to explain how each point of view changes the story.

1. The man who was engaged in being hanged was apparently about thirty-five years of age. He was a civilian, if one might judge from his habit, which was that of a planter. His features were good—straight nose, firm mouth, broad forehead, from which his long, dark hair was combed straight back, falling behind his ears to the collar of his well-fitting frock coat.

   First-person point of view _____

   _____

   _____

   _____

   _____

   _____

   _____

   _____

2. As Peyton Farquhar fell straight downward through the bridge he lost consciousness and was as one already dead. From this state he was awakened—ages later, it seemed to him—by the pain of a sharp pressure upon his throat, followed by a sense of suffocation.

   Third-person omniscient point of view _____

   _____

   _____

   _____

   _____

   _____

   _____

   _____

   _____

   _____

Unit 4: Division, Reconciliation, and Expansion (1850–1914)

"The Gettysburg Address" and **"Second Inaugural Address"** by Abraham Lincoln
"Letter to His Son" by Robert E. Lee

Build Vocabulary

Spelling Strategy Except when creating plurals, use -ss to spell the s sound at the end of a word, as in redress.

Using the Root -archy

A. DIRECTIONS: The following words each contain the word root -archy, meaning "rule" or "government." Combine your knowledge of this root with the meaning of each prefix provided to match the words with their definitions.

____ 1. oligarchy—*oligo-* "few"   a. rule by women

____ 2. matriarchy—*matri-* "mother"   b. rule by only one person

____ 3. monarchy—*mono-* "one", "alone", or "single" c. rule by a faction or small group

____ 4. patriarchy—*patri-* "father"   d. rule by men

Using the Word Bank

consecrate	hallow	deprecated	insurgents	discern
scourge	malice	anarchy	redress	

B. DIRECTIONS: Circle the synonym for the underlined word in each sentence or phrase.

1. . . . we cannot consecrate (bless, profane)

2. . . . we cannot hallow (honor, haunt)

3. Both parties deprecated war (awaited, condemned)

4. . . . shall we discern therein any departure from those divine attributes (demand, recognize)

5. . . . that this mighty scourge of war may speedily pass away. (affliction, miracle)

6. With malice toward none; (spite, spirit)

7. As far as I can judge by the papers, we are between a state of anarchy and civil war. (progress, chaos)

8. I feel the aggression and am willing to take every proper step for redress. (armament, atonement)

C. DIRECTIONS: For each item choose the word that is most nearly *opposite* in meaning to the numbered word. Circle the letter of your choice.

1. DISCERN: a. confuse b. distinguish c. indicate d. agree

2. MALICE: a. spite b. rudeness c. benevolence d. fear

3. ANARCHY: a. disorder b. rivalry c. curvature d. order

4. SCOURGE: a. pest b. reward c. sweeper d. doctor

5. INSURGENTS: a. supporters b. rivals c. rebels d. politicians

"The Gettysburg Address" and **"Second Inaugural Address"** by Abraham Lincoln
"Letter to His Son" by Robert E. Lee

Grammar and Style: Parallel Structure

The use of **parallel structure**, or the expression of similar ideas in similar form, helps to emphasize important concepts. Often, the most memorable excerpts from literature are those that contain examples of parallel structure. Look at this example from "The Gettysburg Address."

> But, in a larger sense, **we cannot** dedicate—**we cannot** consecrate—**we cannot** hallow this ground.

By repeating the phrase "we cannot," Lincoln creates a strong feeling of humility.

A. Practice: Underline each element of parallel structure in the excerpts below.

1. . . . testing whether that nation, or any nation so conceived and so dedicated, can long endure.

2. . . . —that from these honored dead we take increased devotion to that cause for which they gave the last full measure of devotion—that we here highly resolve that these dead shall not have died in vain—that this nation, under God, shall have a new birth of freedom. . . .

3. . . . —and that government of the people, by the people, for the people, shall not perish from the earth.

4. With malice toward none; with charity for all; with firmness in the right . . .

5. . . . one of them would *make* war rather than let the nation survive, and the other would *accept* war rather than let it perish.

B. Writing Application: Rewrite the paragraph below as a short speech introducing the subject of the Civil War. Use at least two instances of parallel structure in your speech.

The Civil War was a unique and terrible time in American history. Although slavery was probably the catalyst that started the war, many other regional factors, including economics, climate, and land, also divided the nation. The land in the North could not support large farms, therefore the northern states turned to trade and industry. This economic trend led to the growth of large cities and a fast-paced urban lifestyle. The southern states relied on agriculture, which resulted in a demand for cheap labor, small communities, and a generally slower pace of life. Friends and families were often divided in their loyalties, and sometimes faced each other on opposite sides of the battlefield. One state, Virginia, even divided itself, with Virginia remaining a Confederate state and West Virginia becoming a Union state.

_____

_____

_____

_____

_____

_____

_____

_____

Unit 4: Division, Reconciliation, and Expansion (1850–1914)

"The Gettysburg Address" and **"Second Inaugural Address"** by Abraham Lincoln
"Letter to His Son" by Robert E. Lee

Reading Strategy: Use Background Knowledge

Background knowledge may include information about the author, about the characters or subjects of the selection, or about the times and events discussed in the selection. Background knowledge can often include personal experience of people and experiences similar to those in the selection. You learned that Robert E. Lee believed in the Union but opposed both slavery and secession. In this activity, you will learn more about Robert E. Lee to understand further the personal conflict he felt.

DIRECTIONS: Read the information below. Then use the facts to explain your understanding of each excerpt from Lee's letter to his son.

- Lee attended the United States Military Academy at West Point in 1825, graduating in 1829.
- In the late 1840s, Lee served in the Mexican War, where he was recognized for his skill and courage.
- Lee's family was a well-established, important family of Virginia. His father was a cavalry commander in the Revolutionary War and a friend of George Washington. Lee admired the first president and named one of his sons George Washington Custis Lee.
- Lee was an honorable and respected man who displayed kindness and humor, and who did not smoke, drink alcohol, or swear.
- Lee did not believe in slavery. Long before the Civil War broke out, he freed the slaves he had inherited.
- Lee felt that Virginia stood for George Washington's principles. He considered the Civil War as a second "Revolutionary War" for independence.

1. How [Washington's] spirit would be grieved could he see the wreck of his mighty labors!

   _____

   _____

2. I feel the aggression [of acts of the North] and am willing to take every proper step for redress. It is the principle I contend for, not individual or private benefit.

   _____

   _____

3. As an American citizen, I take great pride in my country, her prosperity and institutions, and would defend any state if her rights were invaded.

   _____

   _____

4. [The dissolution of the Union] would be an accumulation of all the evils we complain of, and I am willing to sacrifice everything but honor for its preservation.

   _____

   _____

5. I shall mourn for my country and for the welfare and progress of mankind.

   _____

   _____

"The Gettysburg Address" and **"Second Inaugural Address"** by Abraham Lincoln
"Letter to His Son" by Robert E. Lee

Literary Analysis: Diction

Diction, or word choice, gives the writer's voice its unique quality. The writer's diction reflects the audience and purpose of the work.

DIRECTIONS: Read each question and pair of phrases or sentences below. Circle the letter of the phrase or sentence in which the diction suits the indicated writing purpose.

1. Which phrase is better suited for a letter?
   a. Four score and seven years ago . . .
   b. Eighty-seven years ago . . .

2. Which phrase is better suited for a letter?
   a. . . . that this awful war will end soon.
   b. . . . that this mighty scourge of war may speedily pass away.

3. Which phrase is better suited for a public speech?
   a. As a citizen of these United States, . . .
   b. As someone who lives in America, . . .

4. Which phrase is better suited for a letter?
   a. . . . we are stuck between chaos and war.
   b. . . . we find ourselves entrapped between anarchy and civil war.

5. Which phrase is better suited for a letter?
   a. No one will remember or pay attention to today's speeches, . . .
   b. The world will little note, nor long remember what we say here, . . .

6. Which sentence is better suited for a public speech?
   a. These slaves constituted a peculiar and powerful interest.
   b. These slaves were very valuable to some.

7. Which sentence is better suited for a public speech?
   a. We are met on a great battlefield of that war.
   b. Here we are at this great battlefield.

8. Which phrase is better suited for a public speech?
   a. Neither side expected it would be so bad or so long . . .
   b. Neither party expected . . . the magnitude, or the duration . . .

9. Which phrase is better suited for a public speech?
   a. . . . they gave the last full measure of devotion . . .
   b. . . . they died.

10. Which phrase is better suited for a public speech?
    a. . . . will not disappear.
    b. . . . shall not perish from the earth.

11. Which phrase is better suited for a letter?
    a. . . . all thoughts were anxiously directed to an impending civil war.
    b. . . . we were all worried that there might be a civil war.

© Prentice-Hall, Inc.

Unit 4: Division, Reconciliation, and Expansion (1850–1914)

from Civil War Diaries, Journals, and Letters

Build Vocabulary

Spelling Strategy Verbs that end in -ate have noun forms ending in -ion. Drop the final -e before adding the suffix, as in imprecate/imprecation and capitulate/capitulation.

Using the Prefix ob-

A. DIRECTIONS: The prefix ob- means "against" or "toward." Each word that follows contains the prefix ob-. Given the meaning of the other word part, match the words with their definitions.

____ 1. obliterate = ob + littera "letter"   a. to get possession of

____ 2. oblong = ob + longus "long"   b. showing a great willingness to serve or obey

____ 3. obnoxious = ob + noxa "harm"   c. exposed to injury or evil

____ 4. obsequious = ob + sequi "to follow"   d. to blot out or leave no trace

____ 5. obtain = ob + tenere "to hold"   e. longer in one direction than in the other

Using the Word Bank

capitulate	audaciously	foreboding
obstinate	imprecations	serenity

B. DIRECTIONS: Circle the synonym for the underlined word in each sentence or phrase.

1. Anderson will not capitulate. (argue, surrender)

2. Men were more audaciously wise and witty. (noisily, daringly)

3. We had a foreboding that it was to be our last pleasant meeting. (presentiment, pact)

4. If Anderson was obstinate—he was to order the forts on our side to open fire. (stupid, stubborn)

5. . . . if anything, more unruffled than usual in his serenity. . . . (calmness, dress)

C. DIRECTIONS: For each item, choose the word pair that best expresses a relationship similar to that expressed in the numbered pair. Circle the letter of your choice.

1. FOREBODING : EMOTION ::
   a. buyer : consumer
   b. headache : pain
   c. style : manner
   d. prologue : epilogue

2. FLEXIBLE : OBSTINATE::
   a. table : chair
   b. serene : quiet
   c. ecstatic : depressed
   d. invisible: fog

3. BOLDLY : AUDACIOUSLY ::
   a. hurriedly : rapidly
   b. doubtfully : possibly
   c. graciously : meanly
   d. largely: narrowly

4. PEACEFUL : SERENITY ::
   a. calm : scheme
   b. mischievous : seriousness
   c. pious : faith
   d. quiet : chirping

Name _____ Date _____

Grammar and Style: Capitalization of Proper Nouns

The capitalization of proper nouns helps the reader easily identify particular persons, places, things, or ideas. When a proper noun consists of more than one word, capitalize each word except articles, coordinating conjunctions, and prepositions with fewer than four letters.

Examples:

General Ewell's order [specific person]
the crest of Culp's Hill [specific place]
remnant of the Third North Carolina [specific thing]

A. Practice: Rewrite each proper noun with correct capitalization. If there is no proper noun, write *none*.

1. People rejoiced when they heard the emancipation proclamation. _____

2. Many soldiers died in the battle of gettysburg. _____

3. The general's troops camped along a river. _____

4. Shells burst over fort sumter. _____

5. General ulysses s. grant gave the order. _____

B. Writing Application: Rewrite each sentence to replace each underlined common noun with a proper noun. Your proper nouns can be real or imaginary people, places, or things. Be sure to capitalize the proper nouns correctly.

1. The war caused great suffering to the civilian population.

_____

2. Inhabitants of the city lacked food and other supplies.

_____

3. Each morning, the newspaper announced the most recent casualties.

_____

4. The president struggled to make the right decision.

_____

5. The book is a fictionalized account of a spy's activities.

_____

6. A doctor was tending the general's wounds.

_____

Unit 4: Division, Reconciliation, and Expansion (1850–1914)

from Civil War Diaries, Journals, and Letters

Reading Strategy: Distinguish Fact From Opinion

When reading a diary, journal, or letter, it is important to **distinguish fact from opinion**. You can do this by reading carefully and periodically determining which statements can be verified and which statements reflect the writer's personal views.

DIRECTIONS: Read the following excerpts from the selection. Each statement contains both fact and opinion. Identify the elements of fact and opinion in each one.

1. John Manning was pleased as a boy to be on Beauregard's staff while the row goes on.

   Fact: _____

   Opinion: _____

2. Why did that green goose Anderson go into Fort Sumter?

   Fact: _____

   Opinion: _____

3. "Get up, you foolish woman—your dress is on fire," cried a man.

   Fact: _____

   Opinion: _____

4. . . . the flannel shirt was coarse and unpleasant, too large at the neck and too short elsewhere.

   Fact: _____

   Opinion: _____

5. On swept the gallant little brigade . . .

   Fact: _____

   Opinion: _____

6. By the strenuous efforts of the officers of the line and of the staff, order was restored . . .

   Fact: _____

   Opinion: _____

7. Yesterday we fought a great battle and gained a great victory . . .

   Fact: _____

   Opinion: _____

8. The third sheet from the press was grabbed for by several, but I succeeded in procuring so much of it as contained the proclamation, and off I went for life and death.

   Fact: _____

   Opinion: _____

from Civil War Diaries, Journals, and Letters

Literary Analysis: Diaries, Journals, Letters

Diaries and **journals** are private, personal records of events, communications, and observations, and often reveal a writer's innermost thoughts and feelings. Personal **letters** are also often written in an informal style, since there is usually no intent of publication.

DIRECTIONS: Complete each item using information from the selection and what you know about diaries, journals, and letters.

1. Mary Chesnut writes "In addition to our usual quartet (Judge Withers, Langdon Cheves, and Trescot) our two governors dined with us, Means and Manning. These men all talked so delightfully. For once in my life I listened." What information of a personal nature indicates that this excerpt is from a diary or journal? _____

_____

2. How is Mary Chesnut's description of sitting on the roof to watch the firing on Fort Sumter typical of information found in a diary or journal?_____

_____

3. Much of the first paragraph of "Recollections of a Private" discusses Warren Lee Goss's shaving on the morning he went to enlist. What might you learn about Goss from such a description? _____

_____

4. Warren Lee Goss writes "[w]ith a nervous tremor convulsing my system, and my heart thumping like muffled drumbeats, I stood before the door of the recruiting office. . . ." Use a short sentence to describe how Goss felt about enlisting. _____

_____

5. Read Warren Lee Goss's description of his first day of drilling in company. What kind of personality do you think Goss had in civilian life?_____

_____

6. Randolph McKim's account of the Battle of Gettysburg tells of only one small part of the battle. How is this indicative of a diary or journal? _____

_____

7. Stonewall Jackson's letter to his wife tells of a coat. Why doesn't Jackson describe the coat in detail for his wife?_____

_____

8. In his "Reaction to the Emancipation Proclamation," Reverend Henry M. Turner describes a crowd willing to hug President Lincoln to death. What does this description suggest about Turner's feelings for Lincoln?

_____

9. Sojourner Truth writes that "[i]t is hard for the old slaveholding spirit to die. But die it must. . . ." What does this tell of her personal convictions about slavery and freedom?

_____

© Prentice-Hall, Inc.   from Civil War Diaries, Journals, and Letters **131**

"Gulf War Journal" from _A Woman at War_ by Molly Moore

Build Vocabulary: Specialized Vocabulary

Specialized vocabulary often finds its way into everyday speech. Have you ever "waited in the wings" or felt "on the spot"? Both of these phrases come from the world of theater, where they have specific meanings. (The "spot" is the spotlight that highlights a performer, while actors "wait in the wings," or offstage, until it is their time to go on stage.) Recognizing and mastering words and phrases that have both specialized and general usages is an important vocabulary skill. In Molly Moore's "Gulf War Journal," a number of words used in the context of war and journalism can be used in more general ways.

DIRECTIONS: For each listed word or phrase, write a sentence using the term that adapts its specific meaning to a more general context. Then write two definitions for the word: its specialized meaning and its general meaning. Refer to the selection if you need help figuring out the meaning of the word.

1. afterburners: _____

_____

Definitions: _____

_____

2. disinformation: _____

_____

Definitions: _____

_____

3. pool report: _____

_____

Definitions: _____

_____

4. counterattack: _____

_____

Definitions: _____

_____

5. humvee: _____

_____

Definitions: _____

_____

6. flak: _____

_____

Definitions: _____

_____

"Gulf War Journal" from *A Woman at War* by Molly Moore

Thematic Connection: Revealing the Hidden Faces of War

One aspect of wartime is the experiences of the reporters on the scene and the difficulties they face trying to report their stories to the public. This perspective was explored in greater depth than before during the Gulf War. Sometimes, as with the reporting of Peter Arnett of CNN from Baghdad or the capture of CBS correspondent Bob Simon, members of the media themselves became part of the story. Wouldn't it be interesting to turn the tables on a reporter with an interview on how he or she reports on war?

DIRECTIONS: Use the entries below to plan an interview with Molly Moore about her experiences during the Gulf War. First, note some issues or areas of information you would like to investigate. Then use your notes to formulate specific questions.

What I'd Like to Know: _____
_____
_____
_____

Questions for Molly Moore:

1. _____
_____
_____

2. _____
_____
_____

3. _____
_____
_____

4. _____
_____
_____

5. _____
_____
_____

6. _____
_____
_____

Unit 4: Division, Reconciliation, and Expansion (1850–1914)

"The Boys' Ambition" from *Life on the Mississippi* and "The Notorious Jumping Frog of Calaveras County" by Mark Twain

Build Vocabulary

Spelling Strategy The letters *a*, *o*, and *u* following the letter *g* indicate the "hard" sound of *g*, as in *goat* and *garrulous*. The letters *i* and *e* following a *g* often indicate the "soft" sound, as in *cottage*, *prodigious*, and *generous*.

Using the Prefix *mono-*

A. DIRECTIONS: The prefix *mono-* means "alone," "single," or "one." Use the clues given and what you know about the prefix *mono-* to figure out these word puzzles.

1. knowing two languages = *bilingual;*

   knowing one language = _____

2. paralysis of one side of the body = *hemiplegia;*

   paralysis of a single limb = _____

3. a word with four or more syllables = *polysyllable*

   a word with one syllable = _____

4. having three of one type of chromosome = *trisomic*

   having a single chromosome = _____

Using the Word Bank

| transient | prodigious | eminence | garrulous |
| conjectured | monotonous | interminable | ornery |

B. DIRECTIONS: In the blank, write the letter of the Word Bank word that is closest in meaning to the numbered word.

_____ 1. guessed   a. transient

_____ 2. celebrity   b. prodigious

_____ 3. temporary   c. monotonous

_____ 4. bad tempered   d. conjectured

_____ 5. talkative   e. ornery

_____ 6. unvarying   f. interminable

_____ 7. enormous   g. garrulous

_____ 8. endless   h. eminence

"The Boys' Ambition" from *Life on the Mississippi* and **"The Notorious Jumping Frog of Calaveras County"** by Mark Twain

Grammar and Style: Double Negatives

A **double negative** is the use of two negative words when only one is needed.

> **Double negative:** They <u>don't</u> have <u>no</u> business here.

> **Correct:** They <u>don't</u> have <u>any</u> business here.   or   They have <u>no</u> business here.

Double negatives are not acceptable in standard English.

A. Practice: Rewrite each of the following examples in standard English, eliminating the double negatives.

1. "There couldn't be no solit'ry thing mentioned."

   _____

2. "He didn't try no more to win the fight."

   _____

3. "He hadn't no opportunities to speak of."

   _____

4. "He never done nothing for three months."

   _____

5. "I ain't got no frog."

   _____

B. Writing Application: Decide if the sentences below contain double negatives. If the sentence is written correctly, write "correct" on the line that follows it. If the sentence contains a double negative, rewrite it correctly.

1. She cannot have no dog.

   _____

2. I didn't find any witnesses.

   _____

3. They had no business there, neither.

   _____

4. He wouldn't take no bribe from the lawyer.

   _____

5. The sentence did not contain a single negative.

   _____

Unit 4: Division, Reconciliation, and Expansion (1850–1914)

Name _____ Date _____

"The Boys' Ambition" from *Life on the Mississippi* and **"The Notorious Jumping Frog of Calaveras County"** by Mark Twain

Reading Strategy: Understand Regional Dialect

Regional dialect is the informal language people use in everyday speech. Sometimes fiction writers use regional dialect to give readers a picture of certain characters. If you find it hard to understand this language, when you're reading, try reading it aloud.

DIRECTIONS: Read the following excerpts from "The Notorious Jumping Frog of Calaveras County." Write in your own words what you think each one means.

1. ". . . he was the curiousest man about always betting on anything that turned up you ever see, if he could get anybody to bet on the other side; and if he couldn't he'd change sides."

   _____

   _____

   _____

2. "Thish-yer Smiley had a mare—the boys called her the fifteen-minute nag, but that was only in fun, you know, because of course she was faster than that—and he used to win money on that horse, for all she was so slow and always had the asthma, or the distemper, or the consumption, or something of that kind."

   _____

   _____

   _____

3. ". . . to look at him you'd think he warn't worth a cent but to set around and look ornery and lay for a chance to steal something. But as soon as money was up on him he was a different dog; his under-jaw'd begin to stick out like the fo'castle of a steamboat, and his teeth would uncover and shine like the furnaces."

   _____

   _____

   _____

4. ". . . all of a sudden he would grab that other dog jest by the j'int of his hind leg and freeze to it—not chaw, you understand, but only just grip and hang on till they threw up the sponge, if it was a year."

   _____

   _____

   _____

5. "Well, thish-yer Smiley had a yaller one-eyed cow that didn't have no tail, only just a short stump like a bannanner, and—"

   _____

   _____

   _____

"The Boys' Ambition" from *Life on the Mississippi* and "The Notorious Jumping Frog of Calaveras County" by Mark Twain

Literary Analysis: Humor

Humor in literature is writing that is intended to evoke laughter. Western American humorists use a variety of techniques to make their writing amusing. Mark Twain, for example, commonly uses exaggeration, regional dialects, and colorful metaphors.

DIRECTIONS: Decide whether the following passages are humorous because they contain exaggeration, dialect, colorful metaphor, or a combination of these elements. Write your answer on the lines following each passage.

1. "He was the curiousest man about always betting on anything that turned up you ever see. . . ."

   _____

   _____

2. "If he even see a straddle bug start to go anywheres, he would bet you how long it would take him to get to . . . wherever . . . and if you took him up, he would foller that straddle bug to Mexico. . . ."

   _____

   _____

3. " . . . and *always* fetch up at the stand just about a neck ahead, as near as you could cipher it down."

   _____

   _____

4. 'He'd spring straight up and snake a fly off'n a counter there, and flop down on the floor ag'in as solid as a gob of mud."

   _____

   _____

Build Vocabulary

Spelling Strategy In English words, the letter *q* is almost always followed by the letter *u*, as in *querulous*.

Using the Root *-bel-*

The word root *-bel-* means "war," and a word that contains this root probably has something to do with warfare or conflict. For example, the word *antebellum* means "before the war," and specifically refers to the period preceding the Civil War. The word *postbellum*, meaning "after the war," specifically refers to the period following the Civil War.

A. DIRECTIONS: Read each sentence below and fill in the missing adjective, either *antebellum* or *postbellum*.

1. The _____ South had a largely agricultural economy and an easy-paced way of life.

2. The _____ North already believed in industry and modernization.

3. The _____ United States needed to bring together a nation once torn apart.

Using the Word Bank

expatriated	anathema	bellicose	recumbent
equanimity	vociferation	vituperative	querulous

B. DIRECTIONS: Write the Word Bank word that is closest in meaning to the italicized word or phrase in each sentence.

1. "It was her last *abusively spoken* attempt, . . ." _____

2. "Uncle Billy passed rapidly from a *quarrelsome* state into one of stupor, . . ." _____

3. ". . . the *deported* party consisted of . . ." _____

4. "'I'm going,' she said, in a voice of *fault-finding* weakness, . . ." _____

5. "As he gazed at his *resting* fellow exiles, . . ." _____

6. ". . . Uncle Billy included the whole party in one sweeping *curse*." _____

7. ". . . sang with great earnestness and *vehement shouting*." _____

8. ". . . to that calm *composure* for which he was notorious." _____

"The Outcasts of Poker Flat" by Bret Harte

Grammar and Style: Coordinating Conjunctions in Compound Sentences

Conjunctions are words that connect words, phrases, clauses, or sentences. **Coordinating conjunctions** (*and, or, nor, for, so,* and *yet*) connect words, phrases, or clauses of equal weight—particularly in compound sentences.

A. DIRECTIONS: Identify the coordinating conjunctions in the following sentences, and explain the linking or contrasting function that each performs.

1. Two or three men, conversing earnestly together, ceased as he approached, and exchanged significant glances.

   _____

2. Mr. Oakhurst knew that scarcely half the journey to Sandy Bar was accomplished, and the party were not equipped or provisioned for delay.

   _____

3. They had been engaged a long time, but old Jake Woods had objected, and so they had run away.

   _____

4. It was apparently of a jocular nature, for he felt impelled to slap his leg again and cram his fist into his mouth.

   _____

B. DIRECTIONS: Use coordinating conjunctions to combine each of the following groups of sentences into a single compound sentence.

1. John Oakhurst was escorted to the outskirts of town. Two women and a suspected thief were also escorted out of town.

   _____

   _____

2. When he awakens the next morning, Mr. Oakhurst discovers that it has snowed during the night. He also discovers that Uncle Billy has stolen the mules and horses. Uncle Billy has not stolen the provisions.

   _____

   _____

3. Mr. Oakhurst was strong enough to take care of the other outcasts. He was not strong enough to put up a fight against the hardships that they faced.

   _____

   _____

"The Outcasts of Poker Flat" by Bret Harte

Reading Strategy: Question the Text

Questioning the text often helps the reader better understand the selection. By asking questions as you read and then looking for answers, you can help yourself get more out of a selection.

DIRECTIONS: Reread "The Outcasts of Poker Flat" and then write the answer to each question below its excerpt.

1. "It was experiencing a spasm of virtuous reaction, quite as lawless and ungovernable as any of the acts that had provoked it."

   What was the "virtuous reaction?"

   _____

   _____

2. "With the easy good humor characteristic of his class, he insisted upon exchanging his own riding horse, 'Five Spot,' for the sorry mule which the Duchess rode."

   What significance does the trading of "Five Spot" for the mule have in the selection?

   _____

   _____

3. "At noon the Duchess, rolling out of her saddle upon the ground, declared her intention of going no farther, and the party halted."

   How does this singular act ultimately have a major effect on the story?

   _____

   _____

4. "In the fresh, open face of the newcomer Mr. Oakhurst recognized Tom Simson, otherwise known as the 'Innocent' of Sandy Bar. . . . [H]e had run away with Piney Woods."

   Why does the author introduce Tom Simson and Piney Woods to the story?

   _____

   _____

5. "'Piney can stay with Mrs. Oakhurst,' said the Innocent, pointing to the Duchess, . . ."

   What significance does this conversation have on the reader's understanding of the character of Tom Simson?

   _____

   _____

6. "'I reckon now you're used to fine things at Poker Flat,' said Piney. The Duchess turned away sharply to conceal something that reddened her cheeks through its professional tint, . . ."

   Why do you think the Duchess blushed?

   _____

   _____

"The Outcasts of Poker Flat" by Bret Harte

Literary Analysis: Regionalism

Regionalism is a type of literature whose purpose is to display the "local color" of a region, often by showing the distinctive qualities of the people and the physical environment. This is often done through explanation of customs and attitudes, accurate representation of local speech patterns, and a description of the unique environment.

DIRECTIONS: Read each excerpt below. Explain what it shows about Poker Flat and the old West.

1. "There was a Sabbath lull in the air which, in a settlement unused to Sabbath influences, looked ominous."

   _____
   _____
   _____

2. "In that advanced season, the party soon passed out of the moist, temperate regions of the foothills into the dry, cold, bracing air of the Sierras."

   _____
   _____
   _____

3. "A wooded amphitheater, surrounded on three sides by precipitous cliffs of naked granite, sloped gently toward the crest of another precipice that overlooked the valley."

   _____
   _____
   _____

4. "Mr. Oakhurst did not drink. It interfered with a profession which required coolness, impassiveness, and presence of mind, and, in his own language, he 'couldn't afford it.'"

   _____
   _____
   _____

5. "He now proposed to narrate the principal incidents of that poem—having thoroughly mastered the argument and fairly forgotten the words—in the current vernacular of Sandy Bar. . . .Most especially was he interested in the fate of 'Ash-heels,' as the Innocent persisted in denominating the 'swift-footed Achilles.'"

   _____
   _____
   _____

6. ". . . [T]hey found the deuce of clubs pinned to the bark with a bowie knife . . . with a Derringer by his side. . ."

   _____
   _____
   _____

"Heading West" by Miriam Davis Colt
"I Will Fight No More Forever" by Chief Joseph

Build Vocabulary

Spelling Strategy When adding *-ed* to a one-syllable word that ends in a single consonant preceded by a vowel, double the final consonant: *rub* + *-ed* = *rubbed*.

Using the Latin Term *terra firma*

The Latin words *terra firma* mean "firm earth" or "solid ground." *Terra* can also mean "land,"
or "territory," as in words like *terra incognita* ("unknown territory"), or "earth" as in *terra cotta*
("baked earth"), unglazed fired clay or pottery.

A. DIRECTIONS: For each situation below, write a descriptive sentence that contains the term
terra firma, terra incognita, or *terra cotta.*

1. discoveries made by archaeologists digging up an ancient city

    _____

2. an astronaut arriving back on earth after six months in a space station

    _____

3. where the Nez Percé were when the government exiled them

    _____

Using the Word Bank

genial	pervading	terra firma	emigrants
profusion	depredations	nonplused	

B. DIRECTIONS: Rewrite each sentence below, replacing the italicized word or phrase with an appropriate word from the Word Bank.

1. There were *people who moved* from many lands to America.

    _____

2. As far as the eye could see, the prairie was covered by a *great abundance* of wild flowers.

    _____

3. The settlers hoped to find new land with a *mild* climate.

    _____

4. The feeling *prevalent throughout* the Nez Percé camp was despair.

    _____

5. The weary travelers were happy to disembark and find *firm earth* under their feet.

    _____

6. Some settlers were *bewildered* by what they found.

    _____

7. Townspeople often had to protect their property from *plundering* by lawless gangs.

    _____

"Heading West" by Miriam Davis Colt
"I Will Fight No More Forever" by Chief Joseph

Grammar and Style: Sentence Fragments

Many of the entries in Miriam Colt's journal are **sentence fragments**—incomplete sentences that lack a subject, verb, or both. Although sentence fragments are acceptable for taking notes or making quick, informal journal entries, they are not acceptable in finished writing.

Sentence fragment missing subject: Have driven 18 miles today.

Sentence fragment missing verb: The lovely day.

Sentence fragment missing subject and verb: In the far west.

A. Practice: These sentences and sentence fragments are from "Heading West." Read each one. If a sentence is complete, write "correct" in blank following it. If it is a fragment, rewrite it as a complete sentence.

1 "We are making every necessary preparation for our journey, and our home in Kansas."

_____

2. "Go up, up, up, and upstairs to our lodging rooms."

_____

3. "On board steamer 'Cataract,' bound for Kansas City."

_____

4. "Large droves of cattle are driven into town to be sold to emigrants, who like us, are going into the Territory."

_____

5. "Think Mrs. Voorhees will get walking enough crossing this prairie."

_____

B. Writing Application: Rewrite each of these passages from "Heading West" to eliminate all sentence fragments.

1. "Found ourselves in this miserable hotel before we knew it. Miserable fare—herring boiled with cabbage—miserable, dirty beds, and an odor pervading the house that is not at all agreeable. Mistress gone."

_____

_____

_____

2. "One mile from the city, and Dr. Thorn has broke his wagon tongue; it must be sent back to Kansas City to be mended. Fires kindled—women cooking—supper eaten sitting around on logs, stones, and wagon tongues."

_____

_____

_____

"**Heading West**" by Miriam Davis Colt
"**I Will Fight No More Forever**" by Chief Joseph

Reading Strategy: Respond

Effective readers connect what they read with their own experiences, feelings, and ideas. Taking time to notice how you respond to what you are reading not only will increase your enjoyment, but also improve your understanding.

DIRECTIONS: Use the chart below to track your responses to your reading. In the first column, note specific words, phrases, and passages from the selections that had a strong effect on you. In the second column, list ideas, emotions and images that the words evoked. In the third column note how your response added to your understanding.

Words, Phrases, Passages	Ideas, Emotions, Images	Improved Understanding

"Heading West" by Miriam Davis Colt
"I Will Fight No More Forever" by Chief Joseph

Literary Analysis: Tone

Tone is usually revealed through word choice, treatment of characters and events, and —especially in a speech—voice and body language. It is usually described by adjectives such as angry, humorous, or sympathetic.

A. DIRECTIONS: Read each of the following passages. On the line, write the letter of the adjective that best describes the tone.

____ 1. "I want to have time to look for my children and see how many I can find. Maybe I shall find them among the dead."—Chief Joseph
   a. warlike   b. despairing   c. questioning   d. calm

____ 2. "There is no retreat but in submission and slavery! Our chains are forged! Their clanging may be heard on the plains of Boston! The war is inevitable—and let it come! I repeat, sir, let it come! —Patrick Henry, "Speech in the Virginia Convention"
   a. sarcastic   b. objective   c. annoyed   d. challenging

____ 3. "Proceed, great chief, with virtue on thy side.
   Thy ev'ry action let the goddess guide,
   A crown, a mansion, and a throne that shine.
   With gold unfading, WASHINGTON! be thine." —Phyllis Wheatley, "To His
                                                      Excellency, George Washington"

   a. amused   b. victorious   c. yearning   d. scandalized

____ 4. "The grave was made beneath the shade of some noble oaks. It had been carefully watched to the present hour by the Pawnees of the Loup, and is often shown to the traveler and the trader as a spot where a just white man sleeps." —James Fenimore Cooper, *The Prairie*

   a. respectful   b. gloomy   c. critical   d. bitter

B. Directions: Imagine that you are Miriam Davis Colt. On the lines provided, write an entry for "Heading West" that reflects the tone of one of the following the adjectives. Title your entry using the adjective you choose.

   despairing   amused   gloomy   annoyed   critical

_____

_____

_____

_____

_____

_____

_____

_____

_____

"To Build a Fire" by Jack London

Build Vocabulary

Spelling Strategy When a word ending in a *y* preceded by a consonant has a suffix added to it, the *y* is usually changed to an *i*. For example, *peremptory* + *ly* = *peremptorily*.

Using the Latin Root *-ject-*

The Latin root *-ject-* comes from a verb meaning "to throw" and appears in many English words.

A. DIRECTIONS: Read the list of prefixes and their meanings. Then read each sentence and explain how the prefix and the root *-ject-* influence the meaning of the underlined word.

de- = "down"	*ob-* = "in the way"; "against"
e- = "out of"	*sub-* = "under"
in- = "into"	

1. The pilot saved himself by <u>ejecting</u> from the cockpit as the plane went down.

_____

2. We were sure that the coach would <u>object</u> to our missing practice.

_____

3. Jillian became <u>dejected</u> when she learned that she had failed the history test.

_____

4. Paul's doctor gave him an <u>injection</u> of antibiotics to help cure his pneumonia.

_____

5. The emperor was harsh and cruel to his <u>subjects</u>.

_____

Using the Word Bank

conjectural	unwonted	conflagration	peremptorily

B. DIRECTIONS: Each question consists of a related pair of words in CAPITAL LETTERS, followed by four lettered pairs of words. Choose the lettered pair that best expresses a relationship *similar* to that expressed in the numbered pair and circle the letter of your choice.

1. CAMPFIRE : CONFLAGRATION ::
   a. car : truck
   b. spark : match
   c. flurry : blizzard
   d. sun : desert

2. CONJECTURAL : CERTAIN ::
   a. guess : fact
   b. generous : charitable
   c. delicious : tasty
   d. shifting : fixed

3. COMMANDS : PEREMPTORILY ::
   a. awakes : retires
   b. sings : ballads
   c. moves : forward
   d. dances : gracefully

4. UNWONTED : SURPRISING ::
   a. undesired : hating
   b. cruel : frightening
   c. sparse : meager
   d. routine : unusual

"To Build a Fire" by Jack London

Grammar and Style: Adverb Clauses

Adverb clauses are subordinate clauses that modify verbs, adjectives, or other adverbs. They explain or describe *how, when, where, why, under what circumstances,* and *to what extent.*

Adverb clause telling *when:* When he touched a twig, he had to look and see whether or not he had hold of it.

Adverb clause telling *why:* He ran because he was afraid.

A. Practice: Some of these sentences from "To Build a Fire" contain an adverb clause. Read each sentence, and when you find an adverb clause, underline it. Then note whether it tells *how, when, where, why, under what circumstances,* or *to what extent.* For sentences that do not contain an adverb clause, write *none.*

1. "If he fell down it would shatter itself, like glass, into brittle fragments."

   _____

2. "It knew that it was no time for traveling."

   _____

3. "So long as he walked four miles an hour, he pumped that blood, willy nilly, to the surface."

   _____

4. "When all was ready, the man reached in his pocket. . . ."

   _____

5. "It was all pure white, rolling in gentle undulations where the ice jams of the freeze-up had formed."

   _____

6. "As he turned to go on, he spat speculatively."

   _____

7. ". . . [H]e bit them off as well as he could with his teeth."

   _____

B. Writing Application: Combine each pair of simple sentences below into one complex sentence containing an adverb clause. Underline the adverb clause.

1. Spring water lay hidden under the snow. The man tried to avoid walking there.

   _____

   _____

2. The man built a fire right under a snow-laden tree. The snow fell and extinguished the flame.

   _____

   _____

   _____

Unit 4: Division, Reconciliation, and Expansion (1850–1914)

"To Build a Fire" by Jack London

Reading Strategy: Predict

Making predictions about what you are reading based on clues in the text and on your own previous experience can increase your enjoyment of a literary work and help you be a more effective reader. Of course, not all your predictions will match the outcomes in the text. You may have to change your predictions as you read further and discover additional clues.

DIRECTIONS: As you read "To Build a Fire," watch for clues that can help you predict what will happen next. In the chart below, list the clues, your predictions based on those clues, and the actual outcomes from the text.

CLUE	PREDICTION	OUTCOME

Name _____ Date _____

Literary Analysis: Conflict

Conflict is the struggle between two opposing forces or characters. An **internal conflict** is a struggle between conflicting thoughts and emotions within a character's mind. You face an internal conflict, for example, when you want to spend time studying for a test, yet you also want to go to the movie with your friends. An **external conflict** is a struggle between a character and an outside force, such as another character, society, nature, or fate. A pilot trying to land an airplane in strong winds is engaged in an external conflict—person against nature.

DIRECTIONS: Following are brief excerpts from "To Build a Fire." Identify the conflict in each as internal or external. Then name the opposing forces—person against internal self, or person against nature, fate, another character, or society—and briefly explain the conflict.

1. "It was seventy-five below zero. Since the freezing point is thirty-two above zero, it meant that one hundred and seven degrees of frost obtained."

   _____

2. "There was nobody to talk to; and, had there been, speech would have been impossible because of the ice-muzzle on his mouth."

   _____

3. "He tried to keep this thought down, to forget it, to think of something else, he was aware of the panicky feeling that it caused and he was afraid of the panic."

   _____

4. "He spoke to the dog . . . but in his voice was a strange note of fear that frightened the animal. . . . As it came within reaching distance, the man lost his control."

   _____

5. "High up in the tree one bough capsized its load of snow. . . it grew like an avalanche, and it descended without warning upon the man and the fire, and fire was blotted out!"

   _____

6. "He was very careful. He drove the thought of his freezing feet, and nose, and cheeks, out of his mind, devoting his whole soul to the matches."

   _____

7. ". . . it was a matter of life and death. This threw him into a panic, and he turned and ran up the creekbed along the old, dim trail."

   _____

8. "Well, he was bound to freeze anyway, and he might as well take it decently."

   _____

Name _____ Date _____

from _Lonesome Dove_ by Larry McMurtry

Build Vocabulary

This selection uses the word _aggrieved_, showing its meaning in the context. It also makes use of many words associated with horses and the West.

DIRECTIONS: See if you can put _aggrieved_ together with the "western" words. For each "western" word below, write a sentence that uses the word correctly and includes the word _aggrieved_.

1. remuda

_____
_____
_____
_____

2. loped

_____
_____
_____
_____

3. spooked

_____
_____
_____
_____

4. chaparral

_____
_____
_____
_____

5. mesquite

_____
_____
_____
_____

from *Lonesome Dove* by Larry McMurtry

Thematic Connection: Forging New Frontiers

A major theme of *Lonesome Dove* is the difference and tension between the romance and reality of the West. Most of us have, at some time, been exposed to the myth of the cowboy. In this selection, you catch a glimpse of the gulf between myth and reality regarding the Old West.

DIRECTIONS: Use the chart below to organize your thoughts about the difference between myth and reality regarding life in the Old West. Include in the first entry romanticized views about the lives of cowboys, including any books or movies that have contributed to the myth. In the second entry, list aspects of cowboy life that you read about in *Lonesome Dove* and have found in other sources that contradict the myth.

Cowboys: The Myth

_____

_____

_____

_____

_____

_____

_____

_____

_____

_____

_____

_____

Cowboys: The Reality

_____

_____

_____

_____

_____

_____

_____

_____

_____

_____

_____

_____

Unit 4: Division, Reconciliation, and Expansion (1850–1914)

"The Story of an Hour" by Kate Chopin

Build Vocabulary

Spelling Strategy To form the plural of a word ending in a consonant plus *y*, change the *y* to *i* and add *es*: *importunity* becomes *importunities*. For words that end in a vowel plus *y*, simply add *s* to form the plural: *days, monkeys.*

Using the Prefix *fore-*

The prefix *fore-* means "before" in the sense of time, place, or condition.

A. DIRECTIONS: Write the letter of the best definition of each of the following words having the prefix *fore*.

_____ 1. foreleg

_____ 2. forenoon

_____ 3. forecast

_____ 4. forewarn

_____ 5. foreword

_____ 6. foreclosure

a. action taken before a loan is lost

b. part of a book that comes before the main section

c. front leg of any animal having four or more legs

d. prediction made before a weather system arrives

e. another word for the morning, the part of the day before 12 o'clock P.M.

f. give notice before a bad event occurs

Using the Word Bank

forestall	repression	elusive
tumultuously	importunities	

B. DIRECTIONS: Select the Word Bank word that relates best to each situation, and write the word on the line.

1. Mrs. Mallard's previous actions regarding her feelings about her marriage

_____

2. Josephine's whispered pleas at her sister's bedroom door

_____

3. the way Mrs. Mallard's imaginings about the free days ahead of her went through her mind

_____

4. Richards's attempt to keep the shock of seeing her husband alive from Mrs. Mallard

_____

5. the mysterious, unsolvable nature of love

_____

Name _____ Date _____

"The Story of an Hour" by Kate Chopin

Grammar and Style: Appositives and Appositive Phrases

An **appositive** is a noun or pronoun placed near another noun or pronoun to give additional information about the first usage. An appositive that can be dropped from a sentence without changing the meaning of the sentence must be set off with commas or dashes. If the appositive is essential to the meaning of the sentence, it is not set off by commas. When an appositive has its own modifiers, it is an **appositive phrase**.

> **Appositive:** Her husband's friend Richards was there. (Richards is essential to the meaning of the sentence because we need to know which of her husband's friends is meant. No commas are used.)

> **Appositive phrase:** Louise's joy—a feeling of complete freedom from repression—almost overwhelmed her. (The appositive phrase is not essential to the meaning of the sentence. Dashes are used.)

A. Practice: Underline the appositive or appositive phrase in each sentence. Where necessary, add commas.

1. A breeze a delicious breath of rain swept through the house.

2. The well-known author Kate Chopin gave the opening address at the meeting.

3. Louise Mallard felt trapped by marriage a repressive institution.

4. The announcement of Mallard's death was a mistake a serious error with dire consequences.

5. One Victorian author Kate Chopin had strong opinions about the place of women in society.

6. That peddler the one standing under her window stared up at her.

7. The family chose Brently's brother Aaron to speak at Louise's funeral.

B. Writing Application: Combine each pair of sentences into one sentence containing an appositive.

1. Mrs. Mallard found herself whispering a single word over and over. That word was "free."

   _____

2. An oak barrier kept Josephine from seeing what her sister was doing. The bedroom door was the barrier.

   _____

3. She felt unfettered by the restraints of time. She felt like a soaring eagle.

   _____

4. Brently Mallard returned suddenly, as if from the dead. He was Louise's husband.

   _____

5. People said that Mrs. Mallard's heart stopped at the shock of seeing her husband alive. A joy too strong to bear stopped it.

   _____

Unit 4: Division, Reconciliation, and Expansion (1850–1914)

© Prentice-Hall, Inc.   The Story of an Hour **153**

"**The Story of an Hour**" by Kate Chopin

Reading Strategy: Recognize Ironic Details

In literature, as in life, **irony** occurs when there is a contrast between what is stated and what is intended, or between expectations and reality. Authors create irony by supplying details that lead us to expect an outcome different from what actually happens.

DIRECTIONS: Think about "The Story of an Hour" in terms of the ironic details that Chopin has provided—words that led you to think one thing about the events and the characters when actually something else was true. List four of these details below and tell what they led you to expect and what the ironic result was.

Ironic details	What you expected	What actually happened

"The Story of an Hour" by Kate Chopin

Literary Analysis: Irony

Irony is a contrast or a difference between what is stated and what is meant, or between what is expected to happen and what actually happens. **Situational irony** occurs when a result turns out differently than expected. For example, from the actions of Mrs. Mallard and her friends, readers expect that she will be overcome with grief at the news of her husband's death. Instead she exults in her freedom. **Dramatic irony** occurs when readers know something a character does not know. Readers know a few seconds before Mrs. Mallard, for example, that her husband is actually alive. Think of other stories you have read that use irony.

DIRECTIONS: On the lines provided, identify stories you have read that use irony. Quote or summarize a passage that is an example of situational irony and one that is an example of dramatic irony. Then explain the irony in each passage.

1. **Situational irony:** Students should choose a passage that illustrates how the outcome of an action or situation is different from what the reader expects.

   _____
   _____
   _____
   _____
   _____
   _____
   _____
   _____
   _____
   _____
   _____
   _____

2. **Dramatic irony:** Students should choose a passage that illustrates how the readers are aware of something that a character in the story does not know.

   _____
   _____
   _____
   _____
   _____
   _____
   _____
   _____
   _____
   _____
   _____

Unit 4: Division, Reconciliation, and Expansion (1850–1914)

"**April Showers**" by Edith Wharton

Build Vocabulary

Spelling Strategy The suffix -ory is preceded by the letter *t* in many adjectives formed from verbs: *admonitory* from *admonish*, *accusatory* from *accuse*, and *obligatory* from *oblige* are some examples.

Using the Prefix manu-

A. DIRECTIONS: Replace the underlined word or phrase in each sentence with one of the words below, which contain the prefix *man-* or *manu-*, meaning "hand."

manacle	maneuver	manicure	manner

1. Eugene Ionesco's plays are written in the Absurdist mode of expression.

   _____

2. Muriel gave herself a treatment of the hands and fingernails for her birthday.

   _____

3. The police officer slapped a handcuff on the prisoner's wrist.

   _____

4. Impatient customers often slyly work themselves to the head of the line.

   _____

Using the Word Bank

admonitory	retrospective	antagonism
contrition	manuscript	commiseration

B. DIRECTIONS: Fill in each blank with the Word Bank word that best completes the sentence.

1. The museum exhibited all of the artist's early work in a(n) _____ exhibit.

2. The teacher gave the class a(n) _____ wag of her finger.

3. The ancient _____ contained delicate illustrations as well as flawless handwriting.

4. Angela's _____ was apparent from the way she hung her head.

5. Despite the competition, there was no _____ among the contestants.

6. Derek and Marna's _____ concerning their misfortune brought them closer.

"April Showers" by Edith Wharton

Grammar and Style: Gerund Phrases

A **gerund** is an -*ing* form of a verb that is used as a noun. **Gerund phrases** consist of a gerund and its modifiers and complements. Gerunds and gerund phrases can function in a sentence as subjects, direct objects, subject complements, and objects of prepositions. Here are several examples.

Theodora was clever at *making bows*, and could have trimmed hats beautifully, had not all her spare moments been given to literature. [gerund phrase, object of the preposition *at*]

As readers can tell, writing is more than just a hobby for Theodora. [gerund as subject]

She enjoys writing very much. [gerund as direct object of *enjoys*]

A. Practice: Read the following sentences and underline each gerund or gerund phrase. Then identify its use in the sentence: as a subject (S), a direct object (DO), a subject complement (SC), or an object of a preposition (OP).

1. "Never would she lay hands on the sacred structure she had reared; never would she resort to the inartistic expedient of modifying her work to suit the popular taste."

   _____

2. "She had said to herself that after the manuscript had been sent she would have time to look after the children and catch up with the mending; but she had reckoned without the postman."

   _____

3. "After she left, Mrs. Dace looked very sad, and the doctor punished Johnny for warbling down the entry: 'Miss Sophy Brill/Is a bitter pill!' "

   _____

4. Theodora enjoyed signing her autograph for Miss Sophy Brill.

   _____

5. Admitting failure was the hardest part of the whole thing.

   _____

B. Writing Application: Use each of the following gerunds in a sentence.

1. Use the gerund *acting* as a subject.

   _____

2. Use the gerund *dancing* as a direct object.

   _____

3. Use the gerund *riding* as an object of the preposition.

   _____

4. Use the gerund *cooking* as a subject complement.

   _____

© Prentice-Hall, Inc.

"April Showers" by Edith Wharton

Reading Strategy: Anticipate Events

Anticipating events is the emotional equivalent of predicting outcomes. When you antici-pate an event during your reading, you develop expectations of what will happen. You may find yourself having feelings of eagerness, excitement, uncertainty, or even dread and foreboding. You look forward to what will happen just as the characters in the story do.

DIRECTIONS: Use this graphic organizer to help yourself analyze some of the events you antici-pate as you read "April Showers."

Event in the Story	Form of Anticipation	What You Think Will Happen

Name _____ Date _____

"**April Showers**" by Edith Wharton

Literary Analysis: Elements of Plot

Edith Wharton is a master storyteller. In "April Showers" she uses the traditional **plot** structure elements of exposition, conflict, rising action, climax, resolution, and denouement (falling action) to construct a story of great emotional impact. Notice, for example, the way Wharton introduces the character of Theodora in part of the story's exposition.

> "But Guy's heart slept under the violets on Muriel's grave."
> It was a beautiful ending; Theodora had seen girls cry over last chapters that weren't half as pathetic. She laid her pen aside and read the words over, letting her voice linger on the fall of the sentence; then, drawing a deep breath, she wrote across the foot of the page the name by which she had decided to become known in literature—Gladys Glyn.

In this brief passage, the reader finds out quite a bit about the story's central character. We learn that Theodora is romantic and sentimental and perhaps a bit silly. She has great aspirations to become a writer. With very few words, Wharton has sketched out a vivid character.

Exposition is only one of the elements of traditional plot construction. Each element has its own specific and important function.

DIRECTIONS: Read the following excerpts from "April Showers" and decide which plot element each represents.

1. "She woke with a start and a heavy sense of apprehension. The *Home Circle* had refused 'April Showers'." No, that couldn't be it; there lay the precious manuscript, waiting to be posted."

   _____

2. "Girls with more pin money than Theodora had ever dreamed of copied her hats and imitated her way of speaking."

   _____

3. "The week was a long nightmare. Theodora could neither eat nor sleep. She was up early enough, but instead of looking after the children and seeing that breakfast was ready, she wandered down the road to meet the postman, and came back wan and empty-handed, oblivious of her morning duties."

   _____

4. "The horrible truth burst forth upon her: *It was not her story!*"

   _____

5. "And then a bell ringing, a zoological specimen ordered to unlock a safe, her name asked for again, the manuscript, her own precious manuscript tied with Aunt Julia's ribbon, laid on the table before her, and her outcries, her protests, her interrogations, drowned in a flood of bland apology. . . ."

   _____

6. "The doctor paused, and Theodora clung to him in a mute passion of commiseration. It was as if a drowning creature caught a live hand through the murderous fury of the waves."

   _____

"Douglass" and **"We Wear the Mask"** by Paul Laurence Dunbar

Build Vocabulary

Spelling Strategy In English, a *y* is sometimes used inside a word where you might expect an *i: myriad, style, type, pyre, lye.* You will need to memorize such spellings.

Related Words: Forms of *guile*

The word *guile* means "craftiness." The word *beguile* means "to mislead by craftiness or deceit." *Guile* and *beguile* are related words.

A. DIRECTIONS: Form other words from *guile* and *beguile* by adding the suffixes listed. Write the meaning of each word on the lines.

1. *beguile* + *-ed* _____

_____

2. *guile* + *-less* _____

_____

3. *beguile* + *-er* _____

_____

4. *beguile* + *-ing* _____

_____

Using the Word Bank

salient	tempest	stark
guile	myriad	

B. DIRECTIONS: Circle the word that best completes each sentence.

1. The error was salient and stood _____ all the rest.
   a. out from   b. below   c. by   d. to the right

2. The tempest that occurred was more violent than any _____.
   a. game   b. criminal   c. color   d. windstorm

3. The stark trees stood out _____ against the rest of the landscape.
   a. boldly   b. subtly   c. darkly   d. colorfully

4. The guile shown by the con artist demonstrated her level of _____.
   a. brashness   b. trickiness   c. perkiness   d. voicelessness

5. The myriad colors made the room seem like a _____.
   a. paintbrush   b. airbrush   c. rainbow   d. gray color

"Douglass" and **"We Wear the Mask"** by Paul Laurence Dunbar

Grammar and Style: Punctuation of Interjections

An **interjection** is a part of speech that expresses emotion. It is always set off from the rest of a sentence by a comma or an exclamation point, depending on the degree of emotion being expressed. For example, the sentence *Yes! I like it very much* indicates excitement, whereas *Yes, I like it very much* indicates acceptance.

A. Practice: The following four excerpts from the selection contain interjections. Change the expression of emotion in each excerpt by rewriting it with different punctuation.

1. "Ah, Douglass, we have fall'n on evil days,"

   _____

   _____

2. "Nay, let them only see us,"

   _____

   _____

3. "Now, when the waves of swift dissension swarm,"

   _____

   _____

4. "Oh, for thy voice high-sounding o'er the storm,"

   _____

   _____

B. Writing Application: Use the following interjections to create new sentences from each sentence in the list. Punctuate your sentences properly.

   Ah   Hey   No   Oh   Yes

1. I didn't like the movie. _____

2. Why not? _____

3. We met the new neighbor. _____

4. The sky is blue. _____

5. He enjoys playing baseball. _____

6. She cut her hair very short. _____

7. I've been to Mexico. _____

8. I want to go to dinner. _____

9. Let's think of a way to finish the project. _____

10. What do you think? _____

"Douglass" and **"We Wear the Mask"** by Paul Laurence Dunbar

Reading Strategy: Interpret

When reading a poem, you often need to **interpret** the meaning of the poet's words and lines, or "read between the lines"—carefully examining the words for what they say and imply. Interpreting is often easier if you ask yourself questions after every few lines.

DIRECTIONS: Answer these interpretive questions about specific words and lines of Dunbar's poetry. Remember to read into the poet's meaning of every line and word. Refer to the selection if you need to.

1. In "Douglass," who is the "we" in the excerpt "Ah, Douglass, we have fall'n on evil days"?

   _____
   _____
   _____

2. In "Douglass," what is the "awful tide that battled to and fro"?

   _____
   _____
   _____

3. In "Douglass," what does the "shivering bark" signify?

   _____
   _____
   _____

4. In "Douglass," what is the "lonely dark"?

   _____
   _____
   _____

5. Why does Dunbar address the poem "Douglass" to Frederick Douglass, an American abolitionist?

   _____
   _____
   _____

6. What is the mask hiding in "We Wear the Mask"?

   _____
   _____
   _____

7. Why does Dunbar want to "hide our cheeks" and "shade our eyes" in "We Wear the Mask"?

   _____
   _____
   _____

"Douglass" and **"We Wear the Mask"** by Paul Laurence Dunbar

Literary Analysis: Rhyme

Rhyme is the repetition of sounds in the accented syllables of two or more words appearing close to each other. A **true rhyme** consists of words whose vowel sounds and final consonants are the same (*fall, squall*). A **slant rhyme** consists of words whose final consonant sounds match but whose vowel sounds are similar but not exact (*prove, love*). A rhyme that occurs at the ends of lines is called an **end rhyme**. If the rhyme occurs within a single line, it is called an **internal rhyme**.

DIRECTIONS: Read the following lines from the poems. For each item, circle two kinds of rhyme the italicized words form.

1. "This debt we pay to human *guile*;
   With torn and bleeding hearts we *smile*,"
   a. true rhyme   b. slant rhyme   c. end rhyme   d. internal rhyme

2. "We sing, but oh the clay is *vile*
   Beneath our feet, and long the *mile*;"
   a. true rhyme   b. slant rhyme   c. end rhyme   d. internal rhyme

3. "Ah, Douglass, we have fall'n on evil *days*,
   Saw, salient, at the cross of devious *ways*,"
   a. true rhyme   b. slant rhyme   c. end rhyme   d. internal rhyme

4. "Such days as thou, not even thou didst *know*,
   Not ended then, the passionate ebb and *flow*."
   a. true rhyme   b. slant rhyme   c. end rhyme   d. internal rhyme

5. "Saw, salient, at the *cross* of *devious* ways,"
   a. true rhyme   b. slant rhyme   c. end rhyme   d. internal rhyme

6. "And all the *country* heard *thee* with amaze."
   a. true rhyme   b. slant rhyme   c. end rhyme   d. internal rhyme

7. "When thee, the eyes of that harsh long *ago*
   The awful tide that battled to and *fro*;"
   a. true rhyme   b. slant rhyme   c. end rhyme   d. internal rhyme

8. "Now, when the waves of swift dissension *swarm*,
   Oh, for thy voice high-sounding o'er the *storm*,"
   a. true rhyme   b. slant rhyme   c. end rhyme   d. internal rhyme

9. "Oh, for thy voice high-sounding o'er the *storm*,
   The blast-defying power of thy *form*,"
   a. true rhyme   b. slant rhyme   c. end rhyme   d. internal rhyme

10. "And Honor, the strong pilot, lieth *stark*,
    For thy strong arm to guide the shivering *bark*,
    To give us comfort through the lonely *dark*."
    a. true rhyme   b. slant rhyme   c. end rhyme   d. internal rhyme

"Luke Havergal" and **"Richard Cory"** by Edwin Arlington Robinson
"Lucinda Matlock" and **"Richard Bone"** by Edgar Lee Masters

Build Vocabulary

Spelling Strategy In many English words of Greek origin, *ph* is used to spell the "f" sound: *epitaph, trophy, physique.* You must learn which words are spelled using *ph* instead of *f.*

Using the Root *-pose-*

A. DIRECTIONS: The word root *-pose-* means "rest," "place" or "position." It sometimes carries the meaning of the placing or positioning of parts. Define each underlined word below based on its use in the sentence and what you know about the word root *-pose-*.

1. Because the body of the "Iceman" had been buried in snow and ice for thousands of years, it had scarcely begun to decompose.

    _____

    _____

2. Anna was nervous before going on stage, but she tried to compose herself.

    _____

    _____

3. I suppose we could go to the movies Monday night, if there is an early show.

    _____

    _____

4. If you type too fast, you might transpose some letters.

    _____

    _____

Using the Word Bank

imperially	repose	degenerate	epitaph

B. DIRECTIONS: Above each underlined word in the following paragraph, write a synonym from the Word Bank.

During her life, Arliss' accusers claimed she was a corrupt person. But when she died, the community laid her out almost regally in an ornate coffin. Even her enemies maintained a respectful silence as she was lowered into the grave for her final rest. The headstone above her grave bore the legend: "A loyal sister, a wise leader, loved by all."

"**Luke Havergal**" and "**Richard Cory**" by Edwin Arlington Robinson
"**Lucinda Matlock**" and "**Richard Bone**" by Edgar Lee Masters

Grammar and Style: Noun Clauses

A **subordinate clause** contains a subject and verb but cannot stand alone as a sentence. A **noun clause** is a subordinate clause that can function in a sentence as a subject, predicate nominative, direct object, indirect object, or object of a preposition.

Noun clause used as subject: *What concerned Harry* was that he might lose his place.

Noun clause used as predicate nominative: He became *what he had always wanted to be.*

Noun clause used as direct object: Heidi thought *that Peggy would return immediately.*

Noun clause used as indirect object: Send *whoever wants some* a bottle of maple syrup.

Noun clause used as object of a preposition: Eileen heard nothing about *where Danny had gone.*

A. Practice: The passages below are from "Luke Havergal" and "Richard Cory." On the lines provided, identify how the noun clause is used in each excerpt.

1. ". . . wait for <u>what will come</u>." _____

_____

2. "To make us wish <u>that we were in his place</u>." _____

_____

3. "God slays Himself with <u>every leaf that flies</u>," _____

_____

B. Writing Application: Complete each sentence by adding a noun clause in the part of speech specified.

1. Gorillas are _____ (predicate nominative).

2. _____ (subject) is what you get.

3. I do not know _____ (direct object).

4. Please give _____ (indirect object) a sample of the new product.

5. I asked him about _____ (object of a preposition).

"Luke Havergal" and **"Richard Cory"** by Edwin Arlington Robinson
"Lucinda Matlock" and **"Richard Bone"** by Edgar Lee Masters

Reading Strategy: Recognize Attitudes

Language in literature is rarely neutral and objective. It usually presents a particular point of view or outlook on life. In a poem, the point of view is normally that of the speaker, who might be the poet, a fictional or nonfictional character, or an element of nature. By analyzing the language the speaker uses, you can make inferences about his or her **attitude**. To help find clues to the speaker's attitude, ask the following questions as you read a poem:

- Who is the speaker?

- What is the subject of the poem?

- What is the speaker's reason for speaking? What does the speaker hope to accomplish by speaking?

- What does the speaker *not* tell you?

- What biases or prejudices are revealed by the speaker's language?

- What emotion does the speaker express? What emotion does the speaker want you to feel?

DIRECTIONS: Use this chart to help you recognize attitudes in the poems by Edwin Arlington Robinson and Edgar Lee Masters. For each poem, determine who the speaker is and write passages from the poem that express the speaker's attitude in the third column. In the last column, write adjectives that describe the attitude that is illustrated by the clues. An example is provided for you.

Name of poem	Speaker	Clues to speaker's attitude	Attitude suggested by the clues
"Luke Havergal"	A ghost	"There is not a dawn in eastern skies"; "God slays himself with every leaf that flies, /And hell is more than half of paradise." "There is yet one way to where she is, /Bitter, but one that faith may never miss."	pessimistic, despondent, bitter
"Richard Cory"			
"Lucinda Matlock"			
"Richard Bone"			

"Luke Havergal" and **"Richard Cory"** by Edwin Arlington Robinson
"Lucinda Matlock" and **"Richard Bone"** by Edgar Lee Masters

Literary Analysis: Speaker

Often, the **speaker** of a poem is the poet, but when the speaker is a fictional character, as in the poems by Edwin Arlington Robinson and Edgar Lee Masters, the poem may not only communicate a message, but also reveal the attitude of the speaker and possibly the development of his or her character. For example, in "Richard Cory," the speaker looks with envy and admiration on Cory for his wealth and breeding. This provides insight into the character speaking the poem—that he or she is not of the same economic or social class.

Directions: In some poems, the speaker's identity is obvious, but in other poems, such as "Luke Havergal," the speaker's identity and purpose are more mysterious. Read "Luke Havergal" again, and then answer the questions below. Cite examples from the poem to support your answers.

1. What details from "Luke Havergal" provide clues to the speaker's identity?

   _____
   _____
   _____
   _____

2. Do you think the woman whom the speaker mentions is alive or dead? Why or why not?

   _____
   _____
   _____
   _____

3. Is the speaker of this poem providing advice about a physical journey or a supernatural one? How can you tell?

   _____
   _____
   _____
   _____

4. Does the speaker of this poem expect Luke Havergal to find happiness? How can you tell?

   _____
   _____
   _____

5. What do you think happened to Luke Havergal before the speaker began speaking?

   _____
   _____
   _____
   _____

© Prentice-Hall, Inc.

Unit 4: Division, Reconciliation, and Expansion (1850–1914)

Build Vocabulary

Spelling Strategy When adding a suffix beginning with a vowel to a word ending in two consonants, do not change the spelling of the base word: *reverent* + *-ial* = *reverential*.

Using Words from Music

Words from music can often have two meanings—one specific musical meaning and one for use in a nonmusical context.

A. DIRECTIONS: Each sentence below contains a word from music. On the line below the sentence, write either *musical* or *nonmusical* to show how the word is used in the sentence.

1. The team practiced as a <u>prelude</u> to the big game.

   _____

2. His job as the drummer was to keep the <u>beat</u>.

   _____

3. His <u>key</u> didn't fit in the new lock.

   _____

4. When we heard the <u>prelude</u>, we knew the performance had just started.

   _____

5. They played the song in a <u>minor</u> key.

   _____

Using the Word Bank

reverential	tremulously	semi-somnambulant
inert	prelude	jocularity

B. DIRECTIONS: Each sentence includes a word or phrase that means about the same as one of the words in the Word Bank. Underline that word or phrase and write the Word Bank word in the blank.

1. The orchestra began with the overture to the opera. _____

2. Aunt Georgiana was emotional and spoke with a quivering voice.

   _____

3. In the concert hall, she seemed somewhat less unable to move. _____

4. The trip left Aunt Georgiana feeling as though she were partly sleepwalking.

   _____

5. Clark's attempts at light-hearted joking seemed lost on Aunt Georgiana.

   _____

6. Clark had very respectful feelings for his aunt. _____

Name _____ Date _____

Grammar and Style: Reflexive and Intensive Pronouns

· Pronouns that end in -self or -selves are either reflexive or intensive pronouns, depending on how they are used in a sentence. A **reflexive pronoun** refers to the subject of the sentence and is necessary to complete the meaning of the sentence. An **intensive pronoun** simply adds emphasis to the noun or pronoun for which it stands; it can be deleted without changing the meaning of the sentence.

> **Reflexive pronoun:** . . . she had surrendered herself unquestioningly into the hands of a country dressmaker.

> **Intensive pronoun:** . . . her fingers worked mechanically upon her black dress, as though of themselves they were recalling the piano score they had once played.

A. Practice: In the following sentences, identify each pronoun ending in -self or -selves as reflexive or intensive.

1. Sometimes I write myself notes to help me remember things. _____

2. We ourselves want to go to the game. _____

3. The little boy likes to try to tie his shoes himself. _____

4. The children watch themselves in the mirror as they practice dancing._____

5. Mr. and Mrs. Perez just bought themselves a new house._____

6. We gave ourselves too little time for the trip. _____

7. I tried to convince myself that I really needed a new CD. _____

8. Will you do the repair yourself?_____

B. Writing Application: Rewrite each of the following sentences using a reflexive or intensive pronoun correctly.

1. The boys did the work without help from anyone else.

   _____

2. Lakisha bought a new jacket with her own money.

   _____

3. Now that you have bought a present for your sister, what will you get?

   _____

4. We wanted a treat, so we went on a boat ride.

   _____

5. Sometimes I really like to be alone.

   _____

Unit 4: Division, Reconciliation, and Expansion (1850–1914)

Name _____   Date _____

"A Wagner Matinée" by Willa Cather

Reading Strategy: Clarifying

As you read, it is important to **clarify**, or check your understanding, of the details in what you read. You can clarify the details by reading a footnote, looking up a word in the dictionary, rereading a passage to refresh your memory, or reading ahead to find additional details.

DIRECTIONS: Read each phrase from the selection. Answer the question using one clarifying strategy.

1. ". . . the gangling farmer boy my aunt had known, scourged with chilblains . . ."

   What is a chilblain?

   _____

   _____

2. "[Aunt Georgiana] had come all the way in a day coach. . ."

   What was the origin and destination of Aunt Georgiana's trip?

   _____

   _____

3. "One summer, which she had spent in the little village in the Green Mountains where her ancestors had dwelt for generations, . . ."

   Where are the Green Mountains?

   _____

   _____

4. "I suggested our visiting the Conservatory and the Common before lunch, . . ."

   Why would Aunt Georgiana be interested in the Conservatory?

   _____

   _____

5. ". . . with the bitter frenzy of the Venusberg theme and its ripping of strings, . . ."

   What is the significance of the term *Venusberg*?

   _____

   _____

6. "Soon after the tenor began the 'Prize Song,' I heard a quick-drawn breath, and turned to my aunt. Her eyes were closed, but the tears were glistening on her cheeks, . . ."

   Why did the "Prize Song" make Aunt Georgiana cry?

   _____

   _____

"A Wagner Matinée" by Willa Cather

Literary Analysis: Characterization

Most readers enjoy a story more when they feel as if they know the characters as people. **Characterization** is the way in whch a writer reveals a character's personality. A writer can make direct statements about a character, give a physical description, describe the character's actions, and/or tell the character's thoughts and comments.

DIRECTIONS: Read each excerpt from the selection, and write down what each tells you about the character of Aunt Georgiana.

1. "Whatever shock Mrs. Springer experienced at my aunt's appearance she considerately concealed."

   _____

   _____

2. "... a plain, angular, spectacled woman of thirty."

   _____

   _____

3. "... she eloped with him, eluding the reproaches of her family and the criticism of her friends by going with him to the Nebraska frontier."

   _____

   _____

4. ". . . in those days I owed to this woman most of the good that ever came my way, . . ."

   _____

   _____

5. "Don't love it so well, Clark, or it may be taken from you."

   _____

   _____

6. "When the violins drew out the first strain of the Pilgrims' chorus, my Aunt Georgiana clutched my coat sleeve."

   _____

   _____

7. "Poor old hands! They were stretched and pulled and twisted into mere tentacles to hold, and lift, and knead with; . . ."

   _____

   _____

8. "She burst into tears and sobbed pleadingly, 'I don't want to go, Clark, I don't want to go!'"

   _____

   _____

"Cats" by Anna Quindlen

Build Vocabulary

Vivid vocabulary and descriptive words and phrases can add greatly to our understanding and enjoyment of a piece of writing. In her essay, the words Anna Quindlen uses to describe cats help evoke a certain mood and set a certain tone. Descriptive words gain much of their power through their connotations—or the meanings they suggest—whether positive, negative, or neutral.

DIRECTIONS: For each word or phrase below, write a sentence involving a cat. After each sentence, indicate whether the descriptive word or phrase adds a positive, negative, or neutral connotation.

1. tiger gray

   _____

   _____

   _____

2. black

   _____

   _____

   _____

3. slither

   _____

   _____

   _____

4. watchful eyes

   _____

   _____

   _____

5. prowling

   _____

   _____

   _____

6. climbed

   _____

   _____

   _____

"Cats" by Anna Quindlen

Thematic Connection: Living in a Changing World

Alienation is withdrawal, distance, or estrangement. The alienation of the individual is a common theme in literature. You can see in the writings of Willa Cather and Anna Quindlen that alienation can arise from many sources. How are the individuals in these selections alienated from their surroundings? What forms does their alienation take? What larger forces or structures can be the source of alienation?

DIRECTIONS: Alienation can arise from an individual's interaction—or lack of interaction—with larger societal forces or structures. For each of the categories listed below, explain how a person's interaction with it could cause alienation. Cite examples from your reading to support your answer.

Society:

_____

_____

_____

_____

_____

Family:

_____

_____

_____

_____

Career:

_____

_____

_____

_____

Health:

_____

_____

_____

_____

Daily Life:

_____

_____

_____

_____

Unit 4: Division, Reconciliation, and Expansion (1850–1914)

"The Love Song of J. Alfred Prufrock" by T. S. Eliot

Build Vocabulary

Spelling Strategy The adjective suffix -ious is much more common than the suffix -eous. A d comes before -eous in only one English word: hideous. In all other words in which the stem ends in d, the ending is spelled -ious: insidious, perfidious, studious.

Using the Prefix di-

A. DIRECTIONS: Each of the following sentences includes an italicized word that contains the prefix di- (or dis-), meaning "away" or "apart." Fill in the blank with a word or phrase that completes the sentence and reveals the meaning of the italicized word.

1. When the botanist *dissected* the flower, she _____.

2 When an elected official is *divested* of his or her office, it is _____.

3. If a company produces a *diverse* line of products, each product is _____

   _____.

4. If I *divert* a child's attention from something, she will _____.

5. The protesters tried to *disrupt* the meeting, causing it to _____.

Using the Word Bank

insidious	digress	malingers	meticulous	obtuse

B. DIRECTIONS: Replace each bracketed word or phrase with one of the words in the Word Bank.

1. We suspect that the boy often [fakes illness] _____ when he claims he is too sick to go to school in the morning but feels well enough to go to a ball game in the afternoon.

2. Robert was such a [neat and careful] _____ cook that his kitchen was usually spotless.

3. Although Denise hinted that she would like to date him, Ramon seemed too [dense]

   _____ to understand.

4. The constant criticism and teasing that Laverne received from her older brother had a(n)

   [damaging] _____ effect on her self-confidence.

5 Pardon me if I [stray] _____ from the subject, but I have some interesting news.

"The Love Song of J. Alfred Prufrock" by T. S. Eliot

Grammar and Style: Adjectival Modifiers

Adjectival modifiers are phrases or clauses that modify or describe a noun or pronoun. They may begin with a preposition, a present or past participle, a relative pronoun, or the infinitive form of a verb.

These lines from "The Love Song of J. Alfred Prufrock" show four types of adjectival modifiers.

Prepositional phrase: Is it perfume *from a dress*

Participial phrase: I know the voices *dying with a dying fall*

Adjective clause: The yellow fog *that rubs its back upon the window-panes*

Infinitive phrase: There will be time *to murder and create*

A. Practice: Underline the adjectival modifier in each of the following lines from "The Love Song of J. Alfred Prufrock." In the blank, identify the type of adjectival modifier each one is.

1. "Arms that are braceleted and white and bare" _____

2. "My necktie . . . asserted by a simple pin" _____

3. "a bald spot in the middle of my hair" _____

4. "Time to turn back and descend the stair" _____

5. "the smoke that rises from the pipes/Of lonely men" _____

B. Writing Application: Describe each of the nouns below, using the type of phrase or clause identified in parentheses.

1. children's faces (adjective clause)

   _____

2. a room (infinitive phrase)

   _____

3. bright light (prepositional phrase)

   _____

4. loud noises (participial phrase)

   _____

5. bitter taste (prepositional phrase)

   _____

6. gentle breeze (participial phrase)

   _____

7. tempting smell (adjective clause)

   _____

Name _____ Date _____

Reading Strategy: Listening

Listening to the way a poem sounds often can be as important as the words themselves. Writers use sound effects and musical devices to enhance the poem's mood and meaning. One device they sometimes use is **alliteration,** which is the repetition of consonant sounds at the beginning of words or accented syllables. Other effects often used are repetition, rhyme, and rhythm. All of these devices are present in the following excerpt from "The Love Song of J. Alfred Prufrock."

> Time for you and time for me,/ And time yet for a hundred indecisions,/ And for a hundred visions and revisions./ Before the taking of a toast and tea.

Notice the repetition of the word *time.* It suggests that Prufrock is trying to convince himself that there is an abundance of time in which to be indecisive. The rhyming of *indecisions, visions,* and *revisions* gives the lines a fluid internal structure and a pleasing sound. The rhythm flows in beats, evoking the feeling of time passing. The excerpt ends with the alliteration of *t's* giving the line a sharp, prim and proper feel.

These musical qualities occur throughout "The Love Song of J. Alfred Prufrock," and to appreciate them, you must listen as you read.

DIRECTIONS: Read each of the following excerpts aloud. On the lines following each one, note which musical devices are being used. Explain how they contribute to the musicality of the poem.

1. "The yellow fog that rubs its back upon the window-panes,/ The yellow smoke that rubs its muzzle on the window-panes.

   _____

   _____

   _____

2. "And indeed there will be time/ To wonder, 'Do I dare?' And 'Do I dare?'/ Time to turn back and descend the stair,/ With a bald spot in the middle of my hair—"

   _____

   _____

   _____

3. "I have seen the moment of my greatness flicker,/ And I have seen the eternal Footman hold my coat and snicker."

   _____

   _____

   _____

4. "We have lingered in the chambers of the sea/ By sea-girls wreathed with seaweed red and brown/ Till human voices wake us and we drown."

   _____

   _____

   _____

"The Love Song of J. Alfred Prufrock" by T. S. Eliot

Literary Analysis: Dramatic Monologue

A **dramatic monologue** is a poem or speech in a play or novel in which a character speaks his or her thoughts aloud about a crucial event or feeling in the character's life. In "The Love Song of J. Alfred Prufrock," Prufrock is speaking to a silent companion—perhaps a part of himself. What Prufrock says reveals a deep split between what he desires and his ability to achieve his desires. Several times in the poem, Prufrock repeats these questions: "Do I dare?" and "How should I presume?" These repeated lines may suggest that Prufrock wishes to act but is deeply afraid of failure and rejection.

DIRECTIONS: Read the lines from the poem and answer the questions on another sheet of paper. Give examples from the poem as evidence to support your interpretation.

1. In the following lines, what might Prufrock wish he could dare to do?

   Time to turn back and descend the stair, / With a bald spot in the middle of my hair— / (They will say: "How his hair is growing thin!") / My morning coat, my collar mounting firmly to the chin, / My necktie rich and modest, but asserted by a simple pin— / (They will say: "But how his arms and legs are thin!") / Do I dare / Disturb the universe?

2. What could these lines show Prufrock is afraid of? To what does he compare himself? Why is this an apt comparison?

   And I have known the eyes already, known them all— / The eyes that fix you in a formulated phrase, / And when I am formulated, sprawling on a pin, / When I am pinned and wriggling on the wall, / Then how should I begin / To spit out all the butt-ends of my days and ways? / And how should I presume?

3. What might Prufrock want to do at this point? Why is he unable to do it?

   Shall I part my hair behind? Do I dare to eat a peach? / I shall wear white flannel trousers, and walk upon the beach. / I have heard the mermaids singing, each to each.

   I do not think that they will sing to me.

4. What might Prufrock like to do when or before he grows old? Pick one of the actions he describes and suggest what it might symbolize to him.

   And would it have been worth it, after all, / After the cups, the marmalade, the tea, / Among the porcelain, among some talk of you and me, / Would it have been worth while, / To have bitten off the matter with a smile, / To have squeezed the universe into a ball / To roll it towards some overwhelming question. / To say: "I am Lazarus, come from the dead, / Come back to tell you all. I shall tell you all"— / If one, settling a pillow by her head, /
   Should say: "That is not what I meant at all. /
   That is not it, at all."

Imagist Poets

Build Vocabulary

Spelling Strategy The prefix *ad-* often loses the *d* when it is added to a word or word stem beginning with the consonants *p*, *g*, and *c*. In such cases, the consonant is doubled as in *appear*, *aggressor*, *assign*, and *account*.

Forms of *appear*

The following words are based on the verb *appear*, meaning "to come into sight or into being" or "to become understood."

apparent	appearance	apparition

A. DIRECTIONS: Rewrite each sentence by replacing the italicized word or words with one of the words in the box.

1. The *seeming* cause of the accident was a drunk driver.

   _____

2. The *ghostly face* in the hallway mirror made the movie audience scream.

   _____

3. The glamorous young star knew that her *showing* at the charity event was important.

   _____

   _____

Using the Word Bank

apparition	voluminous	dogma

B. DIRECTIONS: Fill in each blank with the word from the Word Bank that fits best.

1. The professor carried on a(n) _____ correspondence with the author whose biography he was writing.

2. Don't accept as _____ the following rules about writing poetry; your own ideas may be just as good.

3. The grieving widow thought she saw a(n) _____ of her late husband standing in the moonlit garden.

C. DIRECTIONS: The items that follow consist of a numbered word followed by five lettered words or phrases. For each item, choose the word that is most nearly *opposite* in meaning to the numbered word. Circle the letter of your choice.

1. voluminous
   a. huge
   b. skimpy
   c. well-read
   d. single
   e. encyclopedic

2. dogma
   a. doubt
   b. skill
   c. feline
   d. belief
   e. doctrine

3. apparent
   a. obvious
   b. undisputed
   c. unknowable
   d. obscure
   e. childlike

Imagist Poets

Grammar and Style: Concrete and Abstract Nouns

A **concrete noun** names a physical thing that can be perceived with one or more of the five senses. An **abstract noun** names something that cannot be seen, heard, smelled, tasted, or touched. An abstract noun can be a quality, a characteristic, or an idea. Some examples of abstract nouns are *beauty*, *strength*, *courage*, and *justice*. The following excerpt is from the poem "The River-Merchant's Wife: A Letter." The concrete noun is underlined, and the two abstract nouns are in italics.

Two small <u>people</u>, without *dislike* or *suspicion*.

A. Practice: Underline the concrete nouns in the lines of poetry that follow. Circle the abstract nouns.

1. "I played about the front gate, pulling flowers."

2. "The leaves fall early this autumn, in wind."

3. "The apparition of these faces in the crowd; / Petals on a wet, black bough."

4. "a red wheel / barrow / glazed with rain / water / beside the white / chickens."

5. "Silver dust / lifted from the earth / higher than my arms reach

6. "O wind, rend open the heat . . . rend it to tatters."

B. Writing Application: Below is a list of abstract nouns. On each line, write a sentence that includes the abstract noun as well as at least one concrete noun. One sentence has already been written for you.

1. strength _____ The movers lifted the huge piano with a strength I found incredible. _____

2. beauty _____

3. love _____

4. courage _____

5. future _____

6. success _____

7. kindness _____

8. justice _____

9. fear _____

10. talent _____

Reading Stategy: Engage Your Senses

One way to enjoy, appreciate, and understand what you read is to engage your senses. Imagine yourself actually seeing, smelling, hearing, tasting, or touching the images presented by the writer. Put yourself at the scene mentally, and experience the images in your mind's eye.

DIRECTIONS: Use this graphic organizer to help yourself engage your senses as you read these poems. From each poem, choose images that appeal to the senses. Write the image in the corresponding box or boxes. Remember that many images can be appreciated by more than one sense.

	See	Hear	Touch	Smell	Taste
"The River-Merchant's Wife: A Letter"					
"In a Station of the Metro"					
"The Red Wheelbarrow"					
"The Great Figure"					
"This Is Just to Say"					
"Pear Tree"					
"Heat"					

Name _____   Date _____

Literary Analysis: Imagist Poetry

The **Imagists** were American poets who became prominent between 1909 and 1918. The major objectives of the Imagist poets were (1) to use everyday language, choosing exact words and avoiding near-exact words, (2) to avoid clichés, (3) to create new rhythms and avoid the old, (4) to exercise absolute freedom in the choice of subjects, (5) to present concrete images, (6) to work toward concentrated language, avoiding anything extra, and (7) to suggest rather than to state directly.

DIRECTIONS: Read each poem or excerpt. Then answer the question.

1. Name three concrete images in this poem.

   so much depends / upon / a red wheel / barrow / glazed with rain / water / beside the white / chickens.

   _____

   _____

   _____

2. List five words in this excerpt that can be seen as exact.

   Among the rain / and lights / I saw the figure 5 / in gold / on a red / fire truck

   _____

   _____

   _____

   _____

3. Which of the objectives of the Imagist poets do you think are achieved in this excerpt? Explain.

   I have eaten / the plums / that were in / the icebox / and which / you were probably / saving / for breakfast

   _____

   _____

   _____

   _____

   _____

   _____

   _____

   _____

   _____

"Winter Dreams" by F. Scott Fitzgerald

Build Vocabulary

Spelling Strategy The adjective-forming suffix -ic often does not affect the spelling of the base word to which it is added. Here are some examples: *pugilistic, antagonistic, futuristic, angelic.*

Using the Root -*somn*-

A. The word *somnolent* combines the adjective-forming suffix -*ent*, which means "that has, says, or does," and the word root -*somn*-, which means "sleep." The word *somnolent*, therefore, means "sleepy." Using the information following each word and what you know about the word root -*somn*-, write the word that best completes each sentence.

insomnia (*in-* = "not")	*somnambulate* (*ambulare* = "to walk")
somniferous (*ferre* = "to bring")	*somniloquy* (*loqui* = "to speak")

1. Whenever Becky would _____, her dog followed her to make sure she didn't get hurt.

2. Barry often found that a warm glass of milk was a _____ bedtime treat.

3. Corinne was so worried about the test that she had _____.

4. Kurt's habit of _____ proved to be embarrassing when he said too much one night.

Using the Word Bank

fallowness	preposterous	fortuitous	sinuous
mundane	poignant	pugilistic	somnolent

B. DIRECTIONS: In each blank, write the letter of the choice that is closest in meaning to the word in italics.

____ 1. a *mundane* activity
    a. marvelous
    b. commonplace
    c. wavy
    d. sneaky

____ 2. a *preposterous* idea
    a. on purpose
    b. perfect
    c. unusual
    d. ridiculous

____ 3. the field's *fallowness*
    a. inactivity
    b. foulness
    c. shallowness
    d. following

____ 4. a *pugilistic* attitude
    a. pug-nosed
    b. piglike
    c. calm
    d. like a boxer

____ 5. a *poignant* moment
    a. picky
    b. painful
    c. poor
    d. wealthy

____ 6. a *fortuitous* event
    a. unlucky
    b. fifth
    c. chance
    d. lazy

____ 7. a *somnolent* mood
    a. shaky
    b. lively
    c. sleepy
    d. thin

____ 8. a *sinuous* turn
    a. wavy
    b. tough
    c. straight
    d. right

"Winter Dreams" by F. Scott Fitzgerald

Grammar and Style: Dashes

Dashes are used to introduce information that either interrupts the flow of the text or requires the reader's immediate attention. Dashes may set off appositions, modifiers, or dramatic phrases. The frequent use of dashes in "Winter Dreams" reflects the jumbled emotions portrayed in the story.

A. Practice: The sentences below are from "Winter Dreams." Insert dashes where necessary by writing a ^ between the words where each dash should be.

1. And one day it came to pass that Mr. Jones himself and not his ghost came up to Dexter with tears in his eyes. . . .

2. There was a general ungodliness in the way her lips twisted down at the corners when she smiled, and in the Heaven help us! in the almost passionate quality of her eyes.

3. He knew that if he moved forward a step his stare would be in her line of vision if he moved backward he would lose his full view of her face.

4. [His parents] persuaded Dexter several years later to pass up a business course at the State university his father, prospering now, would have paid his way for the precarious advantage of attending an older and more famous university in the East. . . .

5. He wanted not association with glittering things and glittering people he wanted the glittering things themselves.

6. One minute he had the sense of being a trespasser in the next he was impressed by the tremendous superiority he felt. . . .

B. Writing Application: Combine each set of phrases or sentences into one sentence by using dashes.

1. "That Judy Jones!" remarked Mr. Hedrick on the next tee, as they waited for her to play on ahead. They waited some moments.

   _____

2. He had a rather priggish notion that he should know more about such things. He was the young and already fabulously successful Dexter Green.

   _____

3. He loved her, and he would love her until the day he was too old for loving. But he could not have her.

   _____

4. Early in that summer morning the sun rose slowly up into the hazy sky. The sun was reddish and swollen.

   _____

5. At three o'clock the teacher instructed everyone to stop writing and pass the tests forward. Ross could not finish answering the final question before three o'clock.

   _____

"Winter Dreams" by F. Scott Fitzgerald

Reading Strategy: Draw Conclusions About Characters

When you read a story, you can **draw conclusions about characters** by combining information from the story with your personal knowledge of human behavior. To draw conclusions, you often need to read between the lines to infer emotions and motivations that are not directly stated.

DIRECTIONS: Read each excerpt from "Winter Dreams." Then answer the question that follows.

1. As so frequently would be the case in the future, Dexter was unconsciously dictated to by his winter dreams.

   Does Dexter always plan his moves carefully and then follow them, or does he sometimes behave impetuously?

   _____

2. "You hit me in the stomach!" declared Mr. Hedrick wildly. / "Did I?" [Judy] approached the group of men. "I'm sorry. I yelled 'Fore!' / ". . . Here I am! I'd have gone on the green except that I hit something."

   How does Judy probably feel about hitting Mr. Hedrick?

   _____

3. [Judy] wore a blue silk afternoon dress, and [Dexter] was disappointed at first that she had not put on something more elaborate.

   What does Judy's behavior towards Dexter on their first date reveal about her?

   _____

4. [Dexter] had been born in Keeble, a Minnesota village fifty miles farther north, and he always gave Keeble as his home instead of Black Bear Village. Country towns were well enough to come from if they weren't inconveniently in sight and used as footstools by fashionable lakes.

   How does Dexter probably feel about his background?

   _____

5. There was a pause. Then [Judy] smiled and the corners of her mouth drooped and an almost imperceptible sway brought her closer to [Dexter], looking up into his eyes.

   How does Judy use her physical attractiveness to her advantage?

   _____

6. When [Judy] assured [Dexter] that she had not kissed the other man, he knew she was lying—yet he was glad that she had taken the trouble to lie to him.

   How does this scene foreshadow the future of Dexter and Judy's relationship?

   _____

7. Even the ultimate falsity of the grounds upon which Judy terminated the engagement that she did not want to "take [Dexter] away" from Irene. . . .

   What does this tell you about Judy's motives for becoming engaged to Dexter?

   _____

Name _____ Date _____

"**Winter Dreams**" by F. Scott Fitzgerald

Literary Analysis: Characterization

To emphasize a character's personality traits, a writer often may build into the story deliberate contrasts and comparisons with other charaters. Fitzgerald uses this technique as he develops the character of Judy in "Winter Dreams."

Answer the following questions, citing details from the story to support your answers.

1. In contrast to Judy's "glittering" personality, what kind of personality does Irene have?

   _____
   _____
   _____
   _____
   _____

2. In which ways is Judy like her father?

   _____
   _____
   _____
   _____
   _____

3. In one passage, Fitzgerald characterizes Judy's house. What is the house like, and how is it different from Judy?

   _____
   _____
   _____
   _____
   _____

4. Fitzgerald's two main characters are not "one-sided." Both of them have qualities that seem contradictory, but each is a totally believable human being. Judy, for example, is both a flighty, insensitive flirt and a forlorn, confused young woman. Now consider the character of Dexter. What is the contrast between his attitude toward Judy and his attitude toward his career? How do these contrasting traits make him seem believable?

   _____
   _____
   _____
   _____
   _____
   _____
   _____
   _____

"The Turtle" from ***The Grapes of Wrath*** by John Steinbeck

Build Vocabulary

Spelling Strategy Many English words are constructed by adding prefixes and suffixes to an English base word: *em-* and *-ment* added to *bank* to form *embankment,* for example. However, some words came into English with the prefix or suffix already embedded. For example, removing *pro-* from *protruded* ("stuck out") does not leave an English base word.

Using the Prefix *pro-*

A. DIRECTIONS: In the following words, the prefix *pro-* means "forward." More information about the origin of several words containing *pro-* is given below. Use the words to complete the sentences.

    project (L. *jacere* means "to throw")

    procrastinate (L. *cras* means "tomorrow")

    promote (L. *movere* means "to move")

1. Rather than finishing his homework on Saturday, Bob decided to _____ and do it on Sunday instead.

2. After Juanita had worked as an assistant manager for two years, her boss decided to _____ her to manager.

3. The slide machine used light to _____ an image onto a large screen.

Using the Word Bank

embankment	protruded

B. DIRECTIONS: Underline the better definition for the italicized word in each sentence or phrase.

1. The highway department built an *embankment* to hold the new interstate. (raised structure, tunnel)

2. A flagpole *protruded* from a column next to the front door of the house. (thrust forward, glistened)

C DIRECTIONS: Each item consists of a related pair of words in capital letters followed by four pairs of words. Choose the pair that best expresses a relationship *similar* to that expressed in the pair in CAPITAL LETTERS.

____ 1. NOSE : PROTRUDED ::
    a. wheel : turned
    b. hat : head
    c. empty : full
    d. shined : sun

____ 2. EMBANKMENT : DIRT ::
    a. wood : table
    b. computer : printer
    c. iceberg : ice
    d. feather : bird

"The Turtle" from *The Grapes of Wrath* by John Steinbeck

Grammar and Style: Parallel Structure

Writers use **parallel structure** to express similar ideas in similar grammatical form. The following example from "The Turtle" uses parallel prepositional phrases beginning with *into* and parallel verb forms followed by the word *in*.

> A red ant ran *into the shell, into the soft skin inside the shell*, and suddenly head and legs *snapped in*, and the armored tail *clamped in sideways.*

A. Practice: The following sentence is from "The Turtle." Underline the parallel verbs that are followed by the same word.

> For a long moment the turtle lay still, and then the neck crept out and the old humorous frowning eyes looked about and the legs and tail came out.

B. Writing Application: Rewrite the following sentences so that they have two parallel verbs. Make sure the words that follow the verbs are parallel as well.

1. The apples were dipped in caramel before chocolate was placed on them.

   _____

   _____

2. The faster train arrived in Seattle before the slower train got to Portland.

   _____

   _____

3. A caterpillar changes into a chrysalis before it becomes a butterfly.

   _____

   _____

4. Marcy's younger sister swung on the swing set before climbing on the monkey bars.

   _____

   _____

5. At night, you should turn on a light before you watch television.

   _____

   _____

6. On the standardized test, Jamie wrote with a pen even though he was told to use a pencil.

   _____

   _____

7. Starting around five o'clock, day will change into evening, and then evening will become night.

   _____

   _____

8. The oak tree twists in the hurricane-force winds as a blade of grass is bent by a light breeze.

   _____

   _____

"The Turtle" from *The Grapes of Wrath* by John Steinbeck

Reading Strategy: Find Clues to Theme

Highly descriptive language and complex syntax can make it difficult to grasp an author's theme, or central message about life. Breaking down a long, difficult sentence into meaningful sections—and restating the sections in your own words—can help you to understand that sentence and gain clues to the theme. When you run across unfamiliar words, use context clues to help define them. Defining individual words will provide you with clues to the theme. Look at this example from "The Turtle."

Steinbeck's Version
Pushing hind legs strained and slipped, boosting the shell along, and the horny head protruded as far as the neck could stretch.

Broken Down and Rephrased
The back legs strained and slipped as they pushed up the hill. / The back legs boosted the shell along. / The horny head stuck out as far as it could.

Unfamiliar word: *Protrude* means "to stick out" because the neck is stretching as far out as possible.

DIRECTIONS: Use this graphic organizer to help you break down long sentences and define unfamiliar words in "The Turtle." Each time you come across a difficult sentence, write sections of the sentences in the top row of boxes and restate the sections in your own words below. Write down any difficult words, and use context clues to define them. A sample has been done for you.

Difficult Words				
Now the going was easy,	and all the legs worked,	and the shell boosted along,	waggling from side to side.	(The turtle moved from side to side as it walked.)
(It was easy to move across the highway.)	(All four legs moved.)	(The turtle moved along.)	(moving from side to side)	

Difficult Words				

"The Turtle" from *The Grapes of Wrath* by John Steinbeck

Literary Analysis: Theme

The **theme** of a work of art is its central insight into life. An author's theme is shown through story events, characters, and even story details. Strong determination to survive is a theme of *The Grapes of Wrath*. The Joad family travels from its home of many generations in Oklahoma to California, where it hopes to establish a new farm. This short chapter, "The Turtle," mirrors that theme; the turtle, like the Joads, travels toward an unknown goal, determined to survive despite all obstacles.

DIRECTIONS: Identify details in "The Turtle" that might be connected to the theme of survival. Explain how each detail relates to the story of the Joads or to the theme of survival in general.

1. Story detail:

   _____
   _____

   How it connects to theme:

   _____
   _____
   _____
   _____
   _____

2. Story detail:

   _____
   _____

   How it connects to theme:

   _____
   _____
   _____
   _____
   _____

3. Story detail:

   _____
   _____

   How it connects to theme:

   _____
   _____
   _____
   _____
   _____

"anyone lived in a pretty how town" and **"old age sticks"** by E. E. Cummings
"The Unknown Citizen" by W. H. Auden

Build Vocabulary

Spelling Strategy Several words that sound as if they begin with *s* actually begin with the letters *ps*: *psychology, psalm, pseudonym*. These words are based on Greek roots that begin with the Greek letter *psi*, which has the sound *sī*.

Using the Root *-psych-*

Psyche is a mythological figure. Her name is the same as the Greek word for "breath" or "soul." The Greek root *-psych-*, which forms the basis of several English words, means "mind" or "soul."

A. Directions: Use each word formed from the root *-psych-* to fill the appropriate blanks in the sentences. Then, without using a dictionary, define each word based on its context in the sentence and what you know about the meanings of its roots.

> psychopath (*-path-* = "suffering, disease")   psychokinesis (*-kinesis-* = "motion")   psychotherapy

1. In the science fiction movie, the heroine was able to make objects leap across the room by her powers of _____.

   _____

2. Two years of _____ helped Samantha get over her fears and work more effectively at her job.

   _____

3. The strange notes left at the crime scenes suggested to police that the criminal was a _____.

   _____

Using the Word Bank

> statistics   psychology

B. Directions: Each sentence has a blank space indicating that a word has been omitted. Choose the lettered word that best completes the meaning of the sentence and write the word in the blank.

1. A knowledge of _____ is important for people who work in teaching, marketing, and sports.
   a. psychosis   b. psychiatry   c. psychodrama   d. psychology

2. Baseball _____ such as batting averages and earned-run averages help management to evaluate the players' performance.
   a. plays   b. statistics   c. riddles   d. negotiations

"anyone lived in a pretty how town" and **"old age sticks"** by E. E. Cummings
"The Unknown Citizen" by W. H. Auden

Grammar and Style: Parentheses

Parentheses, ( ), are generally used to enclose extra information. They are used for slightly different purposes than commas and dashes. Use commas to set off material that is especially closely connected to the rest of a sentence. Use dashes to emphasize the information being set off and to show that the material is of great importance. You should use parentheses when the material is unimportant and interruptive in nature, such as the nonessential bit of information in the following sentence.

E. E. Cummings (I think) uses punctuation sparingly.

A. Practice: Complete each sentence by adding parentheses where necessary.

1. E. E. Cummings' poetic style is at least in my opinion unusual.

2. He began writing poetry so I've read after World War I.

3. You and probably most other people can sometimes recognize a Cummings poem by its un-conventional use of punctuation and grammar.

4. I like his poems because of a playfulness if that's the right word that makes the poems fun to read.

5. W. H. Auden is a more traditional poet you'd have to say than E. E. Cummings.

6. He doesn't if you'll pardon the expression throw grammar and punctuation to the wind.

7. Auden was born in England if I'm not mistaken and came to America in 1939, just before the outbreak of World War II.

8. Prior to leaving England, he and I'm glad of this spoke out against the rise of Nazism in Germany.

9. Much of his work deals with the struggle for individuality a contemporary topic by the people in a conformist society.

10. In 1948, Auden received if my memory serves me the Pulitzer Prize for the narrative poem *The Age of Anxiety*, a work about life in the post-World War II era.

B. Writing Application: Write a review of one of the three poems in this grouping. Give your personal opinions of the style and message of the poem you choose. In your review, include at least three expressions that are set off by parentheses.

_____

_____

_____

_____

_____

_____

"anyone lived in a pretty how town" and **"old age sticks"** by E. E. Cummings
"The Unknown Citizen" by W. H. Auden

Reading Strategy: Relate Structure to Meaning

You can often relate a poem's **structure**—the way it is put together in words, lines, and stanzas—to its **meaning**—the central ideas the poet wants you to take away. For example, the poems of Cummings often break the rules of syntax—the way in which words, phrases, and clauses are arranged to form sentences—to reinforce a message of personal individuality or of the individual person trying to break loose from conventional boundaries or patterns. Both "anyone lived in a how town" and "old age sticks" present patterns or cycles of living that each generation relives in turn (although they try to do otherwise). The regular structure of the stanzas of both poems reinforces the concept of patterns.

DIRECTIONS: For each of the following passages from the three poems, do the following: First, write the meaning of the passage. Secondly, write how one or more of the following structural elements reinforce that meaning: **stanzas, rhymes, rhythm, syntax, capitalization, punctuation.**

1. when by now and tree by leaf
   she laughed his joy she cried his grief
   bird by snow and stir by still
   anyone's any was all to he

   _____

   _____

2. old age sticks
   up Keep
   Off
   signs)&

   youth yanks them
   down (old)
   age
   cries No

   Tres)&(pas)
   youth laughs
   (sing
   old age

   _____

   _____

3. Both Producers Research and High-Grade Living declare
   He was fully sensible to the advantages of the Installment Plan
   And had everything necessary to the Modern Man.
   A phonograph, a radio, a car and a frigidaire.

   _____

   _____

"anyone lived in a pretty how town" and **"old age sticks"** by E. E. Cummings
"The Unknown Citizen" by W. H. Auden

Literary Analysis: Satire

Satire uses the elements of sarcasm and humor to make readers aware of the problems of society. It has great potential as a tool with which to effect social change. Advertisers have recognized the power of this tool, and many advertising campaigns have used satire to promote some ideas and ridicule others, particularly in the area of public service. For example, one anti-smoking campaign featured a series of posters with a caption that read "Smoking Makes You Attractive" but with photographs of smokers who looked disheveled or sick.

Think about how you might plan advertising for each of the following public service campaigns. On the lines below each one, write the satirical slogan you would present; then write two or three sentences in which you explain how you would present the slogan to enhance its satirical value and how you hope the slogan would be effective.

1. A campaign to educate drivers about the importance of obeying traffic signs.

_____

_____

_____

_____

_____

2. A campaign to encourage everyone to have an annual physical checkup.

_____

_____

_____

_____

_____

3. A campaign to get people to stop littering public beaches.

_____

_____

_____

_____

_____

4. A campaign to warn teens about the dangers of drug abuse.

_____

_____

_____

_____

_____

"The Far and the Near" by Thomas Wolfe

Build Vocabulary

Spelling Strategy When -ed is added to a verb to form the past tense, the final e of the base word is dropped: *protrude* becomes *protruded, skate = skated, dance = danced,* and *glide = glided.*

Using the Root -temp-

A. The word *tempo* is based on the word root -temp-, which means "time." Using the information following each word and what you know about the word root -temp-, write the word that best completes each sentence.

temporary (-ary = "relating to")

contemporary (con- = "with")

extemporaneous (ex- = "from"; -ous = "characterized by")

temporal (-al = "of")

1. Thomas Wolfe was a _____ of F. Scott Fitzgerald.

2. Janet's speech at the awards dinner was _____.

3. Looking for a job, Frank went to an agency that placed _____ help.

4. Lost in meditations about the eternal hereafter, James neglected _____ matters.

Using the Word Bank

tempo	sallow	sullen	timorous	visage

B. DIRECTIONS: Complete each sentence with the best word from the list in the box.

1. The angry woman looked dully at the engineer, her face a _____, suspicious mask.

2. With _____ expressions, the women looked fearfully at the engineer.

3. "His heart . . . saw the strange and unsuspected _____ of an earth which had always been within a stone's throw of him, and which he had never seen or known."

4. The woman did not look healthy; "the flesh sagged wearily in _____ folds, and the small eyes peered at him with timid suspicion and uneasy doubt."

5. After he retired, the engineer experienced a slowing in the _____ of his daily life.

"The Far and the Near" by Thomas Wolfe

Grammar and Style: Restrictive and Nonrestrictive Participial Phrases

A **participle** is a form of a verb that acts as an adjective. A **participial phrase** is a group of words beginning with a participle that acts as an adjective. A **restrictive participial phrase** is necessary to the meaning of the sentence and is *not* set off with commas. A **nonrestrictive participial phrase** is not necessary to the meaning and, therefore, *is* set off with commas.

Here is an example of a restrictive participial phrase from "The Far and the Near." The phrase is underlined.

> . . . finally nothing could be heard but the solid clacking tempo of the wheels <u>receding into the drowsy stillness of the afternoon.</u>

In this case, the participial phrase describes the noun *tempo* and is necessary to the meaning of the sentence.

Here is an example of a nonrestrictive participial phrase:

> He had driven his great train, <u>loaded with its weight of lives</u>, across the land ten thousand times.

In this case, the participial phrase describes the noun *train*, but it is not necessary to the meaning of the sentence.

A. Practice: Read the following sentences or sentence parts, and underline each participial phrase. Then identify whether it is restrictive or nonrestrictive.

1. "To one side of the house there was a garden neatly patterned with plots of growing vegetables. . . ." _____

2. " . . . now, schooled by the qualities of faith and courage and humbleness that attended his labor, he had grown old." _____

3. " . . . the vision of the little house and the women waving to him with a brave free motion of the arm had become fixed in the mind of the engineer as something beautiful and enduring." _____

4. "And finally, stammering a crude farewell, he departed." _____

B. Writing Application: Write sentences in which you use participial phrases as directed.

1. Use *swept* in a nonrestrictive participial phrase.

_____

2. Use *planted* in a restrictive participial phrase.

_____

3. Use *posing* in a nonrestrictive participial phrase.

_____

4. Use *written* in a restrictive participial phrase.

_____

Name _____ Date _____

"The Far and the Near" by Thomas Wolfe

Reading Strategy: Predict

The beginning and middle of a short story often contain clues about the story's outcome or about what will happen next. You can use these clues to **predict** what might happen. Some stories contain clues that foreshadow their endings or indicate what will actually happen. However, other stories have surprise endings.

DIRECTIONS: Read each passage from "The Far and the Near." Then write a one-sentence prediction based on the passage.

1. The engineer had grown old and gray in service. He had driven his great train, loaded with its weight of lives, across the land ten thousand times.

   _____

   _____

   _____

2. But no matter what peril or tragedy he had known, the vision of the little house and the women waving to him with a brave free motion of the arm had become fixed in the mind of the engineer as something beautiful and enduring, something beyond all change and ruin, and something that would always be the same, no matter what mishap, grief or error might break the iron schedule of his days.

   _____

   _____

   _____

3. Everything was as strange to him as if he had never seen this town before.

   _____

   _____

   _____

4. But now that he had found it, now that he was here, why did his hand falter on the gate; why had the town, the road, the earth, the very entrance to this place he loved turned unfamiliar as the landscape of some ugly dream? Why did he now feel this sense of confusion, doubt and hopelessness?

   _____

   _____

   _____

5. . . . the door was opened, and a woman stood facing him.
   And instantly, with a sense of bitter loss and grief, he was sorry he had come.

   _____

   _____

   _____

"The Far and the Near" by Thomas Wolfe

Literary Analysis: Climax and Anticlimax

Most short stories have plots based on the following structure: exposition, rising action, climax, falling action, resolution. The **climax** is the high point of a story. If a story is very compelling, the reader may feel anxious to know what will happen to the characters and may feel a sense of relief upon reaching the climax. When a story has an **anticlimax**, the author builds up the reader's expectations for a grand finale only to deflate them with an ending that may seem disappointing or trivial.

DIRECTIONS: Read each passage from "The Far and the Near." Then answer the questions that follow.

1. Every day for more than twenty years, as the train had approached this house, the engineer had blown on the whistle, and every day, as soon as she heard this signal, a woman had appeared on the back porch of the little house and waved to him. At first she had a small child clinging to her skirts, and now this child had grown to full womanhood, and every day she, too, came with her mother to the porch and waved.

   Based on this passage, what kind of impression do you think that the woman has made on the engineer? What might the engineer expect her personality to be like?

   _____

   _____

   _____

2. [The engineer] resolved that one day, when his years of service should be ended, he would go and find these people and speak at last with them whose lives had been so wrought into his own.
      That day came. At last the engineer stepped from a train onto the station platform of the town where these two women lived.

   Based on this passage, what do you expect to happen later in the story? What do you expect the engineer to find out about the women?

   _____

   _____

   _____

3. He knew at once that the woman who stood there looking at him with a mistrustful eye was the same woman who had waved to him so many thousand times. But her face was harsh and pinched and meager; the flesh sagged wearily in sallow folds, and the small eyes peered at him with timid suspicion and uneasy doubt.

   How is this passage anticlimactic when paired with the passages above? What expectations does it disappoint?

   _____

   _____

   _____

"Of Modern Poetry" and **"Anecdote of the Jar"** by Wallace Stevens
"Ars Poetica" by Archibald MacLeish
"Poetry" by Marianne Moore

Build Vocabulary

Spelling Strategy The suffix *-able*—which means "capable of," "fit for," or "worthy of"—is used in nearly 1,200 English adjectives, such as *insatiable*, *available*, and *palpable*. The suffix *-ible*, which means the same things, is used in only about 200 words, such as *eligible*, *fallible*, and *feasible*. Therefore, if you're not sure which ending to use when spelling a word, you would be more likely to spell it correctly using the suffix *-able*.

Using the Root *-satis-*

A. DIRECTIONS: In "Of Modern Poetry," Wallace Stevens uses the word *insatiable* to describe an actor who must constantly perform. The root of *insatiable* is *-satis-*, which means "enough." The prefixes for the three words below are defined in parentheses. For each word, write a sentence in which the meaning of *satis* is demonstrated clearly.

1. *dissatisfy* (*dis-* = "fail," "refuse to") _____

2. *insatiable* (*in-* = "no, not") _____

3. *unsatisfactorily* (*un-* = "the opposite") _____

Using the Word Bank

suffice	insatiable	slovenly	dominion
palpable	derivative	literalists	

B. DIRECTIONS: In the following excerpts from the poems, substitute the correct word from the Word Bank for the bracketed word or words and write it on the blank.

1. "A poem should be [able to be handled] _____ and mute / As a globed fruit."

2. "It took [the power to rule] _____ everywhere."

3. "nor till the poets among us can be / [people who take words at their exact meaning] _____ of / the imagination"

4. "It made the [untidy] wilderness _____ / Surround that hill."

5. "It has to be on that stage / And, like an [unable to be satisfied] _____ actor, slowly and/Without meditation"

6. "When they become so [based on something else] _____ as to become / unintelligible"

7. "The poem of the mind in the act of finding / What will [be adequate]" _____

"Of Modern Poetry" and **"Anecdote of the Jar"** by Wallace Stevens
"Ars Poetica" by Archibald MacLeish
"Poetry" by Marianne Moore

Grammar and Style: Subject Complements

A **subject complement** follows a linking verb and identifies or describes the subject. It can be a noun, a pronoun, or an adjective.

Here is an example of a subject complement from "Of Modern Poetry." The subject complement is underlined.

Its past was a <u>souvenir</u>.

In this case, the subject complement is a noun that identifies the subject.
Here is an example of a subject complement from "Anecdote of the Jar."

The jar was <u>round</u> upon the ground

In this case, the subject complement is an adjective that describes the subject.

A. Practice: Read the following excerpts from the poems and underline each subject complement. Then identify its use in the sentence: as a noun identifying the subject or as an adjective describing the subject.

1. "The actor is / A metaphysician in the dark"

_____

2. "The jar was gray . . ."

_____

3. "A poem should be motionless . . ."

_____

4. ". . . all these phenomena are important."

_____

B. Writing Application: Use each of these words as a subject complement in a sentence.

1. instrument

_____

2. emotional

_____

3. wilderness

_____

4. bird

_____

5. moon

_____

"Of Modern Poetry" and **"Anecdote of the Jar"** by Wallace Stevens
"Ars Poetica" by Archibald MacLeish
"Poetry" by Marianne Moore

Reading Strategy: Paraphrase

Often a poem contains unexpected words and images, which can make it difficult to read and understand. To help make the poem clearer, you can **paraphrase** difficult lines, or restate them in your own words.

DIRECTIONS: Read the following excerpts from the poems in this selection. Then paraphrase each excerpt, or rewrite in your own words, to make it easier to read and understand.

1. Then the theatre was changed / To something else. Its past was a souvenir.
   _____

2. It has to face the men of the time and to meet / The women of the time.
   _____

3. wholly / Containing the mind, below which it cannot descend, / Beyond which it has no will to rise.
   _____

4. The jar was gray and bare. / It did not give of bird or bush, / Like nothing else in Tennessee.
   _____

5. A poem should be palpable and mute / As a globed fruit.
   _____

6. A poem should be motionless in time / As the moon climbs.
   _____

7. A poem should not mean / But be.
   _____

8. Reading it [poetry], however, with a perfect contempt for it, one / discovers in / it after all, a place for the genuine.
   _____

9. these things are important not because a / high-sounding interpretation can be put upon them but / because they are / useful.
   _____

10. and can present / for inspection, imaginary gardens with real toads in / them
    _____

"Of Modern Poetry" and **"Anecdote of the Jar"** by Wallace Stevens
"Ars Poetica" by Archibald MacLeish
"Poetry" by Marianne Moore

Literary Analysis: Simile

A **simile** compares two unlike things using the word *like* or *as*. Through the use of similes, a poet arouses associations in the reader's mind that help communicate an emotion or idea. For example, in "Ars Poetica," Archibald MacLeish compares the wordlessness of a poem with the flight of birds. In the reader's mind, the simile evokes the qualities of birds in flight—soundlessness, grace, and a sense of soaring about the earth.

DIRECTIONS: In the following lines from the poems, the poets use similes. Describe the associations each simile evokes in your mind. Then explain why you think the poet chose each simile.

1. "It [the poem] has to be on that stage / And, like an insatiable actor, slowly and / With meditation, speak words. . ."

   _____

   _____

   _____

   _____

   _____

   _____

   _____

   _____

2. "A poem should be palpable and mute / As a globed fruit."

   _____

   _____

   _____

   _____

   _____

   _____

   _____

   _____

3. "a tree, the immovable critic twitching his skin like a / horse that feels a flea . . ."

   _____

   _____

   _____

   _____

   _____

   _____

   _____

"In Another Country" by Ernest Hemingway
"The Corn Planting" by Sherwood Anderson
"A Worn Path" by Eudora Welty

Build Vocabulary

Spelling Strategy In English words that begin with the letters *gn* or *kn*, the *g* or *k* is not pronounced. Examples include *gnarled, gnaw, gnat, knee, knit,* and *knock.* It is necessary to memorize the spelling of such words.

Using the Root -val-

A. DIRECTIONS: The root -*val*- means "strength" or "value." Keeping that in mind, circle the letter of the one best answer in each of the following items.

1. To *evaluate* students, teachers sometimes
   - a. lecture.
   - b. give tests.
   - c. bring snacks.
   - d. write on the chalkboard.

2. Which of the following objects would be most *valuable* to someone who wanted to sell it?
   - a. a old pair of shoes
   - b. a new refrigerator
   - c. a ceramic cup
   - d. a three-bedroom house

3. *Valiant* is most likely to be an accurate description of a
   - a. bank teller.
   - b. movie star.
   - c. fire fighter.
   - d. car salesperson.

4. A *valid* parking ticket is one that
   - a. is legally binding.
   - b. is not legally binding.
   - c. has already been paid.
   - d. is overdue for payment.

5. An apartment that is currently *available* must be
   - a. large enough for a family of four.
   - b. located at ground level.
   - c. expensive.
   - d. in move-in condition.

6. For what you say to have any *validity*, you must
   - a. speak loudly enough for everyone to hear.
   - b. say what you have to say as quickly as possible.
   - c. tell the truth and provide evidence for your claims.
   - d. speak eloquently, using good grammar and beautiful language.

Using the Word Bank

invalided	grave	limber	obstinate

B. DIRECTIONS: Fill in each blank with the appropriate word from the Word Bank.

1. If the astronauts cannot produce more oxygen for the space station, their situation will be

   _____.

2. The mule, as _____ as ever, refused to move even one inch.

3. After breaking her leg, the dancer was _____ for the rest of the season.

4. Mickey knew that if he practiced every day, he would eventually be
   _____ enough to touch his toes.

"In Another Country" by Ernest Hemingway
"The Corn Planting" by Sherwood Anderson
"A Worn Path" by Eudora Welty

Grammar and Style: Punctuating Dialogue

Direct quotations, which report the exact words of a character, give life to prose. As you read stories that have dialogue, you can hear the words of the characters in your imagination, just as if you were standing there eavesdropping. In direct quotations, **punctuating dialogue** correctly is important. Direct quotations require quotation marks around the character's words. Commas set off the quotation from the rest of the sentence.

"Now comes the trial," said Phoenix.

Phoenix said, "I thank you for your trouble."

Except for the comma that introduces the quotation, periods and commas are placed inside the quotation marks. Question marks and exclamation marks are placed according to the logic of the sentence. In other words, if the character's words are a question or exclamation, the question mark or exclamation mark is placed *inside* the quotation marks. If the entire sentence is a question or exclamation, the question mark or exclamation mark is placed *outside* the quotation marks.

When a writer uses indirect quotations, reporting on what a character said without quoting the exact words, no quotation marks are necessary.

Study these examples:

Character's words are a question or exclamation:

"How old are you, Granny?" he was saying.

She whispered, "Sic him!"

Entire sentence is a question or exclamation:

Did you wonder what the nurse meant when she said, "But it's an obstinate case"?

Indirect quotation:

The boys at first were very polite about my medals and asked me what I had done to get them.

A. Practice: Based on the punctuation, determine whether the character's words or the entire sentence is a question or exclamation. Write "character's words" or "entire sentence" in the blank.

1. The major asked, "Will I play football, too?" _____

2. Did you hear the major reply, "No, I'm afraid not"? _____

3. "Speak grammatically!" the major shouted. _____

4. How horrible it was to hear the major admit, "I cannot resign myself"! _____

5. "Did you hear him say, "before the war, I played football." _____

6. "Good," the doctor answered. "You will play football better than ever!" _____

7. That doctor said "the wound was an accident!" _____

8. Did you really hear the doctor say, "The wound was an accident"? _____

"In Another Country" by Ernest Hemingway
"The Corn Planting" by Sherwood Anderson
"A Worn Path" by Eudora Welty

Reading Strategy: Identify with Characters

Sherwood Anderson included in his writing some characters that are grotesques. Such characters have a one-track mind; they are controlled by a single emotion, concept, or goal.

DIRECTIONS: On the lines after each of the following passages, identify an emotion, a concept, or a goal that the passage suggests. Then write one or two sentences to explain how the character might act if he or she were a grotesque, controlled by the way of thinking that you have identified.

1. The major, who had been the great fencer, did not believe in bravery, and spent much time while we sat in the machines correcting my grammar. He had complimented me on how I spoke Italian, and we talked together very easily. One day I had said that Italian seemed such an easy language to me that I could not take a great interest in it; everything was so easy to say. "Ah yes," the major said. "Why, then, do you not take up the use of grammar?" So we took up the use of grammar, and soon Italian was such a difficult language that I was afraid to talk to him until I had the grammar straight in my mind.

   _____
   _____
   _____
   _____
   _____

2. Neither of the old people had ever been to the city and they were curious and eager. They wanted the drawings explained, and Hal said they were like two children wanting to know every little detail Hal could remember about their son's life in the big city. He was always at them to come there on a visit and they would spend hours talking of that.

   _____
   _____
   _____
   _____
   _____

3. . . . he laughed and lifted his gun and pointed it at Phoenix.
   She stood straight and faced him.
   "Doesn't the gun scare you?" he said, still pointing it.
   "No, sir, I seen plenty go off closer by, in my day, and for less than what I done," she said, holding utterly still.
   He smiled, and shouldered the gun. "Well, Granny," he said, "you must be a hundred years old, and scared of nothing."

   _____
   _____
   _____
   _____
   _____

"In Another Country" by Ernest Hemingway
"The Corn Planting" by Sherwood Anderson
"A Worn Path" by Eudora Welty

Literary Analysis: Point of View

Much of what gives a story its unique tone and personality is point of view. A story's **point of view** is the perspective of its narrator. You can tell the point of view of a story by paying attention to the pronouns that refer to the character whose perspective is being presented.

Point of View	Pronouns
first person	*I, me, we, us*
second person	*you*
third person	*he, him, she, her, it, they, them*

A narrator who uses first-person point of view relates events that happened to him or her personally or that he or she witnessed firsthand. Second-person point of view is rarely used in short stories. Third-person point of view can be limited or omniscient. If a limited third-person point of view is used, an outside narrator relates events that happened from the perspective of one person. An omniscient, or all-knowing, third-person narrator can tell a story switching back and forth among the perspectives of different characters and can tell the reader information that a specific character in the story would be unlikely to know. Occasionally, narrators shift back and forth among different points of view in the course of one short story.

DIRECTIONS: Read each passage and identify whether the point of view is first, second, or third person.

1. Always, though, you crossed a bridge across a canal to enter the hospital. There was a choice of three bridges. On one of them a woman sold roasted chestnuts. It was warm, standing in front of her charcoal fire, and the chestnuts were warm afterward in your pocket. The hospital was very old and very beautiful, and you entered through a gate. . . .

_____

2. The three with the medals were like hunting-hawks; and I was not a hawk, although I might seem a hawk to those who had never hunted; they, the three, knew better, and so we drifted apart.

_____

3. Their one son, Will Hutchenson, was a small but remarkably strong boy. He came to our high school in town and pitched on our town baseball team. He was a fellow always cheerful, bright and alert, and a great favorite with all of us.

_____

4. The path ran up a hill. "Seem like there is chains about my feet, time I get this far," she said, in the voice of argument old people keep to use with themselves. "Something always take a hold of me on this hill—pleads I should stay."

_____

Name_____ Date _____

"Anxiety" by Grace Paley

Build Vocabulary: Exact Verbs

A skillful writer uses exact verbs to make his or her work more interesting and exciting. Sometimes the right choice of verbs can achieve a certain effect or evoke a certain image. You can often use context clues to determine the meaning of unfamiliar words.

DIRECTIONS: Write a definition for the underlined verb in each sentence below. Then write a sentence of your own using the verb.

1. "'Up, u-u-p,' he says and <u>hoists</u> her to his shoulders."

   definition: _____

   sentence: _____
   _____

2. "The little boy sits on top of his father's head for a couple of seconds before <u>sliding</u> to his shoulders."

   definition: _____

   sentence: _____
   _____

3. "The frailer father is uncomfortable; his little girl <u>wiggles</u> too much."

   definition: _____

   sentence: _____
   _____

4. "Once, not too long ago, the tenements were <u>speckled</u> with women like me in every third window up to the fifth story. . . ."

   definition: _____

   sentence: _____
   _____

5. "Son, I must tell you that madmen intend to <u>destroy</u> this beautifully made planet."

   definition: _____

   sentence: _____
   _____

6. ". . . starting now, it had better <u>interfere</u> with any daily pleasure."

   definition: _____

   sentence: _____
   _____

"**Anxiety**" by Grace Paley

Thematic Connection: Facing Troubled Times

Can you imagine Grace Paley's story taking place in a setting other than a big city? Which details specific to the urban setting help explain or make the main characters' actions believable? In Sherwood Anderson's "The Corn Planting," the setting couldn't be more different, although the big city touches the lives of the couple at the center of that story. How does the setting of the two stories contribute to the characters' actions?

DIRECTIONS: Complete the chart below to compare and contrast Grace Paley's "Anxiety" and Sherwood Anderson's "The Corn Planting."

Main Character(s)

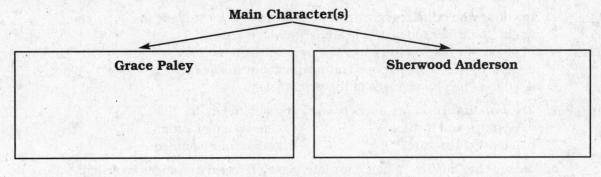

| Grace Paley | Sherwood Anderson |

Setting of Story

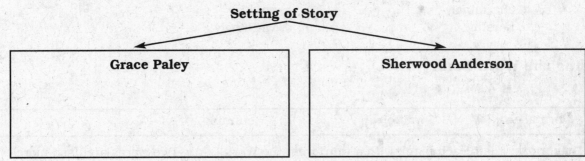

| Grace Paley | Sherwood Anderson |

Ways Setting Affects/Explains Plot Action

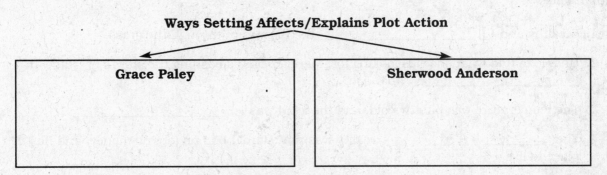

| Grace Paley | Sherwood Anderson |

Ways Setting Affects Anxiety

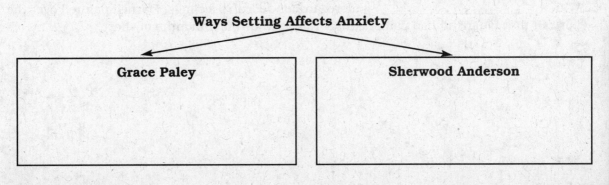

| Grace Paley | Sherwood Anderson |

"Chicago" and **"Grass"** by Carl Sandburg

Build Vocabulary

Spelling Strategy In the words *make, rope, like,* and *brute,* the final e marks the long sound of the preceding vowel. When a suffix beginning with a vowel is added to such words, the final e is usually dropped: *roping, likable, brutal, brutish.*

Related Words: *brutal*

A. DIRECTIONS: Knowing that the word *brutal* means "cruel," "crude," or "harsh," write the letter of the best description of the italicized word in each sentence.

____ 1. An editor who criticizes a writer's work *brutally* is most likely to
    a. give the writer a physical beating.
    b. physically tear up the paper the work is written on.
    c. write unnecessarily severe comments about the work.
    d. suggest helpful changes in the writer's work.

____ 2. "The *brutalization* of prisoners of war" probably refers to
    a. beatings and torture.   c. censorship of letters.
    b. lack of clean water.   d. unfair imprisonment.

____ 3. Because her bus was a half hour late, Sarah growled her anger *brutishly.*
    a. charmingly   c. quietly
    b. harshly   d. whiningly

Using the Word Bank

brutal	wanton	cunning

B. DIRECTIONS: Fill in each blank with a word from the Word Bank. Two words are used more than once.

1. Stealthy and _____, the tiger crept through the grass.

2. Unable to find what she was looking for, Marisa began smashing the store's crystal with _____ abandon.

3. The temperature was bitterly cold, and the wind was _____.

4. The _____ reality was that Harold had no job, no money, and no place to live.

5. With a _____ disregard for Joseph's feelings, Darnell painted over the portrait that his friend had painstakingly rendered through months of effort.

Name _____ Date _____

Grammar and Style: Four Types of Sentences

In English, there are four basic types of sentences: declarative, interrogative, imperative, and exclamatory. You can easily recognize interrogative and exclamatory sentences by their punctuation. **Interrogative sentences** end with a question mark because they ask a question, and **exclamatory sentences** end with an exclamation point because they express a strong emotion. **Declarative sentences** end with a period because they simply make a statement. **Imperative sentences**, however, may end with a period or an exclamation point. These sentences give commands or make requests, but they may also express a strong emotion.

Declarative Sentence: They tell me you are wicked and I believe them. . . .

Interrogative Sentence: Where are we now?

Imperative Sentence: Shovel them under and let me work.

Exclamatory Sentence: . . . under his wrist is the pulse, and under his ribs the heart of the people, laughing!

Practice: In the space next to each sentence, identify the type of sentence it is.

1. "I turn once more to those who sneer at this my city. . . ." _____

2. "Come and show me another city with lifted head singing. . . ." _____

3. "What place is this?" _____

4. "And pile them high at Ypres and Verdun." _____

5. "I am grass." _____

B. Writing Application: Rewrite each of the following sentences to make it into another type of sentence. You may need to change the meaning of a sentence or the point of view from which it is written. For example, the declarative sentence, "[O]n the faces of women and children I have seen the marks of wanton hunger," could be rewritten as an imperative: "Look at the marks of wanton hunger on the faces of the women and children."

1. "I have seen your painted women under the gas lamps luring the farm boys."

   _____

2. "I have seen the gunman kill and go free to kill again."

   _____

3. " . . . here is a tall bold slugger set vivid against the little soft cities."

   _____

4. "Pile the bodies high at Austerlitz and Waterloo."

   _____

5. "Where are we now?"

   _____

Name _____ Date _____

"**Chicago**" and "**Grass**" by Carl Sandburg

Reading Strategy: Respond

For poetry, to be effective, both writer and reader must do some work. The poet's job is to craft his or her message carefully, using tools such as images, rhyme, rhythm, and meter. The reader's job is to respond. As a reader, you can **respond** to a poem by visualizing the images, relating events in the poem to your own knowledge, and forming an opinion of the poem and its message. Your tools are your senses, your background knowledge, and your own gut feelings.

DIRECTIONS: Use this graphic organizer to help you respond to passages from "Chicago" and "Grass." In the first column, write the passage. In the second column, note any senses that might help you respond in a sensory way to the image. In the third column, write down any background knowledge that you need in order to understand the passage. In the last column, write your opinion of the passage or your overall response to it. Do you agree with the passage? Do you disagree? What impression does the passage make on you? One passage has already been done for you.

Passage	Senses	Background Knowledge	My Opinion or Response
"Under the smoke, dust all over his mouth, laughing with white teeth."	Sight—to imagine what the worker looks like; Smell—to imagine the smell of the smoke; Touch—to imagine the feel of the dust on one's skin.	Chicago was an early center of industry in the United States. Someone who worked in a smoky, dusty environment might have worked in a factory.	It's unusual to see a worker laughing in the middle of hard physical labor and harsh working conditions.

"Chicago" and **"Grass"** by Carl Sandburg

Literary Analysis: Apostrophe

Apostrophe is the literary technique of directly addressing a person or thing as if that person or thing were present. This technique is frequently used in romantic poetry or funeral songs in which the speaker of the poem directly addresses the loved one, or death. For example, the clown in Shakespeare's play *Twelfth Night* addresses his love, "O mistress mine! where are you roaming?" In *Much Ado About Nothing*, a group of singers open a funeral song with, "Pardon, Goddess of the night, / Those that slew thy virgin knight;" / In a more modern example, the poet Sandburg is using apostrophe on lines such as this one from "Chicago":

Hog Butcher for the world, . . . They tell me you are wicked. . .

DIRECTIONS: Read "Chicago." Then answer the questions below.

1. List three clues that show that Sandburg is using apostrophe in this poem.

_____

_____

_____

_____

_____

2. Who is being addressed in "Chicago"?

_____

_____

3. Suppose that the speaker of "Chicago" is responding to a previous conversation. What would that conversation have been like? Who would have participated in it?

_____

_____

_____

_____

_____

4. How might the structure of this poem have been different if Sandburg had *not* used the technique of apostrophe?

_____

_____

_____

_____

_____

"The Jilting of Granny Weatherall" by Katherine Anne Porter

Build Vocabulary

Spelling Strategy The suffix *-ety* or *-ity*, changes an adjective into a noun, often with other spelling changes in the word. For example, *pious* becomes *piety*, *anxious* becomes *anxiety*, *illegal* becomes *illegality*, *creative* becomes *creativity*, and *accountable* becomes *accountability*.

Using the Prefix *dys-*

A. DIRECTIONS: The word *dyspepsia* combines the prefix *dys-*, meaning "difficult" or "bad," and the word root *pepsis*, meaning "digestion". The word *dyspepsia*, therefore, means "indigestion." The prefix *dys-* is often used in medical terminology. Using the information following each word and what you know about the prefix *dys-*, write the letter of the definition on the line next to the word it defines.

____ 1. *dyscrasia* (*krasis* = a mixing)

____ 2. *dysgraphia* (*graphia* = writing)

____ 3. *dyskinesia* (*kin[e]sis* = motion)

____ 4. *dyslexia* (*lexis* = speech)

____ 5. *dysphagia* (*phag[ein]* = to eat)

____ 6 *dysphonia* (*ph[o]n[e]* = voice)

____ 7. *dyspnea* (*pnein* = breathing)

a. impairment of the ability to read

b. difficulty in swallowing

c. impairment of the ability to write

d. an abnormal imbalance in some part of the body, especially in the blood

e. shortness of breath

f. impairment of the ability to produce speech sounds

g. impairment of body movement

Using the Word Bank

piety	frippery	dyspepsia

B. DIRECTIONS: Choose the word that best completes the meaning of each sentence and write it in the blank.

1. Their frippery was evident in their _____ furnishings.
   a. gaudy   c. old
   b. functional   d. dark

2. His piety was demonstrated by his desire to _____ .
   a. spend   c. pray
   b. sleep   d. play

3. When her dyspepsia would act up, her _____ would hurt badly.
   a. back   c. head
   b. elbow   d. stomach

"The Jilting of Granny Weatherall" by Katherine Anne Porter

Grammar and Style: Imperative Sentences

An **imperative sentence** states a request or gives an order. The subject in an imperative sentence is not stated; rather, it is understood. In the following example from "The Jilting of Granny Weatherall," the word *You*, or a character's name, is implied in the italicized sentence.

Don't tell me what I'm going to be. I'm on my feet now, morally speaking. It's Cornelia. I had to go to bed to get rid of her.

A. Practice: Read the following excerpts from the selection. Underline each imperative sentence or sentence fragment.

1. " 'Well, Missy, excuse me,' Doctor Harry patted her cheek. 'But I've got to warn you, haven't I?' "

2. "Don't let good things rot for want of using. You waste life when you waste good food. Don't let things get lost. It's bitter to lose things."

3. " 'There, wait a minute, here we are!' John, get the doctor now, Hapsy's time has come. But there was Hapsy standing by the bed in a white cap. 'Cornelia, tell Hapsy to take off her cap. I can't see her plain.' "

B. Writing Application: Rewrite each example to make it an imperative sentence. If it is already an imperative sentence, write "Correct."

1. "I'd have you respect your elders, young man."

   _____

2. "Get along and doctor your sick."

   _____

3. "Come in, children, don't stay out in the night air."

   _____

4. "I want you to pick all the fruit this year and see that nothing is wasted."

   _____

5. "I want you to find George."

   _____

6. "Give Father Connolly a chair."

   _____

7. "Now, Ellen, you must believe what I tell you. . . ."

   _____

8. "Cornelia, you're to have the amethyst set. . . ."

   _____

"The Jilting of Granny Weatherall" by Katherine Anne Porter

Reading Strategy: Clarify Sequence of Events

Granny Weatherall recalls that her father was interviewed by a newspaper reporter when he was 102 years old. Imagine that a reporter comes to interview Mrs. Weatherall just before she lapses into her final illness. The reporter wants to tell in sequence the major events of this woman's life and poses the sequential questions below. The reporter hopes to get Granny Weatherall's feelings, as well as facts.

Reply to each of the reporter's questions as if you were Granny Weatherall. Be sure to use the first person *I* in your answers.

1. What did you look like when you were twenty years old?

   _____

   _____

   _____

2. What kind of relationship did you have with your husband?

   _____

   _____

   _____

3. As a young widow, what tasks did you take on alone?

   _____

   _____

   _____

4. How would you describe your relationship with your children when they were young? How has that relationship changed?

   _____

   _____

   _____

5. You seem to be very unconcerned about death. Could you please explain your reasons for this attitude?

   _____

   _____

   _____

6. During this interview, you've frequently muttered the name "George." Please explain who George is and tell us why he is so important.

   _____

   _____

   _____

"The Jilting of Granny Weatherall" by Katherine Anne Porter

Literary Analysis: Stream of Consciousness

The **stream-of-consciousness** technique in literature is based on real-life thinking processes. You probably realize that your thoughts often jump around. An ordinary sight, a certain sound, or a flash of memory can serve as a trigger, causing your thoughts to drift to the past or evoking a series of images that are yours alone.

A. DIRECTIONS: In Porter's story, the following triggers cause Granny's thoughts to drift. For each one, write one or two sentences that discuss the thoughts, feelings, and images that come to Granny's mind.

1. the sight of Doctor Harry

   _____

   _____

2. jobs to do tomorrow

   _____

   _____

3. the distance of her daughter Lydia

   _____

   _____

4. the feel of the pillow

   _____

   _____

5. the arrival of Father Connolly

   _____

   _____

B. DIRECTIONS: From the list above, choose the trigger you find most interesting. Using the stream-of-consciousness technique, write a paragraph from the perspective of another character, either a character in the story or a character of your own choosing. Show how the trigger evokes thoughts, feelings, and images in the character's mind.

_____

_____

_____

_____

_____

_____

_____

_____

_____

"Race at Morning" and **"Nobel Prize Acceptance Speech"** by William Faulkner

Build Vocabulary

Spelling Strategy Nouns meaning "state or quality of" or "place of" often end in *-ery*: *slavery, trickery, refinery, brewery, distillery*. In contrast, the ending *-ary* is usually reserved for nouns designating a person or thing related to or connected with something: *functionary, actuary, statuary*; or for adjectives meaning "related to" or "connected with": *budgetary, auxiliary, dietary.*

Using the Suffix *-ery*

A. DIRECTIONS: Combine the italicized word with the suffix *-ery*. Write the new word in the blank.

1. Hunting was a great relief after the long months of *drudge* working in the cotton fields.
   _____

2. The deer showed great *brave* as it turned and raced back along the route it had come.
   _____

3. The dogs led the hunters back toward the *fish* at the head of the bayou._____

4. As he followed the dogs, he munched on bagels he'd bought at the *bake* that morning.
   _____

5. The deer used *trick* to confuse the dogs and throw them off its scent.
   _____

Using the Word Bank

bayou	distillery	buck	moiling
switch	scrabbling	swag	glade

B. DIRECTIONS: Write the word from the Word Bank that best completes each sentence.

1. The_____ snorted defiantly and shook its antlers.

2. The guppies began jumping and_____ rapidly near the surface of the water as the woman dropped fish food into the aquarium.

3. The_____ was much warmer than the surrounding woods because the bright sunlight beat down directly on the open grassy area.

4. The fisher paddled quietly across the_____.

5. The boy was down on all fours,_____ up the banks of the steep ravine.

6. The truck from the_____ stopped in front of the tavern and unloaded a supply of alcoholic beverages.

7. The child made a comfortable hideout in a_____ of grapevines hanging from the tree.

8. The boy had a mark on his face from a_____ that had struck him as he ran through the dense woods.

Name _____ Date _____

"Race at Morning" and **"Nobel Prize Acceptance Speech"** by William Faulkner

Grammar and Style: Correct Use of Irregular Verb Forms

Most verbs form their past tense and past participle by adding *-d* or *-ed* to the present tense. These are called regular verbs. Irregular verbs, however, form their past tense and past participle in unusual ways.

	Present Tense	**Past Tense**	**Past Participle**
REGULAR VERBS	look	looked	looked
	help	helped	helped
IRREGULAR VERBS	keep	kept	kept
	give	gave	given
	cut	cut	cut
	sing	sang	sung

In "Race at Morning," the narrator is uneducated and often uses irregular verbs incorrectly. For example:

> And sho enough, as soon as we *come* to the bayou we *seen* his foot in the mud where he had come up out of the river last night. . . .

Written with correct irregular verb forms, the sentence would read as follows:

> And sho enough, as soon as we *came* to the bayou we *saw* his foot in the mud where he had come up out of the river last night. . . .

If you are uncertain about the correct form of an irregular verb, check a dictionary or grammar book.

A. Practice: Underline the irregular verbs in the paragraph below. Circle those verbs that are used incorrectly.

> William Faulkner lived most of his life in the town of Oxford, Mississippi, where he wrote many of his best-known novels and short stories. He chose a wide range of serious themes for his fiction. Many of his novels concern tragic situations, but Faulkner had a strong sense of humor, which sometimes surfaces in even his most tragic stories. He give free rein to his humor in stories such as "Spotted Ponies." Set in the fictional county of Yoknapatawpha, this story tell about some horses that run wild in a small town.

B. Writing Application: Rewrite the following sentences. Write the correct past or past participle for each italicized verb.

1. Faulkner *say* that the Nobel Prize was not presented to him but to his writing.

_____

2. He *mean* that his work, not his life, was exceptional.

_____

3. Faulkner had *spend* much of his life working long hours.

_____

"Race at Morning" and **"Nobel Prize Acceptance Speech"** by William Faulkner

Reading Strategy: Break Down Long Sentences

William Faulkner often strings ideas together in very long sentences. In "Race at Morning," this style gives the impression that the narrator is relating events without planning the story or editing what he says. The style makes the story seem natural and immediate, but it can also confuse the reader. One way to figure out the meaning of long sentences is to break them down into smaller units of meaning. Then analyze each sentence by asking yourself questions about the characters, the action, and the setting. Look at this example from "Race at Morning." Notice that slashes are used to indicate the smaller units of meaning.

"Mister Ernest!" I hollered, and then clumb down to the bayou and scooped my cap full of water / and clumb back and threw it in his face, / and he opened his eyes and laid there on the saddle cussing me.

1. What characters are featured in this sentence? (the narrator and Mister Ernest)

2. Where does the action take place? (the bayou)

3. What are the characters doing, or what is happening around them? (The narrator addresses Mister Ernest, gets a cap of water from the bayou, and throws it in the man's face. Mister Ernest then cusses the narrator.)

DIRECTIONS: Use the same strategy for these long sentences that are difficult to understand. First break the sentence into smaller units of meaning. Then ask yourself the questions that follow.

1. We come to a place where the bayou had narrowed down to about twelve or fifteen feet, and Mister Ernest said, "Look out, I'm going to touch him," and done it; I didn't even have time to freshen my holt when we was already in the air, and then I seen the vine—it was a loop of grapevine nigh as big as my wrist, looping down right across the middle of the bayou—and I thought he seen it, too, and was jest waiting to grab it and fling it over our heads to go under it, and I know Dan seen it because he even ducked his head to jump under it

a. Which characters are featured in this sentence?

_____

_____

b. Where does the action take place?

_____

_____

c. What are the characters doing, or what is happening around them?

_____

_____

_____

"Race at Morning" and **"Nobel Prize Acceptance Speech"** by William Faulkner

Literary Analysis: Dialect

Dialect is a regional variation in the way a language is spoken. The variation may be a difference in the choice of words or the way in which words are pronounced, or it may be the use of nonstandard grammatical constructions or syntax. Every region of the United States has its own dialect. In "Race at Morning," Faulkner uses a Southern dialect. Notice the examples of dialect in this passage.

> Then Mister Ernest loaded the gun and *give* me the stirrup, and I got up behind him and we *taken* the fire road up toward the bayou, the four big dogs dragging Simon along in front with his single-barrel *britch*-loader slung on a piece of plow line across his back, and the puppies moiling along in *ever'body's* way.

The narrator doesn't use the standard past tense forms of *give* and *take* but uses *give* in place of *gave* and *taken* in place of *took*. The narrator changes the pronunciation of *breechloader*, which is a type of gun, to *britch-loader*. He also shortens the word *everybody's* to *ever'body's*.

DIRECTIONS: Read the following passages from "Race at Morning" and underline the examples of dialect. Then rewrite the passage in standard English.

1. "Which is jest what we never aimed for him to do this time."

   _____

2. "Eagle must 'a' been looking right up that big son of a gun's tail until he finally decided he better git on out of there."

   _____

   _____

3. "I don't know hos he done it. I just had a glimpse of him. He looked big as a elephant, with a rack on his head you could cradle a yellin' calf in."

   _____

   _____

4. " 'Mister Ernest!' I hollered, and then clumb down to the bayou and scooped my cap full of water and clumb back and throwed it in his face, and he opened his eyes and laid there on the saddle cussing me."

   _____

   _____

   _____

5. "If we could jest ketch Dan; not that he would have went them fifteen miles back to camp, because, if anything, he would have went on by hisself to try to help Eagle ketch that buck."

   _____

   _____

   _____

Build Vocabulary

Spelling Strategy The one-syllable word *full* is spelled with two *l*'s. However, longer words ending with the suffix *-ful*, such as *rueful* and *stressful*, are spelled with only one *l* at the end.

Using the Root *-lum-*

A. DIRECTIONS: The following words contain the root *-lum-*, meaning "light." Look carefully at each word and its definition; then write a sentence in which you use the word. Pay close attention to the part of speech of each word.

1. *luminary, n,* a person of prominence or brilliant achievement

_____

_____

2. *luminary, adj,* giving off light

_____

_____

3. *luminous, adj,* emitting or reflecting steady, suffused, or glowing light

_____

_____

4. *luminosity, n,* the quality or state of being luminous

_____

_____

5. *illuminate, vt,* 1: to enlighten spiritually or intellectually 2: to supply or brighten with light

_____

_____

Using the Word Bank

poise	rueful	luminary

B. DIRECTIONS: Fill in each blank with the vocabulary word that best completes the sentence.

1. The moon cast its _____ glow against the night sky.

2. In the poem " 'Out, Out—,' " the young boy's first expression of shock about his accident is a _____ laugh.

3. The neighbor in the poem "Mending Wall" shows his _____ with the repeated comment "Good fences make good neighbors."

Name _____ Date _____

Grammar and Style: Uses of Infinitives

An **infinitive** is a common verb form that consists of the base verb preceded by the word *to*. Infinitives can function in a sentence as nouns, adjectives, or adverbs. The following line from Robert Frost's "Birches" contains an example of an infinitive used as a noun. The underlined infinitive is the direct object of the verb *prefer*.

I should prefer <u>to have</u> some boy bend them. . . .

The following line from "Stopping by Woods on a Snowy Evening" contains an infinitive used as an adverb, modifying *gives*.

He <u>gives</u> his harness bells a shake/<u>To ask</u> if there is some mistake.

An **infinitive phrase** consists of an infinitive plus its complements or modifiers.

A. Practice: Read the following sentences and underline the infinitive or infinitive phrase. Then in the blank, identify how it is used in the sentence: as a noun (N), an adjective (ADJ), or an adverb (ADV).

_____ 1. "I'd like to get away from earth a while/And then come back to it and begin over."

_____ 2. "As he swung toward them holding up the hand,/Half in appeal, but half as if to keep/The life from spilling. . . ."

_____ 3. "No more to build on there."

_____ 4. "My little horse must think it queer/To stop without a farmhouse near"

_____ 5. "I have passed by the watchman on his beat/And dropped my eyes, unwilling to explain."

B. Writing Application: Rewrite each of these sentences, replacing the underlined verb with an infinitive. Add or change other words in the sentence as necessary. The first one has been done for you.

1. Robert Frost <u>gave</u> many speeches during his lifetime.

   Robert Frost was asked to give many speeches during his lifetime.

2. He often <u>wrote</u> about New Englanders and the rural landscape of the eastern part of the United States.

   _____

3. "Mending Wall" is about two neighbors <u>putting</u> up a fence between their property.

   _____

4. "Stopping by Woods on a Snowy Evening" is about a man pausing <u>and reflecting</u> on the beauty of nature.

   _____

5. Robert Frost often <u>presented</u> himself as a folksy, jovial farmer.

   _____

Robert Frost's Poetry

Reading Strategy: Reading Blank Verse

Many of Robert Frost's poems are written in blank verse. With this type of poetry, it is a good idea to read the words aloud and track each sentence from beginning to end, rather than to pause at the end of each poetic line. By reading the poem as a group of sentences, readers can help themselves interpret and enjoy the rich meanings and the more subtle nuances of the words.

A. DIRECTIONS: Reread the following passage from Robert Frost's poem "Acquainted with the Night." Then answer the questions below.

> I have stood still and stopped the sound of feet
> When far away an interrupted cry
> Came over houses from another street,
>
> But not to call me back or say good-by;
> And further still at an unearthly height
> One luminary clock against the sky
>
> Proclaimed the time was neither wrong nor right.

1. How many lines are there in the passage? _____

2. How many sentences are there in the passage? _____

B. DIRECTIONS: As you read the six Frost poems, use this chart to note first the number of sentences in each one. Then remember to read the poems by pausing only at the ends of the sentences.

Poem	Number of Sentences
"Birches"	
"Mending Wall"	
" 'Out, Out—' "	
"Stopping by Woods on a Snowy Evening"	
"Acquainted with the Night"	
"The Gift Outright"	

Robert Frost's Poetry

Literary Analysis: Blank Verse

Robert Frost was a versatile poet equally skilled at writing in rhymed and unrhymed formats. In his poem "Stopping by Woods on a Snowy Evening," for example, he uses the technique of rhyming first, second, and fourth lines until the final stanza which has end rhymes on all four lines:

> The woods are lovely, dark and deep,
> But I have promises to keep,
> And miles to go before I sleep,
> And miles to go before I sleep.

Despite this formal rhyme scheme, the poem has an unforced musical quality that reveals both the speaker's joy at the beauty of nature and his wistfulness at the many obligations he must fulfill before his day is done.

However, in "The Gift Outright," "Birches," and " 'Out, Out—'," Frost writes in quite a different style. These poems are written in **blank verse**, which is composed of unrhymed lines of **iambic pentameter**. The basic unit of this type of meter is the iamb, which is made up of one unstressed syllable immediately followed by a stressed syllable. In iambic pentameter there are five iambs per poetic line. This meter recreates the flow of human speech patterns. Poems written in iambic pentameter, therefore, lend themselves especially to being read aloud.

DIRECTIONS: Read the following excerpt from Robert Frost's poem "Birches." Underline each stressed syllable. Then read the excerpt aloud to observe especially the poem's rhythm.

> And so I dream of going back to be.
>
> It's when I'm weary of considerations,
>
> And life is too much like a pathless wood
>
> Where your face burns and tickles with the cobwebs
>
> Broken across it, and one eye is weeping
>
> From a twig's having lashed across it open.

"The Night the Ghost Got In" by James Thurber
from _Here Is New York_ by E. B. White

Build Vocabulary

Spelling Strategy Many words spell the "f" sound with a _ph_: _claustrophobia, blasphemy, physical, symphony, phrase_. These words are derived from Greek words that have the Greek letter _phi_.

Using the Root _-terr-_

The root _-terr-_ comes from the Latin word _terra_, meaning "earth." Many English words are formed from _-terr-_ with a variety of suffixes and prefixes.

A. DIRECTIONS: Fill each blank in the sentences below with one of the listed words. Then explain how the meaning is related to that of _-terr-_. Use a dictionary if necessary.

terrace	terrestrial	terrier	territorial

1. Kelp is not a _____ plant because it grows in the ocean.

_____

2. The wolf is a _____ animal because it defends the area where it lives.

_____

3. The hunter waited as his _____ dug into the underground burrow.

_____

4. Sliding doors opened onto a _____ at the back of the house.

_____

Using the Word Bank

intuitively	blaspheming	aspiration
subterranean	claustrophobia	cosmopolitan

B. DIRECTIONS: Select the Word Bank word that is related best to each situation or thing and write it in the blank.

1. a series of caves located under the base of a mountain _____

2. someone trapped in a broken-down elevator _____

3. a homeowner accidentally hitting his thumb with a hammer _____

4. a student practicing hours every day to become a pianist_____

5. a restaurant serving foods of many nations _____

6. a detective following a hunch to question a minor suspect_____

"The Night the Ghost Got In" by James Thurber

from *Here Is New York* by E. B. White

Grammar and Style: Commas in Series

Writers sometimes string together details in a *series*—three or more parallel items linked together by commas. A conjunction such as *and* or *or* often comes before the final item. Some writers leave out the comma before that conjunction. However, to make your writing clear, you should always include a comma before the conjunction. Study these examples from the selections:

Thurber: Instantly the steps began again, circled the dining-room table like a man running, **and** started up the stairs toward us . . . .

White: . . . the great walls and towers rising, the smoke rising, the heat not yet rising, the hopes and ferments of so many awakening millions rising. . . .

A. Practice: Read the sentences below. Write *correct* on the line after each passage in which commas are correctly used. In the others, insert commas in the appropriate places.

1. ". . . [D]oors were yanked open drawers were yanked open windows were shot up and pulled down furniture fell with dull thumps." _____

2. "They began to ransack the floor: pulled beds away from walls tore clothes off hooks in the closets pulled suitcases and boxes off shelves." _____

3. "[T]hey sit in stalled subways without claustrophobia they extricate themselves from panic situations by some lucky wisecrack they meet confusion and congestion with patience and grit. . . ." _____

4. ". . . he buys a bunch of pussy willows, a Mazda bulb, a drink, a shine—all between the corner where he steps off the bus and his apartment." _____

B. Writing Application: Read each group of sentences. Then combine them to form a single sentence made up of a series of items. Insert commas in the correct places.

1. As I left for the airport, I turned on my alarm system. Then I danced out the door and slammed it joyfully behind me. I suddenly realized I had left all my keys on the kitchen counter.

   _____

   _____

2. A stuffed woodchuck in a lifelike pose dominated the shelf. The shelf also held a ceramic mug bearing the image of a long-forgotten politician. There was an assortment of dusty quartz crystals. Six or seven tiny plastic dolls were scattered like casualties on a battlefield. Last but not least, there was a grimy ball of aluminum foil the size of a human head.

   _____

   _____

3. Evelyn began to imagine herself on vacation: she would relax for nine days free of her boss's snarls. She could read novels in the sun. She could eat romantic dinners on moonlit terraces. She would get painfully sunburned and suffer stomach upsets from the rich food. She would come home after six days.

   _____

   _____

"The Night the Ghost Got In" by James Thurber
from *Here Is New York* by E. B. White

Reading Strategy: Recognize Hyperbole

Hyperbole is a deliberate exaggeration or overstatement, often used for comic effect. By enlarging on details or stretching the reader's credence, the writer can create amusing characters and situations. Often, these lively exaggerations are juxtaposed with a mild, understated commentary that serves to highlight the ridiculous parts of the story.

On the lines following each of the passages from *"The Night the Ghost Got In,"* write what is exaggerated in the passage and how the exaggeration adds to the humor of the story.

1. " 'Awp,' he said, in the low, hopeless tone of a despondent beagle—"

   _____
   _____
   _____
   _____

2. " 'Nothing,' he said, gruffly, but he was, in color, a light green."

   _____
   _____
   _____
   _____

3. "Bodwell was at the window in a minute, shouting, frothing a little, shaking his fist. 'We'll sell the house and go back to Peoria,' we could hear Mrs. Bodwell saying. "

   _____
   _____
   _____
   _____

4. " 'There were two or three of them,' mother said, 'whooping and carrying on and slamming doors.' "

   _____
   _____
   _____
   _____

5. "He bounded out of bed wearing a long flannel nightgown over long woolen underwear, a nightcap, and a leather jacket around his chest."

   _____
   _____
   _____
   _____

"The Night the Ghost Got In" by James Thurber

from *Here Is New York* by E. B. White

Literary Analysis: Informal Essay

You would probably agree that informal essays are fun to read because of their casual style, everyday language, and informal organization. Their subjects are usually clearly defined and down-to-earth. In **informal essays**, authors chat, digress as the spirit moves them, express their opinions, and reveal their personalities.

DIRECTIONS: Read the following passages from "The Night the Ghost Got In" and "Here Is New York." Briefly describe what makes each passage characteristic of an informal essay. Use extra paper if you need to.

1. "Glass tinkled into the bedroom occupied by a retired engraver named Bodwell and his wife. Bodwell had been for some years in rather a bad way and was subject to mild 'attacks.' Most everybody we know or lived near had *some* kind of attacks."

   _____

   _____

   _____

   _____

2. "One of them found an old zither that Roy had won in a pool tournament. 'Looky here, Joe,' he said, strumming it with a big paw. The cop named Joe took it and turned it over. 'What is it?' he asked me. 'It's an old zither our guinea pig used to sleep on,' I said. It was true that a pet guinea pig we once had would never sleep anywhere except on the zither, but I should never have said so. Joe and the other cop looked at me a long time. They put the zither back on a shelf."

   _____

   _____

   _____

   _____

3. "Every time the residents brush their teeth, millions of gallons of water must be drawn from the Catskills and the hills of Westchester. When a young man in Manhattan writes a letter to his girl in Brooklyn, the love message gets blown to her through a pneumatic tube—pfft—just like that."

   _____

   _____

   _____

   _____

4. "In summer the city contains (except for tourists) only diehards and authentic characters. No casual, spotty dwellers are around, only the real article. And the town has a somewhat relaxed air, and one can lie in a loincloth, gasping and remembering things."

   _____

   _____

   _____

   _____

from *Dust Tracks on a Road* by Zora Neale Hurston

Build Vocabulary

Spelling Strategy In many words, the "j" sound is spelled -*dg*-. Examples include *knowledge*, *judgment*, *fudge*, *pudgy*, and *ledger*.

Using the Root -*graph*-

The root -*graph*- comes from a Greek word meaning "write." In English, this root appears in a variety of words.

A. DIRECTIONS: Write each word listed below in the blank following the situation to which it is most closely related.

lithograph (*litho-* = stone)	*graphology*
calligraphy (*calli-* = beautiful)	*graphic*

1. the study of handwriting to analyze personalities _____

2. a reporter describing a crime in clear and vivid detail _____

3. a picture created from an image drawn on a stone plate _____

4. an invitation written in a decorative script _____

Using the Word Bank

foreknowledge	brazenness	caper
exalted	geography	avarice

B. DIRECTIONS: Match each word in the left column with its definition in the right column.

____ 1. foreknowledge	a. filled with joy or pride; elated
____ 2. brazenness	b. an extreme desire for wealth; greed
____ 3. caper	c. awareness of something before it happens
____ 4. exalted	d. study of the earth
____ 5. avarice	e. prank
____ 6. geography	f. shamelessness; boldness

Name _____ Date _____

from *Dust Tracks on a Road* by Zora Neale Hurston

Grammar and Style: Parallelism in Coordinate Elements

Parallel grammatical elements in a sentence may be linked by coordinating conjunctions—
and, *but*, *or*, and *nor*. Parallel elements are of the same type—nouns, verbs, adjectives, adverbs,
clauses, or phrases. They are also the same in structure.

> You will find something *significant* and *enjoyable* in most mythological stories.

In the example, *significant* and *enjoyable* are equivalent elements—they are both adjectives
with the same structure.

> Jerry preferred *walking* and *to run* over riding.

Walking and *to run* are not parallel: one is the gerund form of a verb and one is the infinitive
form of a verb.

> Jerry preferred *walking* and *running* over *riding*.

A. Practice: Read the sentences below. Circle the coordinating conjunction(s) and underline
the parallel coordinate elements.

1. "I was fifth or sixth down the line."

2. "Last thing, I was given a handkerchief to carry, warned again about my behavior, and
   sent off. . . ."

3. "I seemed to remember seeing Thor swing his mighty short-handled hammer as he sped
   across the sky in rumbling thunder, lightning flashing from the tread of his steeds and the
   wheels of his chariot."

4. "The clothes were not new, but they were very good."

5. "Not one time did David stop and preach about sins and other things."

B. Writing Application: Read each group of sentences. Then combine them to form a single
sentence with a coordinating conjunction to link parallel elements.

1. The two white ladies who visited her school had fingers that were long. Their fingers were
   also white. However, they were pink near the tips.

   _____

2. Zora liked to read mythological stories. She also enjoyed studying geography. She liked
   game playing.

   _____

3. Zora didn't know whether she would get a reward. She didn't know whether she would
   be whipped.

   _____

4. For her visit to the ladies, Zora was thoroughly scrubbed in a tub of sudsy water. She
   dressed in a gingham dress. Then her mother inspected her from head to toe.

   _____

   _____

Name _____ Date _____

from *Dust Tracks on a Road* by Zora Neale Hurston

Reading Strategy: Analyze How a Writer Achieves Purpose

Writers usually have one or more **purposes** in mind when they write. The words, characters, events, and details of their works are chosen to achieve their purposes or goals. In her autobiography, Zora Neale Hurston wrote to describe her own personal experiences, her own character, and the vital African American community in which she grew up.

DIRECTIONS: The first column of the chart below lists summaries of scenes, events, and comments from Zora Neale Hurston's autobiography. Read the summaries and, in the second column, record your analysis of the author's purpose in choosing each scene. Then choose two more scenes, events, or comments, summarize them in the first column, and analyze their purpose in the second. If necessary, use extra paper.

Scene, Event, or Comment of Writer	Analysis of Writer's Purpose
1. Zora marvels at the fingers of the white women with their pink tips.	
2. The white ladies ask Zora to read from a magazine when she visits them in their hotel.	
3. Zora finds Hercules a moving hero because he chooses duty over pleasure. She likes David because he is a strong, active character.	
4.	
5.	

Name _____ Date _____

from *Dust Tracks on a Road* by Zora Neale Hurston

Literary Analysis: Social Context in Autobiography

Zora Neale Hurston's autobiography, *Dust Tracks on a Road*, is clearly written from the point of view of an adult reflecting on her childhood in the segregated South. Although she remembers these early events in great detail, she makes it clear that her interpretation happened long after the incidents occurred. She is able to fit her own story into the social context of the time period in which she grew up. For example, in the second paragraph Hurston comments on the white travelers' allowing her to accompany them a short way: "I know now that I must have caused a great deal of amusement among them, but my self-assurance must have carried the point, for I was always invited to come along." As a child she was not aware of why asking to walk along with white people was frowned upon by her family, but as an adult, she places her behavior in a social context and sees how her actions were very unusual among African Americans at that time.

By combining narration and reflection on the social situation, autobiographers not only reveal something about themselves and their social context, they also lead us to contemplate our own social context and its influence upon us.

DIRECTIONS: For each of the following quotations, discuss what Zora Neale Hurston reveals about the social context of her writing. Then briefly explain how each quotation might relate to something in your current social context.

1. "Git down offa dat gate-post! You li'l sow, you! Git down! Setting up dere looking dem white folks right in de face! They's gowine to lynch you, yet. And don't stand in dat doorway gazing out at 'em neither. Youse too brazen to live long."

_____

_____

_____

2. The village seemed dull to me most of the time. If the village was singing a chorus, I must have missed the tune.

_____

_____

_____

3. The whites that came down from the North were often brought by their friends to visit the village school. A Negro school was something strange to them, and while they were always sympathetic and kind, curiosity must have been present.

_____

_____

_____

4. Usually, the visitors gave warning a day ahead and we would be cautioned to put on shoes, comb our heads, and see to ears and fingernails.

_____

_____

_____

"Refugee in America," "Ardella," "The Negro Speaks of Rivers," and **"Dream Variations"** by Langston Hughes
"The Tropics in New York" by Claude McKay

Build Vocabulary

Spelling Strategy *Lulled* is the past tense of the verb *lull*, which ends in two *l*'s. One-syllable words such as *lull* and *roll* have two *l*'s because the words have only a single vowel. One-syllable words such as *seal* and *peal* have only one *l* because the words have two vowels.

Using the Root *-lib-*

A. DIRECTIONS: The word root *-lib-* derives from *liber*, the Latin word for "free."

Complete each of the sentences below with one of the words or phrases in the box. To help figure out which word or phrase to use, determine which part of speech—noun, verb, adverb—is missing in the sentence.

liberalize	liberal arts	liberally	libertarian

1. Since basketball games often did not end until about 11:00 P.M., Anthony began a campaign to _____ the curfew laws.

2. Literature, philosophy, and history are considered to be part of the _____ because studying them helps students to develop their general ability to think and reason.

3. Scowling at the steamed broccoli, Maura poured cheese sauce over it _____ .

4. A person who believes that liberty should be absolute and unrestricted is a _____ .

Using the Word Bank

lulled	dusky	liberty

B. DIRECTIONS: In each blank, write the letter of the one best answer.

____ 1. A baby would most likely be lulled to sleep by
   a. a deep bellow.   b. a sharp screech.   c. a loud yell.   d. a soft song.

____ 2. It is *dusky* outside when
   a. it is completely dark.   c. the sun is high in the sky.
   b. it is almost dark.   d. the sun is behind clouds.

____ 3. A prisoner who is told that he is at *liberty* to go may safely assume that
   a. he may leave and go wherever he wants to.
   b. he may leave if he keeps in touch with authorities.
   c. he is only free to go home and go to work.
   d. he must stay in prison.

"Refugee in America," "Ardella," "The Negro Speaks of Rivers," and **"Dream Variations"** by Langston Hughes
"The Tropics in New York" by Claude McKay

Grammar and Style: Verb Tenses: Past and Present Perfect

The **past tense** shows an action or condition that began or ended at a given time in the past. No helping verb is used when forming the past tense. The **present perfect tense** shows an action or condition that occurred at an indefinite time in the past or that began in the past but continues in the present. The helping verb *has* or *have* is placed before the past participle of the main verb when forming the present perfect tense.

A. Practice: For each item, underline the words used to express the tense. Then circle the verb tense used in the sentence.

1. "I've known rivers ancient as the world. . . ."   PAST or PRESENT PERFECT

2. "I built my hut near the Congo. . . ."   PAST or PRESENT PERFECT

3. "and it lulled me to sleep."   PAST or PRESENT PERFECT

4. "I heard the singing of the Mississippi. . . ."   PAST or PRESENT PERFECT

5. "I've seen its muddy bosom. . . ."   PAST or PRESENT PERFECT

6. "My soul has grown deep like the rivers."   PAST or PRESENT PERFECT

B. Writing Application: Write two short sentences—one in the past tense and one in the present tense—using each of the words below.

1. rivers

   (past)_____

   (present perfect) _____

2. home

   (past)_____

   (present perfect) _____

3. history

   (past)_____

   (present perfect) _____

4. pride

   (past)_____

   (present perfect) _____

"Refugee in America," "Ardella," "The Negro Speaks of Rivers," and **"Dream Variations"** by Langston Hughes
"The Tropics in New York" by Claude McKay

Reading Strategy: Make Inferences About the Speaker

Often, a poem's speaker isn't stated directly. Rather, the reader must **make inferences**, or draw conclusions, about the speaker's identity, attitudes, feelings, and experiences. To make these inferences, the reader must pay close attention to the words, ideas, and details in the poem.

DIRECTIONS: Reread each poem in the selection. Use the graphic organizer below to help you determine the attitudes, feelings, and experiences of the speaker for each poem. Write down words, ideas, and details from each poem that help you make inferences about the speaker. Then tell what inferences the clues helped you to make.

Poem	Words, Ideas, or Details	Inference About the Speaker
"Refugee in America"		
"Ardella"		
"The Negro Speaks of Rivers"		
"Dream Variations"		
"The Tropics in New York"		

"Refugee in America," "Ardella," "The Negro Speaks of Rivers," and **"Dream Variations"** by Langston Hughes

"The Tropics in New York" by Claude McKay

Literary Analysis: Speaker

The **speaker** is the voice of a poem. There are several possibilities as to who the speaker may be: the author, another person, an imaginary person, a group of people, an animal, or an object. Often, clues from the poem can help the reader figure out who the speaker is.

DIRECTIONS: Reread each poem in the selection. Decide who the speaker is for each poem. Then tell what clues helped you figure out who the speaker is.

"Refugee in America" by Langston Hughes

Who is the speaker of the poem? _____

How do you know?

_____

"Ardella" by Langston Hughes

Who is the speaker of the poem? _____

How do you know?

_____

"The Negro Speaks of Rivers" by Langston Hughes

Who is the speaker of the poem? _____

How do you know?

_____

"Dream Variations" by Langston Hughes

Who is the speaker of the poem? _____

How do you know?

_____

"The Tropics in New York" by Claude McKay

Who is the speaker of the poem? _____

How do you know?

_____

"From the Dark Tower" by Countee Cullen
"A Black Man Talks of Reaping" by Arna Bontemps
"Storm Ending" by Jean Toomer

Build Vocabulary

Spelling Strategy The letter g changes in pronunciation depending on what letter follows it. For a "hard" sound, such as that in *gone*, g is usually followed by a, h, o, or u: *gate, ghost, gun, goat, beguile*. For a "soft" sound, as in *gem*, g is usually paired with e, i, or y: *gem, giant, gym, cottage*. A common exception is the word *get*.

Using the Root -cre-

A. Directions: The word *increment*, meaning "an increase, as one of a series," contains the root -cre-, which means "to grow." Each of the defined words below contains the word root -cre-. Rewrite each definition using the word *grow* or one of its forms.

1. *concrescence*—a merging together of parts or cells

   _____

2. *create*—to cause to come into existence

   _____

3. *recreation*—any form of play that causes refreshment in the body or mind

   _____

Using the Word Bank

increment	countenance	beguile
stark	reaping	glean

B. Directions: Choose the word that best completes the meaning of each sentence and write it in the blank.

1. He did not countenance their behavior; that is to say, he would not _____ their talking and laughing in class.
   a. like   b. acknowledge   c. understand   d. tolerate

2. The room was stark, as its furnishings were _____.
   a. few   b.lavish   c. bright   d. ornamental

3. Although she gleaned in the field all day, the amount she _____ was small.
   a. dug   b. plucked   c. collected   d. saw

4. The dance beguiled, or_____, the audience.
   a. bored   b. angered   c. delighted   d. puzzled

5. Late in the summer, the farmer was reaping, or_____, his crops.
   a. harvesting   b. planting   c. tending   d. pruning

6. The patron's yearly_____helped the city's homeless population.
   a. pay check   b. taxation   c. pension   d. donation

"From the Dark Tower" by Countee Cullen
"A Black Man Talks of Reaping" by Arna Bontemps
"Storm Ending" by Jean Toomer

Grammar and Style: Placement of Adjectives

The **placement of adjectives** can help set a mood in writing. Usually, adjectives precede the words they modify. However, for reasons of style, emphasis, or variety, they may be placed after the words they modify. When placed after the modified words, adjectives sometimes need to be set off with commas.

A. Practice: Underline the adjectives, circle the words they modify, and indicate whether the adjectives are placed before or after the modified words.

1. "We shall . . . Not always countenance, abject and mute. . . ." _____

2. "That lesser men should hold their brothers cheap . . ." _____

3. "And there are buds that cannot bloom at all . . . but crumple, piteous, and fall. . . ."

   _____

4. "I planted safe against this stark, lean year." _____

5. "I scattered seed enough to plant the land. . . ." _____

6. "my children glean in fields . . . and feed on bitter fruit." _____

7. "Great, hollow, bell-like flowers . . ." _____

8. "Full-lipped flowers . . . dripping rain . . ." _____

B. Writing Application: Write a sentence using each of the nouns below and an adjective of your choice. Place the adjective either before or after the noun as indicated. The first sentence is written for you as an example.

1. thunder (before)

   I heard loud thunder just before the rain fell. _____

2. grain (before)

   _____

3. field (after)

   _____

4. flower (after)

   _____

5. house (before)

   _____

6. night (after)

   _____

Unit 5: Disillusion, Defiance, and Discontent (1914–1946)

"From the Dark Tower" by Countee Cullen
"A Black Man Talks of Reaping" by Arna Bontemps
"Storm Ending" by Jean Toomer

Reading Strategy: Connect to Historical Context

The three poets featured in this selection were part of the cultural movement known as the Harlem Renaissance. This movement took place in the 1920s, mainly in Harlem, New York.

In the early 1900s, many Southern blacks moved to northern cities to escape discrimination, brutality, and crop losses. However, few found a good life there. Many found themselves working again as laborers or servants and living in poor, crowded, areas. Racial conflicts were common.

The Harlem Renaissance featured literature that showed black confidence and pride as well as literary skill. Many of these writers wrote about common experiences in the lives of African Americans throughout the country.

DIRECTIONS: Reread the three poems in the selection and answer the following questions.

1. How does knowing about life in the northern cities help you to understand "From the Dark Tower"?

   _____

   _____

   _____

   _____

2. How does knowing about how blacks in America lived—in the past and at the time this poem was written—help you to understand "A Black Man Talks of Reaping"?

   _____

   _____

   _____

3. How does knowing that the Harlem Renaissance produced literature that showed black confidence and pride, as well as literary skill, help you to understand "Storm Ending"?

   _____

   _____

   _____

4. Compare the authors' treatment of the subject of life in America for African Americans.

   _____

   _____

   _____

   _____

"From the Dark Tower" by Countee Cullen
"A Black Man Talks of Reaping" by Arna Bontemps
"Storm Ending" by Jean Toomer

Literary Analysis: Metaphor

A **metaphor** is an implied comparison between two seemingly dissimilar things. By using a metaphor, the author can evoke images that may help to communicate his or her message.

DIRECTIONS: Reread the poem "A Black Man Talks of Reaping." Briefly describe the metaphor in the poem on the lines provided. Underline words and images used to support the metaphor in the poem. Make notes in the margins identifying the images and emotions the metaphor evokes.

Metaphor: _____

_____

_____

A Black Man Talks of Reaping by Arna Bontemps

I have sown beside all waters in my day.

I planted deep, within my heart the fear

that wind or fowl would take the grain away.

I planted safe against this stark, lean year.

I scattered seed enough to plant the land

in rows from Canada to Mexico

but for my reaping only what the hand

can hold at once is all that I can show.

Yet what I sowed and what the orchard yields

my brother's sons are gathering stalk and root;

small wonder then my children glean in fields

they have not sown, and feed on bitter fruit.

"i yearn" by Ricardo Sánchez

Build Vocabulary: Vivid Vocabulary

A skillful writer makes use of vivid vocabulary to make his or her work more interesting and exciting. Sometimes even simple words can achieve a certain affect or evoke a certain image.

DIRECTIONS: Write a definition for the underlined word as it is used in each sentence below. Then write a sentence of your own using the word in that sense.

1. The poet's words, spoken in his native language, seemed to <u>glide</u> off his tongue.

   definition: _____

   sentence: _____

   _____

2. The little boy dashed and <u>darted</u> through the plaza.

   definition: _____

   sentence: _____

   _____

3. This spice adds <u>zest</u> to our cooking.

   definition: _____

   sentence: _____

   _____

4. The strange language and music <u>assailed</u> the tourists' ears.

   definition: _____

   sentence: _____

   _____

5. Maria <u>yearned</u> for the sights and smells of the land of her birth.

   definition: _____

   sentence: _____

   _____

6. A few puffy clouds floated by, seeming to <u>caress</u> the tall mountains.

   definition: _____

   sentence: _____

   _____

"i yearn" by Ricardo Sánchez

Thematic Connection: From Every Corner of the Land

The sentiments expressed in the poem "i yearn" could be echoed by Americans of many different backgrounds. The United States has been described as a melting pot of many people, but perhaps it might be more accurate today to call our country a quilt of diversity. We live in what is probably the most diverse country in the world. Learning about other cultures or showcasing facts about your own culture is an effective way to break down the walls of ignorance and anxiety that divide people.

DIRECTIONS: Get together with a classmate or group of classmates who share your cultural background. Brainstorm for ideas about traditions and customs you would like to share with other students. Use the entries on the sheet below to help you come up with ideas, and plan how you will present your ideas to the class.

1. What culture or country will your presentation be about?

   _____

2. List ideas you have concerning costumes, food, music, dance, and other traditional aspects of your culture.

   _____
   _____
   _____
   _____
   _____
   _____

3. Decide what aspects of your culture you want to include in your presentation.

   _____
   _____
   _____
   _____
   _____
   _____

4. Decide who in your group will be responsible for which parts of your presentation.

   _____
   _____
   _____
   _____
   _____
   _____

"The Life You Save May Be Your Own" by Flannery O'Connor

Build Vocabulary

Spelling Strategy When adding a suffix to a word that ends in *w*, never double the *w*. The Word Bank word *guffawing* illustrates this rule.

Using the Root *-sol-*

A. DIRECTIONS: The root *-sol-* comes to English from the Latin adjective *solus*, meaning "alone." Use each of the following words in a sentence to demonstrate your understanding of its meaning.

1. solitary _____

2. sole _____

3. solely _____

Using the Word Bank

desolate	listed	ominous
ravenous	morose	guffawing

B. DIRECTIONS: Use one of the Word Bank words as you write each sentence according to the instructions given. Use the context of the sentence instructions to determine which word to use.

1. Write a sentence about something that tilts.

   _____

   _____

2. Write a sentence about someone who has a distinctive laugh.

   _____

   _____

3. Write a sentence about the isolated setting of a story.

   _____

   _____

4. Write a sentence about someone who is gloomy or sullen.

   _____

   _____

5. Write a sentence about someone who is extremely eager about something.

   _____

   _____

6. Write a sentence about a situation that is threatening or sinister.

   _____

   _____

Name _____ Date _____

Grammar and Style: Subjunctive Mood

In modern English, there are three moods, or ways in which a verb can express an action or condition: *indicative*, *imperative*, and *subjunctive*. The indicative mood is used to make factual statements and ask questions. The imperative mood is used to give orders or directions. The subjunctive mood is used (1) in clauses beginning with *if* or *that* to express an idea contrary to fact, and (2) in clauses beginning with *that* to express a request, demand, or proposal.

Verbs in the subjunctive mood differ from verbs in the indicative mood in two significant ways. First, in the present tense subjunctive, a third-person singular verb does not have the usual *-s* or *-es* ending. Secondly, in the present tense, the subjunctive mood of *be* is *be*, and in the past tense, it is *were*, regardless of the subject.

Certain verbs in English are more prone to appear in the subjunctive mood than others. These include the following: *ask, demand, determine, insist, move, order, prefer, propose, request, require, suggest.*

A. DIRECTIONS: Each of the following sentences should contain a verb in the subjunctive mood. Cross out the verb that appears in the incorrect form and write the correct form on the line provided.

1. He held the burning match as if he was studying the mystery of flame.

   _____

2. The mother preferred that Mr. Shiftlet slept in the car rather than in the house.

   _____

3. If Mr. Shiftlet was lying, do you think he would have done all that work around the farm?

   _____

4. A fat moon appeared in the branches of a tree as if it was going to roost there with the chickens. _____

5. Lucynell, the mother, insisted that her daughter was with her at all times.

   _____

B. DIRECTIONS: Use each of the following phrases in an original sentence about "The Life You Save May Be Your Own." Each sentence should contain a verb in the subjunctive mood.

requested that _____

_____

if Lucynell were _____

_____

that Mr. Shiftlet be _____

_____

wondered if _____

_____

"The Life You Save May Be Your Own" by Flannery O'Connor

Reading Strategy: Make Predictions

As you read a selection, you often wonder how a story will end. One strategy for understanding the way a story unfolds is to pause and make predictions about what will happen. Often a story contains hints that foreshadow things to come.

DIRECTIONS: On the lines following each excerpt, record what predictions you might make about the rest of the story.

1. "Although the old woman lived in this desolate spot with only her daughter and she had never seen Mr. Shiftlet before, she could tell, even from a distance, that he was a tramp and no one to be afraid of."

   _____

   _____

2. "The old woman watched from a distance, secretly pleased. She was ravenous for a son-in-law."

   _____

   _____

3. "'Saturday, the old woman said, 'you and her and me can drive into town and get married.'"

   _____

   _____

4. "'I'm only saying a man's spirit means more to him than anything else. I would have to take my wife off for the weekend without no regards at all for cost. I got to follow where my spirits says to go.'"

   _____

   _____

5. "As they came out of the courthouse, Mr. Shiftlet began twisting his neck in his collar. He looked morose and bitter as if he had been insulted while someone held him."

   _____

   _____

6. "'Give it to her when she wakes up,' Mr. Shiftlet said. 'I'll pay for it now.'"

   _____

   _____

"The Life You Save May Be Your Own" by Flannery O'Connor

Literary Analysis: Grotesque Characters

Flannery O'Connor included in her writing some characters that are **grotesques**. Such characters have a one-track mind; they are controlled by a single emotion, concept, or goal.

On the lines after each of the following passages, identify an emotion, a concept, or a goal that the passage suggests. Then write one or two sentences to explain how the character might act if he or she were a grotesque, controlled by the way of thinking that you have identified.

1. "Is she your baby girl?" he asked.

"My only," the old woman said, "and she's the sweetest girl in the world. I would give her up for nothing on earth. She's smart too. She can sweep the floor, cook, wash, feed the chickens, and hoe. I wouldn't give her up for a casket of jewels."

"No," he said kindly, "don't ever let any man take her away from you."

"Any man come after her," the old woman said, " 'll have to stay around the place."

_____

_____

_____

_____

2. He had raised the hood and studied the mechanism and he said he could tell that the car had been built in the days when cars were really built. You take now, he said, one man puts in one bolt and another man puts in another bolt and another man puts in another bolt so that it's a man for a bolt. That's why you have to pay so much for a car: you're paying all those men. Now if you didn't have to pay but one man, you could get you a cheaper car and one that had had a personal interest taken in it, and it would be a better car.

_____

_____

_____

_____

3. Mr. Shiftlet felt that the rottenness of the world was about to engulf him. He raised his arm and let it fall again to his breast. "Oh Lord!" he prayed. "Break forth and wash the slime from this earth!"

_____

_____

_____

_____

"The First Seven Years" by Bernard Malamud

Build Vocabulary

Spelling Strategy When you hear the "j" sound in the middle of a word, that sound is al-most always produced by the letter g. The word *diligence* is an example.

Using the Root -liter-

A. DIRECTIONS: Explain how the meaning of each of the following words is related to the root word *-liter-*, meaning "letter."

1. literate (*adj.*)_____

_____

2. literature _____

_____

Using the Word Bank

discern	diligence	connivance
illiterate	unscrupulous	repugnant

B. DIRECTIONS: Answer the following questions to demonstrate your understanding of the Word Bank words.

1. What is Feld's *connivance*?

_____

_____

2. Why does Feld think Max has *diligence* and Miriam does not?

_____

_____

3. Why are Sobel and Miriam *not* described as *illiterate*?

_____

_____

4. What might an *unscrupulous* employee have done to Feld?

_____

_____

5. What did Feld think he could *discern* that Miriam could not?

_____

_____

6. Why was the idea of sending Miriam to Sobel's boarding house *repugnant*?

_____

_____

Name _____ Date _____

"The First Seven Years" by Bernard Malamud

Grammar and Style: Correct Use of *who* and *whom*

Who and **whom** are pronouns that replace the names of persons. Because these pronouns begin clauses, the first step in deciding which is correct is to isolate the clause and to ignore the rest of the sentence. After you've isolated the clause, think about the role that the pronoun will play. If it plays a nominative role (subject or predicate nominative), use *who.* If it plays an objective role (direct object or object of a preposition), use *whom. Whoever* and *whomever* follow the same rules.

A. DIRECTIONS: First, underline the clauses containing *who* or *whom* in each of the following sentences. Then circle the correct pronouns by asking yourself what roles the pronouns play in the clauses.

1. Feld could not turn his thoughts from Max the college boy, (*who, whom*) he so respected because of the sacrifices he made to further his education.

2. What possible harm could it cause for a working girl (*who, whom*) met only loud-mouthed salesmen and illiterate shopping clerks?

3. Sobel was a Polish refugee (*who, whom*) loved to read the classics.

4. When Max entered the shop one winter day, Feld scarcely recognized (*who, whom*) he was.

5. Since Max asked to see a photograph, he must not have known (*who, whom*) Miriam was.

6. Feld, (*who, whom*) had looked forward to anticipating how it would go with his daughter and Max, instead had a great worry on his mind.

7. Sobel turned into an excellent assistant (*who, whom*) rebuilt shoes as well as his employer did.

8. Sobel was also a man in (*who, whom*) Feld could place his trust.

9. Feld had to get to the store before his new assistant, a dark, speechless man (*who, whom*) Feld would not trust with the key.

10. Miriam claimed that Max was a materialist (*who, whom*) had no soul.

11. "She knows (*who, whom*) I am and what is in my heart," Sobel said of Miriam.

12. Sometimes the person we are seeking is the person (*who, whom*) is standing right beside us.

13. Sobel turns out to be the man (*who, whom*) Miriam will marry after all.

14. Would you hire a man (*who, whom*) might fall in love with your daughter?

15. More importantly, do you think Sobel is a man (*who, whom*) Miriam can love?

B. DIRECTIONS: Write two original sentences containing the pronoun *who.* Then write two sentences containing the pronoun *whom.*

1. _____

2. _____

3. _____

4. _____

Name _____ Date _____

Reading Strategy: Identify With Characters

When you think that a story or book is really good, it is probably because you are able to **identify with the characters**. That means that you can understand their ideas, their actions, their motives—maybe you have even had the very same ideas and motives.

Making an effort to identify with characters can help you gain understanding and come away with more meaning from a story. Perhaps when you read "The First Seven Years," you identified most with Miriam because she is near your age. The other characters also have feelings and ideas with which you may identify, and you should be sure not to overlook them.

DIRECTIONS: Consider the characters' thoughts, ideas, and actions listed in the first column of this table. In the middle column is a question to help you identify with the character. Use the right column to make a connection to your own life in terms of an emotion, an idea, or an event.

Event from Story	Question	My Connection
Feld was annoyed that his helper was so insensitive that he wouldn't for a minute cease his pounding.	Have you ever been in a thoughtful mood and been annoyed by someone around you making noise?	
Miriam said she wanted to get a job and be independent.	Have you ever told a parent that you want to be in-dependent?	
Max embarrassedly explained what he wanted done to his old shoes.	Have you ever been embarrassed about asking a question or seeking help?	
Sobel broke the last, tore his coat from the hook, and rushed out into the snow.	Have you ever gotten angry and stormed out of the room?	
Though Feld needed Sobel's help, he decided to let him stew for a week.	Have you ever allowed some-one to stew after a disagreement?	

Name _____ Date _____

"The First Seven Years" by Bernard Malamud

Literary Analysis: Epiphany

Characters in literature sometimes have a sudden flash of insight, which is called an **epiphany**. At the moment of epiphany, the character may realize something significant about himself or herself, about another character, or about life in general.

DIRECTIONS: On the lines below each of the following quotations, explain why that moment in the story does or does not represent a true epiphany for Feld, the shoemaker.

1. Neither the shifting white blur outside, nor the sudden deep remembrance of the snowy Polish village where he had wasted his youth could turn his thoughts from Max the college boy . . .

   _____
   _____
   _____
   _____

2. An old wish returned to haunt the shoemaker: that he had had a son instead of a daughter . . .

   _____
   _____
   _____
   _____

3. Maybe he could awaken in her a desire to go to college; if not—the shoemaker's mind at last came to grips with the truth—let her marry an educated man and live a better life.

   _____
   _____
   _____
   _____

4. That night the shoemaker discovered that his new assistant had been all the while stealing from him, and he suffered a heart attack.

   _____
   _____
   _____
   _____

5. Feld had a sudden insight. In some devious way, with his books and commentary, Sobel had given Miriam to understand that he loved her.

   _____
   _____
   _____
   _____

Name _____ Date _____

Build Vocabulary

Spelling Strategy When adding a prefix to a word, do not change the spelling of the word, regardless of the prefix or the first letter of the word—for example, *un-* + *fathomable* creates the Word Bank word *unfathomable*.

Using the Root -sim-

A. DIRECTIONS: Complete each of the following sentences to demonstrate your understanding of the italicized word. Keep in mind that the root *-sim-* means "alike" or "the same."

1. There is a *similarity* among my friends because _____
   _____
   _____.

2. The writer used a *simile* to show _____
   _____
   _____.

3. The flight *simulator* seemed realistic because _____
   _____
   _____.

Using the Word Bank

mottled	assimilate	unfathomable
egregious	proprietorial	evanescent

B. DIRECTIONS: Choose the Word Bank word that best completes the meaning of each sentence. Write the word in the blank.

1. The man's motive was merely _____; his concern was for the condition of the chest, not for its contents or its significance.

2. Gordon's request was somewhat _____, since never before had he expressed interest in his grandparents' belongings.

3. The main character hints that he feels his son's mishandling of his life is _____, but allows that Gordon is young and still finding his way.

4. A number of the items in the chest are described as _____, which is evidence of their age.

5. The main character discovers that life occurs in phases, which may be lasting or _____.

6. The main character's wife is unable to _____ the brown chest or any of the other furniture into her home.

"The Brown Chest" by John Updike

Grammar and Style: Beginning Sentences With Adverb Clauses

Regardless of whether a piece of writing is fiction or nonfiction, humorous or serious, sentences should differ in length and in structure. In particular, writers can vary **sentence beginnings** to add interest to their writing.

One way to begin a sentence is with an **adverb phrase**, a prepositional phrase that modifies a verb, an adjective, or an adverb. Remember that adverbs and adverbial constructions tell *how, when, where, why, to what extent,* or *under what condition.*

> *During the 1920's,* the main character's father played football. [The adverb phrase modifies the verb *played* and tells *when.*]

Another way to begin a sentence is with an **adverb clause**, a kind of subordinate clause. Adverb clauses always begin with subordinating conjunctions, such as *after, although, as soon as, because, before, if, since, unless, when, wherever, why* and *while.*

> *Wherever he goes,* the man takes the brown chest with him. [The adverb clause modifies the verb *takes* and tells *where.*]

> *Since Morna is shy,* she speaks only to Gordon. [The adverb clause modifies the verb *speaks* and tells *under what condition* she speaks to Gordon.]

A. Practice: Indicate whether each sentence begins with an adverb phrase or an adverb clause by writing *phrase* or *clause* on the blank provided. Then circle the word the phrase or clause modifies.

1. Outside the guest-bedroom door, the upstairs hall broadened to be almost a room.

   _____

2. If she had never done this, the room would have become haunted. _____

3. On the side, wavy stripes of paint had run down. _____

4. On that moving day, the chest was placed in the attic of the new house.

   _____

5. As soon as Morna saw the chest, she was intrigued. _____

B. Writing Application: Follow the instructions to write sentences that begin with adverb phrases and adverb clauses. Use events and characters in "The Brown Chest" as the subjects of your sentences.

1. Begin a sentence with an adverb phrase that tells *when.*

   _____

2. Begin a sentence with an adverb phrase that tells *where.*

   _____

3. Begin a sentence with an adverb clause that tells *why.*

   _____

4. Begin a sentence with an adverb clause that tells *when.*

   _____

"The Brown Chest" by John Updike

Reading Strategy: Break Down Long Sentences

Good writers know that varying sentence length, as well as structure, makes their writing more engaging. As you read a long sentence, break it down to make sure you know what the writer is saying. One way to **break down long sentences** is to pay special attention to punctuation. Commas, dashes, colons, and semicolons will help you separate a sentence into manageable parts.

Another way to break down long sentences is to look for repeated or parallel words or phrases. These, too, will help you divide a sentence into meaningful parts. Finally, paraphrasing a sentence—putting it in your own words—will help you capture the most important idea or ideas.

DIRECTIONS: Use the strategies discussed here to break down each of the following sentences from "The Brown Chest." In each sentence, circle punctuation that helps create meaningful parts. Underline repeated or parallel words or phrases. Then paraphrase the sentence. Your paraphrase may be more than one sentence long.

1. The entire front of the house had this neglected quality, with its guest bedroom where guests hardly ever stayed; it held a gray-painted bed with silver moons on the headboard and corner posts shaped at the top like mushrooms, and a little desk by the window where his mother sometimes, but not often, wrote letters and confided sentences to her diary in her tiny backslanting hand.

   _____

   _____

   _____

   _____

   _____

2. Outside the guest-bedroom door, the upstairs hall, having narrowly sneaked past his grandparents' bedroom's door, broadened to be almost a room, with a window all its own, and a geranium on the sill shedding brown leaves when the women of the house forgot to water it, and curtains of dotted swiss he could see the telephone wires through, and a rug of braided rags shaped like the oval tracks his Lionel train went around and around the Christmas tree on, and, to one side, its front feet planted on the rag rug, with just enough space left for the attic door to swing open, the chest.

   _____

   _____

   _____

   _____

3. Heaps and rows of overgrown stones and dumps of rusty cans and tinted bottles indicated that other people in fact had been here, people like those who had posed in their Sunday clothes in the gilded albums, but the traces they left weren't usable, the way city sidewalks and trolley-car tracks were usable.

   _____

   _____

   _____

   _____

   _____

Name _____ Date _____

"The Brown Chest" by John Updike

Literary Analysis: Atmosphere

Have you ever wondered why scary stories are set in dark places? It's because dark places cause feelings of anxiety in the reader. The writer uses the setting to generate the atmosphere of suspense. Fiction writers use details about setting, events, and characters to create a story's **atmosphere**, or mood. The atmosphere is the feeling or feelings a story causes the reader to feel.

DIRECTIONS: Examine each passage as directed and identify the atmosphere it creates. Explain what words, phrases, or ideas contribute to the atmosphere.

1. Review the first two paragraphs of the story, which describe the main character's first house. What atmosphere does Updike create?

   _____

   _____

   _____

   _____

   _____

   _____

2. Review the fifth paragraph, which begins, "The new house . . ." What is the atmosphere of this, the main character's second home?

   _____

   _____

   _____

   _____

   _____

   _____

3. Reread the paragraph that begins, "Now his barn felt haunted." What atmosphere does the author create with respect to the main character's present dwelling?

   _____

   _____

   _____

   _____

   _____

4. Finally, what is the atmosphere of the story's final paragraph?

   _____

   _____

   _____

   _____

   _____

"**Hawthorne**" by Robert Lowell
"**Gold Glade**" by Robert Penn Warren
"**The Light Comes Brighter**" by Theodore Roethke
"**Traveling Through the Dark**" by William Stafford
"**The Adamant**" by Theodore Roethke

Build Vocabulary

Spelling Strategy When adding a suffix to a word ending in one consonant preceded by two vowels, do not double the final consonant: *brood + -ing = brooding.*

Using Related Words: *exhaust*

A. DIRECTIONS: Complete each sentence with one of the following words related to the word *exhaust: exhausted, exhaustively, exhaustible.*

1. Our current use of fossil fuels is depleting _____ energy sources.

2. At the end of their twelve-hour shifts, the relief workers were _____.

3. The environmental group _____ researched all sides of the issue.

Using the Word Bank

brooding	furtive	meditation
declivity	vestiges	exhaust

B. DIRECTIONS: For each pair of numbered words, choose the lettered pair of words that best expresses a similar relationship. Circle the letter of your choice.

1. BROODING : WORRYING ::
   a. building : erecting
   b. virus : infection
   c. serious : thoughtful
   d. architect : blueprint

2. FURTIVE : SPY ::
   a. eager : impatient
   b. actor : dramatic
   c. impressive : ordinary
   d. instructive : teacher

3. MEDITATION : QUIET ::
   a. energetic : sloth
   b. sunlight : bright
   c. profitable : expensive
   d. creation : destroyer

4. DECLIVITY : INCLINE ::
   a. sorrowful : grieving
   b. hill : peak
   c. emptiness : fullness
   d. earthiness : sky

5. VESTIGES : TRACES ::
   a. flowers : fragrant
   b. edifices : buildings
   c. determine : discover
   d. spice : cinnamon

6. EXHAUST : POLLUTION ::
   a. ocean : salty
   b. disaster : fatality
   c. airplane : propeller
   d. grass : vegetation

"**Hawthorne**" by Robert Lowell
"**Gold Glade**" by Robert Penn Warren
"**The Light Comes Brighter**" by Theodore Roethke
"**Traveling Through the Dark**" by William Stafford
"**The Adamant**" by Theodore Roethke

Grammar and Style: Subject and Verb Agreement

Subjects and verbs must agree in number, even when they are separated by intervening words. Look at the subject and verb in the following example:

The *water* stored in narrow pools *escapes* / In rivulets.

Note that the verb *escapes* agrees with the single subject *water*, not with the plural noun *pools* that immediately precedes the verb.

A. Practice: Underline the subject in each of the following sentences. Then circle the verb form in parentheses that agrees with the subject.

1. The leaves of the hickory tree (*shines / shine*) like gold.

2. Drivers on the narrow canyon road sometimes (*hit / hits*) deer.

3. The customs house where Hawthorne worked (*stands / stand*) in Salem.

4. The last vestiges of snow (*disappears / disappear*) from the leaves.

5. Truth, like the strongest of diamonds, (*remains / remain*) solid.

6. The boulders beneath the water (*was / were*) slick and treacherous.

B. Writing Application: Write your answers, including the complete italicized phrase, to the following questions.

1. In "Hawthorne," what is distinctive about *the beards of Longfellow and other writers*?

_____

_____

2. How does the speaker in "Hawthorne" describe *the eyes of Hawthorne*?

_____

_____

3. In "Traveling Through the Dark," how does the speaker describe *the parking lights from the car*?

_____

_____

4. In "The Light Comes Brighter," what happens to *the last vestiges of snow*?

_____

_____

"Hawthorne" by Robert Lowell
"Gold Glade" by Robert Penn Warren
"The Light Comes Brighter" by Theodore Roethke
"Traveling Through the Dark" by William Stafford
"The Adamant" by Theodore Roethke

Reading Strategy: Paraphrase

When you **paraphrase**, you restate someone else's language in your own words. Paraphrasing can be especially helpful when reading poetry, which often contains complex and sophisticated language and ideas. Compare the following lines from "Gold Glade" and a paraphrase of those lines:

Warren's lines: The glade was geometric, circular, gold, / No brush or weed breaking that bright gold of leaf-fall.

Paraphrase: The glade lay in a perfect circle and gave off a golden, autumnal glow.

DIRECTIONS: Paraphrase each of the following lines or passages. Write your paraphrases on the lines provided.

from "Gold Glade"

1. But high over high rock and leaf-lacing, sky / Showed yet bright, and declivity wooed / My foot by the quietening stream

_____

_____

from "Hawthorne"

2. On State Street / a steeple with a glowing dial-clock / measures the weary hours, / the merciless march of professional feet.

_____

_____

from "The Light Comes Brighter"

3. The sun cuts deep into the heavy drift, / Though still the guarded snow is winter-sealed, / At bridgeheads buckled ice begins to shift, / The river overflows the level field.

_____

_____

from "The Adamant"

4. Thought does not crush to stone. / The great sledge drops in vain. / Truth never is undone; / Its shafts remain.

_____

_____

"Hawthorne" by Robert Lowell
"Gold Glade" by Robert Penn Warren
"The Light Comes Brighter" by Theodore Roethke
"Traveling Through the Dark" by William Stafford
"The Adamant" by Theodore Roethke

Literary Analysis: Diction and Style

Style refers to the way in which a writer puts ideas into words. Poetic style is established through the writer's use of tone, rhythm, sound devices, figurative language, symbols, punctuation and capitalization, line length and arrangement, stanza format, and **diction**, or word choice.

DIRECTIONS: Determine if and/or how each poet uses each style element listed. Complete the following chart by writing a word or phrase that describes each poet's use of each style element.

Style Element	Lowell	Warren	Roethke	Stafford
Tone				
Rhythm				
Sound Devices				
Figurative Language				
Symbols				
Punctuation and Capitalization				
Line Length and Arrangement				
Stanza Format				
Diction				

"Average Waves in Unprotected Waters" by Anne Tyler

Build Vocabulary

Spelling Strategy When adding a suffix starting with either a vowel or a consonant to a word ending in two consonants, retain the consonants; for example, *bunt + -ing = bunting; thank + -ful = thankful.*

Using the Prefix *trans-*

A. DIRECTIONS: Knowing that the prefix *trans-* means "across," "over," or "through," match each word in the left column with its definition in the right column.

____ 1. transfix   a. to go beyond set limits

____ 2. transgress   b. to pierce through with a pointed weapon

____ 3. transmit   c. to send across from one person or place to another

Using the Word Bank

orthopedic	transparent	stocky	staunch	viper

B. DIRECTIONS: For each Word Bank word, choose the word or phrase that is most nearly *similar* in meaning. Circle the letter of your choice.

1. orthopedic

    a stiff   b. corrective   c. plain   d. voluntary

2. transparent

    a. hollow   b. airy   c. unclouded   d. light colored

3. stocky

    a. solid   b. large   c. gangly   d. reliable

4. staunch

    a. offensive   b. firm   c. unreasonable   d. proven

5. viper

    a. vicious person b. liar   c. amphibian   d. suspicious individual

"Average Waves in Unprotected Waters" by Anne Tyler

Grammar and Style: Correct Use of Adjectives and Adverbs

Use an adjective to modify a noun or a pronoun. Use an adverb to modify a verb, an adjective, or another adverb. For instance, in the following sentence, the adverb *anxiously* modifies the verb *waited.*

She *waited anxiously* for the doctor.

Use a predicate adjective, rather than an adverb, after a linking verb such as the verb *be* or one of its forms. You must use an adjective because you are modifying the subject of the sentence, not the verb. In the following sentence, the adjective *average* modifies the subject *waves.*

The *waves* were *average.*

A. Practice: Circle the correct modifier. Then write the complete sentence on the line. Draw an arrow from the modifier to the word being modified.

1. Bet's dress hung (*loose, loosely*) from her thin shoulders.

_____

_____

2. Even as a baby, Arnold slept (*fitful, fitfully*).

_____

_____

3. Bet wanted Arnold to look (*good, well*) when he arrived at the hospital.

_____

_____

4. Bet felt (*terrible, terribly*) about leaving Arnold.

_____

_____

5. In the cab, she cried (*open, openly*).

_____

_____

B. Writing Application: Write a paragraph in which you describe how Bet came to care for Arnold on her own. Incorporate words from each of the following pairs of words: *foolish, foolishly; angry, angrily; resigned, resignedly.*

_____

_____

_____

_____

_____

_____

Name _____ Date _____

"Average Waves in Unprotected Waters" by Anne Tyler

Reading Strategy: Order Events

Writers usually present story events in chronological order, the order in which events occur. Sometimes, however, the sequence of events is interrupted with a flashback, a scene or an event from an earlier time. As you read, pay attention to the order of events and recognize flashbacks to help you order events in the story.

A. DIRECTIONS: Order the following events from the story. Write the events in order on the numbered lines, beginning with the earliest one.

Bet and Arnold board the train.

Bet frantically inquires about the train schedule.

Avery leaves Bet and Arnold.

Bet insists that the driver wait for her return.

A doctor diagnoses Arnold's handicap.

1. _____

2. _____

3. _____

4. _____

5. _____

B. DIRECTIONS: Fill in the following diagram with story events in chronological order.

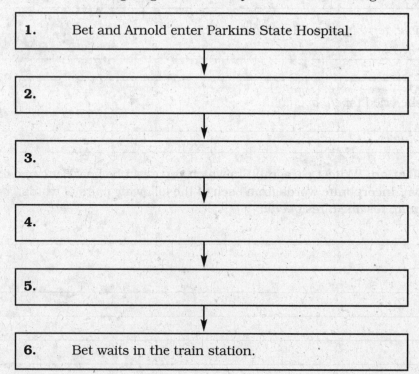

1.	Bet and Arnold enter Parkins State Hospital.
2.	
3.	
4.	
5.	
6.	Bet waits in the train station.

"Average Waves in Unprotected Waters" by Anne Tyler

Literary Analysis: Foreshadowing

Writers use **foreshadowing** to hint at events that occur later in the story. On the lines following each passage, explain briefly how subsequent events are foreshadowed in the passage.

1. Small though he was, he was strong, wiry; he was getting to be too much for her.

   _____
   _____
   _____
   _____
   _____

2. He looked at the suitcase suspiciously, but only because it was new.

   _____
   _____
   _____
   _____
   _____

3. But her voice was all wrong. He would pick it up for sure.

   _____
   _____
   _____
   _____
   _____

4. Maybe she [Mrs. Puckett] felt to blame that he was going. But she'd done the best she could: babysat him all these years and only given up when he'd grown too strong and wild to manage.

   _____
   _____
   _____
   _____

5. But she couldn't stop herself; she had to tell him before she forgot. "Listen," she said, "I want you to wait for me right in the driveway. I don't want you to go on away."

   _____
   _____
   _____
   _____
   _____

from *The Names* by N. Scott Momaday
"Mint Snowball" by Naomi Shihab Nye
"Suspended" by Joy Harjo

Build Vocabulary

Spelling Strategy Many words end in *-ent* or *-ence*—for example, *dependents, dependence*. However, you should make a point of memorizing the exceptions that end in *-ant* or *-ance*, such as *flamboyant* and *flamboyance*.

Using the Prefix *con-*

A. DIRECTIONS: Knowing that *con-* (or *com-*) means "with" or "together," complete this sentence by placing the appropriate word in each blank: *communicate, confident, combination*.

The young Momaday felt _____ that he could
_____ the difficult _____ of stunt moves to Pecos.

Using the Word Bank

supple	concocted	flamboyant	elixir
permeated	replicate	revelatory	confluence

B. DIRECTIONS: Circle the letter of the word that best completes the meaning of the sentence.

1. The mysterious _____ was thought to cure arthritis, back pain, and the common cold.

   a. flamboyant   b. supple   c. elixir   d. confluence

2. Indeed, after drinking the strange medicine, my aching muscles felt _____ and youthful.

   a. supple   b. flamboyant   c. revelatory   d. confluence

3. Because no one knows the secret ingredients, we are unable to _____ the recipe.

   a. concocted   b. permeated   c. revelatory   d. replicate

4. The druggist _____ the treat in secret, so that no one saw which ingredients were included.

   a. permeated   b. replicate   c. concocted   d. supple

5. The _____ of bold, fresh taste with comforting sweetness made the dessert especially delicious.

   a. supple   b. confluence   c. replicate   d. elixir

6. I think it was the added scoops of vanilla ice cream in the Mint Snowball that made the dessert _____.

   a. supple   b. revelatory   c. permeated   d. flamboyant

7. When the druggist made the Mint Snowball, the scent of mint _____ the drugstore.

   a. permeated   b. elixir   c. replicate   d. confluence

8. Associating the taste of the Mint Snowball with a sense of loss was a _____ experience for Nye.

   a. supple   b. revelatory   c. flamboyant   d. concocted

from *The Names* by N. Scott Momaday
"Mint Snowball" by Naomi Shihab Nye
"Suspended" by Joy Harjo

Grammar and Style: Elliptical Clauses

In an **elliptical clause**, one or more words are omitted because they are understood. In the following sentence from Harjo's essay, the elliptical clause appears in italics.

I became acutely aware of the line *[that] the jazz trumpeter was playing* . . .

Because the relative pronoun *that* is understood, it can be omitted from the clause.

A. Practice: Underline each elliptical clause. On the blank, write the clause with the understood word or words included.

1. Momaday did not enjoy riding the stallion as much as riding Pecos.

   _____

2. Momaday won more races than anyone else.

   _____

3. The Mint Snowball tasted better than an ice cream sundae.

   _____

4. Jazz is the first music Harjo remembers.

   _____

B. Writing Application: Rewrite each sentence, omitting any word or words that are understood.

1. On the back of his horse, Momaday could see more of the world than he had ever seen before.

   _____

   _____

   _____

2. Eventually, Momaday sold the horse that he had named Pecos.

   _____

   _____

   _____

3. Nye's "pathetic" sprigs of mint cannot compare to her grandfather's sprigs of mint.

   _____

   _____

   _____

4. Harjo remembers riding in the black Cadillac that her father owned.

   _____

   _____

   _____

from *The Names* by N. Scott Momaday
"Mint Snowball" by Naomi Shihab Nye
"Suspended" by Joy Harjo

Reading Strategy: Relate to Your Own Experiences

The writers of these essays describe experiences that have great personal significance. You can better understand the writers and their ideas if you look for ways in which the essays relate to your own experiences.

DIRECTIONS: Write your answers to the following questions.

1. At age thirteen, Momaday received a horse from his parents. What event can you relate from your own experience?

   _____

   _____

2. What significance did your experience have?

   _____

   _____

3. How does recalling your experience help you understand Momaday's?

   _____

   _____

4. Nye mourns the loss of her great-grandfather's recipe for the Mint Snowball. What personal experience with loss helps you relate to Nye's loss?

   _____

   _____

5. What similar emotion or idea connects Nye's experience to your own?

   _____

   _____

6. Harjo first heard jazz "around the time [she] acquired language, or even before that time." What is your earliest memory from childhood?

   _____

   _____

7. What significance does this early memory have for you?

   _____

   _____

8. How does your experience help you relate to Harjo's?

   _____

   _____

from *The Names* by N. Scott Momaday

"Mint Snowball" by Naomi Shihab Nye

"Suspended" by Joy Harjo

Literary Analysis: Anecdote

An **anecdote** is a brief account of an entertaining or interesting event or experience. Although many anecdotes are told purely for amusement, they can also be used to make a point. In an essay, a writer might recount an anecdote and then draw a conclusion or make a generalization based on the account.

A. DIRECTIONS: Answer the following questions about the anecdotes related by Momaday, Nye, and Harjo.

1. What point does Momaday make with his anecdote about trading horses with Pasqual?

   _____

   _____

2. What dual purpose does Momaday's anecdote about learning to mount Pecos while running serve? Explain.

   _____

   _____

3. How do Momaday's anecdotes support his statement that "I knew where the journey was begun, that it was itself a learning of the beginning, that the beginning was infinitely worth the learning"?

   _____

   _____

4. Why does Nye relate the anecdote about her great-grandfather selling the Mint Snowball recipe?

   _____

   _____

5. How does Harjo's anecdote about hearing jazz for the first time relate to the title of her essay, "Suspended"?

   _____

   _____

B. DIRECTIONS: On the following lines, write an anecdote that illustrates a moment when you discovered something important about yourself.

_____

_____

_____

_____

_____

_____

"Everyday Use" by Alice Walker

Build Vocabulary

Spelling Strategy When adding a suffix starting with either a vowel or a consonant to a word that ends in two consonants, retain the consonants. For example, the Word Bank word *oppress* plus the suffixes *-ed, -es,* and *-ive = oppressed, oppresses, oppressive.*

Using the Roots *-doc-/-doct-*

The roots *-doc-* and *-doct-* mean "teach." The Word Bank word *doctrines,* which means "ideas, beliefs, or rules that are taught," is formed from the root *-doct-*.

A. DIRECTIONS: Complete each of the following sentences by choosing the best word for each sentence. Use context clues and what you know about the meaning of *-doc-/-doct-* to make your selection.

docent	doctorate	doctrinaire	documented

1. She received her _____ in veterinary science from the state university.

2. Wanting a record of their family reunion, the Hernandez family _____ the event on videotape.

3. The _____ who teaches our honors class is not a regular faculty member.

4. The tutor's inflexible and _____ methods did not inspire his students.

Using the Word Bank

furtive	lye	oppress	doctrines

B. DIRECTIONS: Choose the word or phrase that is most nearly *opposite* in meaning to each numbered Word Bank word. Circle the letter of your choice.

1. furtive
   a. shifty
   b. hidden
   c. honest
   d. annoying

2. lye
   a. liquid
   b. garbage
   c. deodorizer
   d. cleanser

3. oppress
   a. enslave
   b. control
   c. punish
   d. free

4. doctrines
   a. beliefs
   b. doubts
   c. creeds
   d. theories

"Everyday Use" by Alice Walker

Grammar and Style: Sentence Fragments

A **sentence fragment** is a group of words that is punctuated as a sentence but lacks a subject, a verb, or both and fails to express a complete thought. Sometimes writers use sentence fragments to create for the reader the specific rhythms of a character's thoughts or spoken dialogue. Following is one of the sentence fragments that appears in "Everyday Use."

Sentence fragment: But a real smile, not scared.

This sentence fragment lacks a verb. If a verb were added to create a complete sentence, the sentence might read, "But a real smile, not scared, spread across her face."

A. Practice: Each of the following sentence fragments appears in "Everyday Use." On the lines provided, identify the missing part or parts of speech. Then rewrite the sentence to include the subject, verb, or both. Make sure the revised sentence expresses a complete thought.

1. Dee next.

   _____

   _____

2. A dress down to the ground, in this hot weather.

   _____

   _____

3. A dress so loud it hurts my eyes.

   _____

   _____

4. Earrings gold, too, and hanging down to her shoulders.

   _____

   _____

5. Bracelets dangling and making noises when she moves her arm up to shake the folds of the dress out of her armpits.

   _____

   _____

B. Writing Application: Write a paragraph to follow the last paragraph of "Everyday Use." Include three sentence fragments in your paragraph to capture the narrator's thought and speech patterns.

_____

_____

_____

_____

_____

_____

_____

"**Everyday Use**" by Alice Walker

Reading Strategy: Contrasting Characters

Good writers use specific details to depict characters. In depicting characters who are very different, writers use contrasting details. For example, recall the ways in which the three female characters in "Everyday Use" are dressed:

The narrator: I wear flannel nightgowns to bed and overalls during the day.

Maggie: her thin body enveloped in pink skirt and red blouse

Dee: A dress down to the ground, in this hot weather. A dress so loud it hurt my eyes. There are yellows and oranges enough to throw back the light of the sun. . . . Earrings gold, too, and hanging down to her shoulders.

Nowhere does Alice Walker come out and write, "The narrator was practical; Maggie was plain, simple, and solid; Dee, on the other hand, was flashy and bold." Instead of making such "telling" remarks, Walker shows us how the characters are different by using specific and concrete details and letting us draw our own conclusions.

Below are several specific details, some drawn from "Everyday Use." After each, describe a contrasting detail. (It, too, may be from "Everyday Use.") An example is given.

Example: The mother opened her arms and ran across the room to embrace her daughter.

Answer: Her arms folded across her chest, the mother stared at her daughter from across the room.

1. He smiles broadly; his teeth shiny white as pearls.

   _____

   _____

2. She cooked the freshly killed pork over an open fire.

   _____

   _____

3. She hung back in the kitchen, her scarred hands hidden in the folds of her tattered skirt.

   _____

   _____

4. She rifled through the trunk to find the precious quilts.

   _____

   _____

5. She talked a blue streak over the sweet potatoes and the rest of the meal.

   _____

   _____

"**Everyday Use**" by Alice Walker

Literary Analysis: Character's Motivation

You get to know and understand characters in literature the same way you get to know people in real life. You listen to what they say and to what other characters say about them. You see what they look like and watch what they do. From these details, you draw conclusions about characters. If a writer is good, the details will be consistent; that is, they will lead you to conclusions that make sense and that don't contradict each other. In "Everyday Use," for example, Alice Walker offers the following details about Dee (Wangero):

What she says: "No, I don't want those!"

What she does: She rifles through the trunk.

What she looks like: She wears gold earrings hanging to her shoulders.

What others say about her: Hesitation was no part of her nature.

What conclusions can you draw? There are several: Dee is bold; she is brassy; she doesn't hide her feelings; she is brusque.

Beyond these conclusions are your own opinions or judgments about the character. You might feel that Dee is offensive and inconsiderate, or you may feel that she is forthright and honest. Your opinions of characters depend upon your own personal values and experiences with people.

DIRECTIONS: Here is a list of specific details from "Everyday Use." What character trait do you think each detail shows? Write your answer on the line.

1. They swept the hard clay clean and lined the edges with tiny grooves.

   _____

   _____

2. She wears flannel nightgowns to bed and overalls during the day.

   _____

   _____

3. She shuffled along with her chin on her chest, watching every step her feet made.

   _____

   _____

4. She wore a stunning long-sleeved dress down to the ground even in hot weather.

   _____

   _____

5. "Wa-su-zo-Tean-o!" she says, using an African greeting.

   _____

   _____

6. Her hand is limp and cold, and she keeps trying to pull it away from him.

   _____

   _____

from *The Woman Warrior* by Maxine Hong Kingston

Build Vocabulary

Spelling Strategy When adding the suffix *-ly* or *-less* to a word ending in *l*, or when adding *-ness* to a word ending in *n*, keep all the letters of the word; for example, *sudden* + *-ness* forms *suddenness*, and *hysterical* + *-ly* forms the Word Bank word *hysterically*.

Using the Root *-aud-*

The word *inaudibly* contains the root *-aud-*. This root comes from the Latin word *audire*, which means "to hear." The Word Bank word *inaudibly*, therefore, means "in a manner that cannot be heard." Most words containing the root *-aud-* are related to sound and hearing.

A. Directions: Read each of the following descriptions. On the line provided, write the word containing the root *-aud-* that is being described.

audit	audible	audience	audiovisual	audiology

1. a kind of presentation that involves both hearing and sight _____

2. a branch of science that deals with hearing _____

3. to attend a class as a listener, rather than as an active participant

   _____

4. a group of people gathered to hear a concert, speech, or play _____

5. loud and clear enough to be heard _____

Using the Word Bank

hysterically	encampment	inaudibly	gravity	oblivious

B. Directions: Choose a lettered word pair that best expresses a relationship *similar* to that expressed in the numbered pair. Circle the letter of your choice.

1. HYSTERICALLY : CALMLY ::
   a. cheer : gloom
   b. fortunate : luck
   c. discourage : encourage
   d. courageously : cowardly

2. ENCAMPMENT : TEMPORARY ::
   a. cabin : shelter
   b. entrapment : enclose
   c. house : permanent
   d. vacation : retreat

3. INAUDIBLY : FAINTLY ::
   a. sincerely : frankly
   b. swift : slow
   c. gradual : movement
   d. lively : animate

4. GRAVITY : PROBLEM ::
   a. friendly : relationship
   b. excitement : surprise
   c. clearly : transparent
   d. complicated : problem

5. OBLIVIOUS : UNAWARE ::
   a. gigantic : impressive
   b. attentive : neglectful
   c. abundant : plentiful
   d. hopelessness : sorrow

Name _____ Date _____

from *The Woman Warrior* by Maxine Hong Kingston

Grammar and Style: Punctuating a Quotation Within a Quotation

Always use single quotation marks to enclose a **quotation within a quotation**. For example:

"My son and daughter said, 'Come, Mother. The plane's landed early.'"

Place commas and periods inside the closing single quotation marks and place colons and semicolons outside. Place question marks and exclamation points inside or outside, depending on which words they are punctuating. Read the following examples:

"When Moon Orchid arrives, she might say, 'I am happy to be in America'; or she might say 'I miss China,'" Brave Orchid said.

Brave Orchid said, "I heard my niece call, 'Mama!'"

"Did you hear Moon Orchid say, 'You are an old woman'?" Brave Orchid asked.

A. Practice: Read the following paragraph and insert single quotation marks wherever they are needed.

Brave Orchid told her husband, "I saw Moon Orchid and exclaimed, You're an old woman!

My sister responded, You're an old woman, too. On the way home, Moon Orchid then

asked me, How did you get so old?" Brave Orchid asked her husband, "Have you ever

seen someone after many years and thought I can't believe how much you have changed?"

B. Writing Application: Write a paragraph in which you quote Brave Orchid's niece describing some of the conversation she has with her aunt as they wait for Moon Orchid. Use single quotation marks to indicate quotations within quotations.

_____
_____
_____
_____
_____
_____
_____
_____
_____
_____
_____
_____
_____
_____
_____
_____

from _The Woman Warrior_ by Maxine Hong Kingston

Reading Strategy: Apply Background Information

When you read a piece of literature, **background information** can often help you to gain a better understanding of characters, important details, cultural and historical references, and central ideas in the piece. You can gather background information from a variety of sources, including a book jacket, an introduction, footnotes, an author biography, or even from your own personal experiences. In this text, background information for selections is provided by the author biography, by the Background for Understanding, and by footnotes. Think about how background information helped your understanding as you read the selection from _The Woman Warrior_.

DIRECTIONS: Answer the following questions, based on background information provided in your textbook about this selection.

1. Why did Maxine Hong Kingston name her book _The Woman Warrior_? To which characters in this selection from the book might the title refer?

   _____
   _____

2. Where is Ellis Island? Why is Brave Orchid able to compare the experience of immigrants arriving by plane in San Francisco to the experience of immigrants arriving by sea at Ellis Island years ago?

   _____
   _____

3. Why did Brave Orchid leave China to begin a new life in the United States?

   _____
   _____

4. After leaving for the United States, why did Moon Orchid first fly to Hong Kong? Why could she not leave from her province in mainland China?

   _____
   _____

5. Why is Brave Orchid's son in Vietnam? Why did Brave Orchid encourage him to move to Canada?

   _____
   _____

6. Why do Brave Orchid and her children have a difficult time relating to one another? How does this fact relate to the experience Maxine Hong Kingston was trying to capture by writing _The Woman Warrior_?

   _____
   _____

© Prentice-Hall, Inc.

from *The Woman Warrior* by Maxine Hong Kingston

Literary Analysis: Memoirs

Most **memoirs** are similar to autobiographies. They are usually first-person nonfiction narratives describing significant experiences and events in the life of the writer. Maxine Hong Kingston's *The Woman Warrior*, subtitled *Memoirs of a Girlhood Among Ghosts*, has features that are both similar to and different from those of typical memoirs.

DIRECTIONS: Answer the following questions to examine the ways in which this selection from *The Woman Warrior* is both similar to and different from a standard memoir.

1. What is the narrative point of view of the selection? Is this point of view typically used in memoirs? Explain.

   _____

   _____

   _____

   _____

   _____

2. On whose personal impressions of events does the piece focus? Describe two passages in the selection that reveal this person's unique perspective.

   _____

   _____

   _____

   _____

   _____

3. What are two significant experiences, moments, or events described by the selection? Why are they significant to both the person who is the focus of the piece and to the writer of the piece?

   _____

   _____

   _____

   _____

   _____

4. Explain why features of *The Woman Warrior* are different from those of standard memoirs. Why do you think Maxine Hong Kingston chose this unique style for her memoirs? In what way does this style help to convey her central message?

   _____

   _____

   _____

   _____

   _____

"Antojos" by Julia Alvarez

Build Vocabulary

Spelling Strategy For words ending in silent *e*, drop the e before adding a suffix beginning with a vowel. For example, the suffix -*ed* added to the word *enunciate* forms the Word
Bank word *enunciated*.

Words From Spanish

A *machete* is a large, heavy knife used to cut down vegetation. The word is taken directly
from Spanish, in which it has the same meaning. Many other words in English come
from Spanish.

A. DIRECTIONS: The following words are derived from Spanish. Consult a dictionary, and then
write down their different meanings. Tell which words are taken directly from Spanish, like
machete, and which have been changed slightly.

1. hammock _____

2. plaza _____

3. patio _____

4. cocoa_____

Using the Word Bank

dissuade	loath	appease	machetes
collusion	docile	enunciated	

B. DIRECTIONS: For each Word Bank word, choose the word or phrase that is *most similar* in
meaning. Circle the letter of your choice.

1. dissuade

   a. persuade   b. destroy   c. discourage   d. encourage

2. loath

   a. reluctant   b. anxious   c. sure   d. slow

3. appease

   a. apply   b. control   c. provoke   d. satisfy

4. machetes

   a. artillery   b. shovels   c. knives   d. machines

5. collusion

   a. argument   b. conspiracy   c. disruption   d. interpretation

6. docile

   a. harmful   b. angry   c. obedient   d. foolish

"Antojos" by Julia Alvarez

Grammar and Style: Absolute Phrases

An **absolute phrase** is made up of a noun or noun phrase and a participle or participle phrase. It has no grammatical connection to any element in the rest of the sentence, and it does not modify one word or phrase but the whole sentence. It stands absolutely by itself. An absolute phrase, which can appear at the beginning, middle, or end of a sentence, is always set off with a comma or commas. In the following sentences, the absolute phrases appear in italics.

It was an old army bus, *the official name brushed over with paint.*

The road widening, the hills began to plane out into a high plateau.

A. Practice: For each of the following sentences, underline the absolute phrase. If there is no absolute phrase, write *none* after the sentence.

1. Her engine turned off, she heard the sound of another motor. _____

2. She tried the radio again, but all she could hear was static. _____

3. A patient soul, she joked with her aunts. _____

4. They lead sheltered lives, their air-conditioned car taking them from one safe place to another. _____

5. The boy smiled, his head ducking behind his mother. _____

B. Writing Application: Rewrite each of the following sentences, adding an absolute phrase. Your sentences should be about characters and events in "Antojos."

1. The road ahead was rough.

_____

_____

2. They searched through the grove.

_____

_____

3. They approached the car.

_____

_____

4. One man lay beneath the car.

_____

_____

5. Jose walked down the road alone.

_____

_____

"Antojos" by Julia Alvarez

Reading Strategy: Identify With a Character

When you **identify with a character** in a literary selection, you put yourself in the character's place and think about what you have in common with him or her in terms of background, attitudes, or behavior. Identifying with a character increases your enjoyment and understanding of a story.

DIRECTIONS: Examine how well you can identify with the character of Yolanda by filling in the following chart. Answer the questions in the chart, thinking about what similarities in background, personality, and attitudes you do or do not share with Yolanda.

What is Yolanda's family background?	**What is your family background?**
What is Yolanda's attitude toward warnings not to travel by herself?	**What would be your attitude toward such warnings?**
What is Yolanda's attitude toward the children who gather around her car?	**What would your attitude toward the children be?**
How does Yolanda feel and behave when the men appear carrying machetes?	**How would you feel in the same situation?**
How does Yolanda treat Jose when he returns from the Miranda place in tears? How does she seem to feel about him?	**How would you treat Jose? How might you feel about him?**

"Antojos" by Julia Alvarez

Literary Analysis: Plot

The **plot** of a story carries it along. In many stories, the structure of the plot itself reflects the story's meaning. For example, when Alvarez uses a flashback to interrupt the chronological order of the story, she reveals her relationship with her aunts at the beginning of the story and also demonstrates her desire to see the country her own way.

The traditional plot structure consists of these elements:

- Exposition: introduction to the settings, characters, and situation or conflict.
- Rising Action: a series of events that builds interest or suspense
- Climax: the high point of interest or suspense during which the outcome is decided
- Resolution and Falling Action: the point following the climax at which issues are resolved and questions are answered.

As you read "Antojos," look for the ways that the elements of plot create the story.

DIRECTIONS: For each element of plot in the left column, find an example from the story and record it in the right column.

Plot Element	Example from Story
Exposition	
Rising Action	
Climax	
Resolution and Falling Action	

"Freeway 280" by Lorna Dee Cervantes
"Who Burns for the Perfection of Paper" by Martín Espada
"Hunger in New York City" by Simon Ortiz
"Most Satisfied by Snow" by Diana Chang
"What For" by Garrett Hongo

Build Vocabulary

Spelling Strategy The sound *shun* in a suffix is usually formed by the letter combinations *sion*, *tion*, or *ssion*. For example, the noun form of the verb *automate* is the Word Bank word *automation*.

Using the Prefix *auto-*

The Word Bank word *automation*, which refers to manufacturing conducted with self-operating machinery, contains the prefix *auto-*, from the Greek word *autos*, meaning "self."

A. Directions: Fill in each blank with a word from the following list: *autobiography, autocrat, automatic.*

1. An _____ is a self-willed and domineering ruler.

2. The story of your life, written or dictated by yourself, is your _____.

3. Something that moves or operates by itself is _____.

Using the Word Bank

crevices	automation	pervade	liturgy
conjure	calligraphy	trough	

B. Directions: Choose the Word Bank word that best completes the meaning of each sentence. Circle the letter of your choice.

1. The poet listened to the drone of the priest's _____.

   a. liturgy   b. calligraphy   c. trough   d. automation

2. Sharp paper cuts slits in the skin thinner than the _____ of the hands.

   a. calligraphy   b. trough   c. crevices   d. liturgy

3. Words on the invitations were written in _____ .

   a. liturgy   b. calligraphy   c. trough   d. crevices

4. The beautiful ceremony could _____ money from listeners.

   a. automate   b. pervade   c. trough   d. conjure

5. Every morning, fog seemed to _____ the atmosphere.

   a. pervade   b. conjure   c. arrange   d. automate

6. City factories were changed by the _____ of machinery.

   a. calligraphy   b. automation   c. liturgy   d. crevices

Name _____ Date _____

"**Freeway 280**" by Lorna Dee Cervantes
"**Who Burns for the Perfection of Paper**" by Martín Espada
"**Hunger in New York City**" by Simon Ortiz
"**Most Satisfied by Snow**" by Diana Chang
"**What For**" by Garrett Hongo

Grammar and Style: Participial Phrases

A **participial phrase** is a participle and the words that modify or complete it. The entire phrase functions as an adjective, modifying a noun or pronoun. When placing a participial phrase in a sentence, make it clear which word the phrase is modifying. To do this, place the phrase as close as possible to the modified noun or pronoun. For example, read the following sentences:

I notice legal pads *glued with the sting of hidden cuts.*

Sitting beside the freeway, I think about las casitas.

My Grandmother, *stirring curry into a thick stew,* sang beautiful songs.

A. Practice: For each of the following sentences, underline the participial phrase and draw an arrow to the noun or pronoun it modifies.

1. Living a child's life, I was fascinated by many things.

2. My grandfather, slapping *hana* cards on a mat, told me stories of war.

3. I lived for the red volcano dirt staining my toes.

4. Dusted with blasts of sand, my father always walked to the laundry sink to scrub after a long day.

5. I wanted to heal his sores created by work and war.

B. Writing Application: Write a sentence that uses each of the following participial phrases. Remember to place each phrase close to the noun or pronoun being modified so that each sentence is clear. Try to base the subject of your sentences on the poem "Hunger in New York City."

1. covered in concrete

_____

2. blazing in the sun

_____

3. burdened with oil

_____

4. hungering for words and wisdom

_____

5. plagued by hunger

_____

"Freeway 280" by Lorna Dee Cervantes
"Who Burns for the Perfection of Paper" by Martín Espada
"Hunger in New York City" by Simon Ortiz
"Most Satisfied by Snow" by Diana Chang
"What For" by Garrett Hongo

Reading Strategy: Summarize

To **summarize** a poem is to restate briefly its main points. Summarizing as you read a poem or after you finish reading a poem can help you have a clearer understanding of the poem.

DIRECTIONS: Practice your summarizing skills by writing brief summaries of each of the following excerpts from the poems you've read.

1. **"Freeway 280"**

   Las casitas near the gray cannery, / nestled amid wild abrazos of climbing roses / and man-high red geraniums / are gone now. The freeway conceals it / all beneath a raised scar. / But under the fake windsounds of the open lanes, / in the abandoned lots below, new grasses sprout, / wild mustard remembers, old gardens / come back stronger than they were

   _____

   _____

   _____

   _____

   _____

2. **"Who Burns for the Perfection of Paper"**

   Ten years later, in law school, / I knew that every legal pad / was glued with the sting of hidden cuts, / that every open lawbook / was a pair of hands / upturned and burning.

   _____

   _____

   _____

   _____

3. **"Hunger in New York City"**

   Hunger crawls into you / . . . It comes to you, asking / for food, words, wisdom, young memories / of places you ate at, drank cold spring water, / or held somebody's hand, / or home of the gentle, slow dances, / the songs, the strong gods, / the world you know. / . . . And the concrete of this city, / the oily wind, the blazing windows, / the shrieks of automation cannot, / truly cannot, answer for that hunger . . .

   _____

   _____

   _____

   _____

   _____

"Freeway 280" by Lorna Dee Cervantes
"Who Burns for the Perfection of Paper" by Martín Espada
"Hunger in New York City" by Simon Ortiz
"Most Satisfied by Snow" by Diana Chang
"What For" by Garrett Hongo

Literary Analysis: Voice

A poem's unique **voice** comes from its style, its tone, and the individual personality of its speaker. Reading closely, you will find that every poem has a particular voice. Think about the different voices of the poems you have read. In what way does each poet express a unique style, tone, and personality?

DIRECTIONS: As you read the five poems, make notes describing the style, tone, and personality of each speaker. Include details from the poems that emphasize or help create the speaker's voice.

Poem	Voice
"Freeway 280"	
"Who Burns for the Perfection of Paper"	
"Hunger in New York City"	
"Most Satisfied by Snow"	
"What For"	

from *The Mortgaged Heart* by Carson McCullers
"Onomatopoeia" by William Safire
"Coyote v. Acme" by Ian Frazier

Build Vocabulary

Spelling Strategy A suffix can change a word's part of speech, as well as its spelling. For example, adding the *-ic* ending to the noun *aesthete* changes the noun to an adjective and drops the final *e*: *aesthete + -ic = aesthetic.*

Using the Root *-ten-*

A. DIRECTIONS: Knowing that the word root *-ten-* means "to stretch tightly," circle the letter of the best synonym for each word.

1. *extend*   a. multiply   b. spread out   c. distribute   d. repeat

2. *intense*   a. tall   b. arrogant   c. strong   d. minimal

3. *tendon*   a. socket   b. band   c. rod   d. game

Using the Word Bank

pristine	corollary	aesthetic	maverick
contiguous	precipitate	caveat	tensile

B. DIRECTIONS: Choose the lettered pair that best expresses a relationship *similar* to that expressed in the pair that includes the Word Bank word. Circle the letter of your choice.

1. PRISTINE : FLAW ::
   a. hesitant : delay
   b. confused : understandable
   c. cruel : charity
   d. intelligence : ignorant

2. COROLLARY : INFERENCE ::
   a. whole : part
   b. ending : beginning
   c. popularity : choice
   d. death : mortality

3. AESTHETIC : ART ::
   a. dinosaur : archaeology
   b. meteorological : weather
   c. automobiles : traffic
   d. panic : calm

4. MAVERICK : DISOBEY ::
   a. counselor : discourage
   b. example : disgrace
   c. explorer : discover
   d. believer : discount

5. CONTIGUOUS : ADJACENT ::
   a. open : acceptance
   b. relaxation : restful
   c. anxious : tense
   d. honorable : shameful

6. PRECIPITATE : SLUGGISH ::
   a. cluttered : ransack
   b. chill : humidity
   c. productive : laziness
   d. excited : bored

7. CAVEAT : WARNING ::
   a. punishment : sentence
   b. stanza : poem
   c. joyous : pleased
   d. formal : casual

8. TENSILE : STRETCH ::
   a. capable : unable
   b. flammable : burn
   c. agile : gymnast
   d. fragile : broken

from *The Mortgaged Heart* by Carson McCullers
"Onomatopoeia" by William Safire
"Coyote v. Acme" by Ian Frazier

Grammar and Style: Pronouns With Appositives

The form of the pronoun in an appositive must match the form of the noun or group of words that it renames or defines. To help you choose the proper pronoun form, drop the noun or noun phrase the pronoun replaces as you say the sentence aloud. Look at the following example from "The Mortgaged Heart":

> . . . we *Americans* are always seeking.

When a pronoun renames a subject, always use the subjective form. Use the objective form for a pronoun that renames an object.

A. Practice: To complete the following sentences, circle the correct form of the pronoun in parentheses.

1. Two writers, (*he, him*) and Thoreau, sought to understand their lives through their surroundings.

2. McCullers considers (*we, us*) Americans to be mavericks.

3. Some columnists, Safire and (*she, her*), are syndicated in many newspapers.

4. I've watched these cartoon characters, the Road Runner and (*he, him*), for years.

5. (*We, Us*) teenagers still enjoy their antics.

B. Writing Application: Rewrite each sentence, either replacing the italicized words with the appropriate pronoun or adding a pronoun as indicated in parentheses.

1. The students, Roger and *Marcus*, read their essays aloud.

   _____

   _____

2. The teacher praised some students, Annie and *Jane* and *Terrance*, for their analytical skills.

   _____

   _____

3. Two new students, *Margaret* and Walter, expressed interest in joining the debating team.

   _____

   _____

4. (*insert pronoun*) debaters could use their analytical skills.

   _____

   _____

from *The Mortgaged Heart* by Carson McCullers
"Onomatopoeia" by William Safire
"Coyote v. Acme" by Ian Frazier

Reading Strategy: Identify Line of Reasoning

To identify an author's line of reasoning, first identify the main point. Then ask yourself how the writer justifies or explains this point to the reader. Begin by summarizing the essay's main point, and then summarize the writer's argument or reason for presenting it.

DIRECTIONS: Identify lines of reasoning by writing logical arguments and supporting facts or examples in the boxes beneath the main points.

1. "The Mortgaged Heart" by Carson McCullers

Main Point

The "nature of American loneliness" is a "quest for identity."

Line of Reasoning

2. "Coyote v. Acme" by Ian Frazier

Main Point

Acme Company must be held accountable for Mr. Wile E. Coyote's personal injuries.

Line of Reasoning

from *The Mortgaged Heart* by Carson McCullers
"Onomatopoeia" by William Safire
"Coyote v. Acme" by Ian Frazier

Literary Analysis: Essays

Essays are brief prose discussions of specific topics. Among the many types of essays are the **analytical essay**, which attempts to analyze, or consider each part of a topic; the **satirical essay**, which uses irony, ridicule, or sarcasm to comment on a topic; and the **expository essay**, which explains or provides information about a topic.

DIRECTIONS: Determine the type of each of the following essays. Then provide two examples from each essay that demonstrate its type.

Essay	Type	Representative Elements
"The Mortgaged Heart"		1. 2.
"Onomatopoeia"		1. 2.
"Coyote v. Acme"		1. 2.

"Straw Into Gold" by Sandra Cisneros
"For the Love of Books" by Rita Dove
"Mother Tongue" by Amy Tan

Build Vocabulary

Spelling Strategy If a word of more than one syllable ends in a single consonant preceded by a single vowel, and the accent is *not on the last syllable*, do *not* double the final consonant before adding a suffix beginning with a vowel: *nomad* + *-ic* = *nomadic*.

Using the Roots *-scrib-* and *-script-*

A. DIRECTIONS: Knowing that *-scrib-* and *-script-* mean "write," use each of the following words in an original sentence that demonstrates the root's meaning.

1. inscribe _____

2. manuscript _____

Using the Word Bank

nomadic	transcribed	empirical	benign
semantic	quandary	nascent	

B. DIRECTIONS: For each of the following items, choose the Word Bank word that best completes the meaning of the sentence. Circle the letter of your choice.

1. The biology students _____ the instructor's words in their notebooks.

    a. nomadic   b. transcribed   c. empirical   d. benign

2. She explained that, unlike ants that build colonies in one location, army ants are _____.

    a. nomadic   b. benign   c. semantic   d. transcribed

3. One doesn't need _____ training to figure out that the name *army ants* refers to ants that move in large groups.

    a. nomadic   b. transcribed   c. nascent   d. semantic

4. Although a few ants have poisonous stings, most ant bites are _____.

    a. transcribed   b. semantic   c. benign   d. empirical

5. Through the glass wall of the ant farm, students observed an ant that moved from side to side, in an apparent _____.

    a. nomadic   b. empirical   c. quandary   d. benign

6. The instructor stressed the importance of _____ evidence over facts learned from second-hand sources.

    a. benign   b. semantic   c. nomadic   d. empirical

7. The student's _____ interest in biology drove him to learn more about ants.

    a. nascent   b. nomadic   c. benign   d. transcribed

"Straw Into Gold" by Sandra Cisneros
"For the Love of Books" by Rita Dove
"Mother Tongue" by Amy Tan

Grammar and Style: Varying Sentence Structure

A healthy variety of sentence structures can make your writing vital and engaging. Simple sentences contain one independent clause and convey ideas concisely and directly. Compound sentences, which contain two or more independent clauses, and complex sentences, which contain an independent clause and one or more subordinate clauses, can enhance the flow of ideas.

A. Understanding Style: Write the types of sentence structures used in each of the following quotations. Then explain how each writer's sentence structure affects her prose.

1. Henry, the second oldest and my favorite [brother], appears often in poems I have written and in stories which at times only borrow his nickname, Kiki. He played a major role in my childhood. We were bunkbed mates. We were co-conspirators. We were pals.
   —Sandra Cisneros, "Straw Into Gold"
   _____
   _____

2. What I remember most about long summer days is browsing the bookshelves in our solarium to see if there were any new additions. I grew up with those rows of books; I knew where each one was shelved and immediately spotted newcomers.—Rita Dove, "For the Love of Books"
   _____
   _____

3. The talk was going along well enough, until I remembered one major difference that made the whole talk sound wrong. My mother was in the room.—Amy Tan, "Mother Tongue"
   _____
   _____

B. Writing Application: Varying your sentence structure, write a paragraph in which you describe your most memorable experience with reading or language.

_____
_____
_____
_____
_____
_____
_____
_____
_____
_____
_____

"Straw Into Gold" by Sandra Cisneros
"For the Love of Books" by Rita Dove
"Mother Tongue" by Amy Tan

Reading Strategy: Evaluate a Writer's Message

As essay writers, Cisneros, Dove, and Tan want to convey messages to their audience. As readers, we must not only understand these messages but also evaluate them. To do so, we must look carefully at the evidence the writers provide, consider alternative interpretations, and ultimately draw conclusions about each message.

DIRECTIONS: For each writer and essay listed, write your answer to the questions in the chart.

Evaluation Questions	Cisneros, "Straw Into Gold"	Dove, "For the Love of Books"	Tan, "Mother Tongue"
1. What is the writer's main idea?			
2. What evidence supports the main idea?			
3. What are possible disagreements?			
4. What is your evaluation of the writer's message?			

Name _____ Date _____

"Straw Into Gold" by Sandra Cisneros
"For the Love of Books" by Rita Dove
"Mother Tongue" by Amy Tan

Literary Analysis: Reflective Essay

In a **reflective essay**, the writer uses an informal tone to describe personal experiences or key events. This type of essay can reveal the writer's feelings about these experiences as well as his or her values and personality.

DIRECTIONS: Write your answers to the following questions.

1. What personal experience does Cisneros describe in the beginning of her essay? What other personal experience does it bring to mind for her?

   _____

   _____

2. What feelings does Cisneros associate with these experiences?

   _____

   _____

3. What is revealed about Cisneros's personality or values in the story she relates?

   _____

   _____

4. What books and writers does Dove remember reading as a child?

   _____

   _____

5. What do Dove's reading tastes reveal about her values?

   _____

   _____

6. What do Dove's recollections about reading reveal about her childhood?

   _____

   _____

7. What do Tan's experiences with her mother reveal about her personality?

   _____

   _____

8. What do Tan's experiences with her mother reveal about her values?

   _____

   _____

"The Rockpile" by James Baldwin

Build Vocabulary

Spelling Strategy If a word ends in two consonants, it is not necessary to change the two consonants when adding a suffix: *engross + -ed = engrossed.*

Using the Prefix *mal-*

A. DIRECTIONS: The prefix -*mal* means "bad." For each word or phrase that follows, write a synonym that contains the prefix *mal-*.

1. poorly adjusted _____

2. misshapen _____

3. stinking _____

4. work or function improperly_____

Using the Word Bank

intriguing	benevolent	decorously	latent	engrossed
jubilant	arrested	malevolence	perdition	

B. DIRECTIONS: Choose the word or phrase that is most nearly *opposite* in meaning to the word in the Word Bank. Circle the letter of your choice.

1. intriguing:
   a. boring   b. confusing   c. colorful   d. common

2. benevolent:
   a. unaware   b. stingy   c. careless   d. saintly

3. decorously:
   a. hastily   b. rudely   c. strenuously   d. determinedly

4. latent:
   a. dormant   b. tardy   c. invisible   d. evident

5. engrossed:
   a. forgetful   b. preoccupied   c. uninterested   d. serene

6. jubilant:
   a. happy   b. sad   c. skillful   d. jumpy

7. arrested:
   a. began   b. released   c. stopped   d. continued

8. malevolence:
   a. willingness   b. aid   c. acceptance   d. kindness

9. perdition:
   a. relief   b. intuition   c. salvation   d. focus

"**The Rockpile**" by James Baldwin

Grammar and Style: Restrictive and Nonrestrictive Adjective Clauses

An **adjective clause** is a subordinate clause used as an adjective to modify a noun or pronoun. A **restrictive adjective clause** is necessary to complete the meaning of the noun or pronoun it modifies. In the following example the restrictive adjective clause, shown in italics, modifies the noun *boys*.

He was afraid of the rockpile and of the boys *who played there*.

A **nonrestrictive adjective clause** provides additional but not necessary information. It is set off from the rest of the sentence with commas. The following example shows a nonrestrictive adjective clause that modifies the noun *boy*.

Once a boy, *whose name was Richard*, drowned in the river.

A. Practice: Underline the adjective clause in each sentence. On the blank before each sentence, write *N* if the adjective clause is nonrestrictive and *R* if it is restrictive.

____ 1. . . . she had just left some sinful place, which she dared not name, as, for example, a movie palace.

____ 2. She looked back at Gabriel, who had risen . . .

____ 3. John began drawing into his schoolbook a newspaper advertisement that featured a new electric locomotive.

____ 4. He turned back to Roy, who had lain quietly sobbing, eyes wide open and body held rigid. . . .

B. Writing Application: Write a paragraph in which you describe a street scene in your community. Use at least one restrictive adjective clause and one nonrestrictive adjective clause in your description.

_____

_____

_____

_____

_____

_____

_____

_____

_____

_____

_____

_____

_____

_____

Name _____ Date _____

"**The Rockpile**" by James Baldwin

Reading Strategy: Identify Cause and Effect

When you **identify cause and effect** relationships in fiction, you can take several approaches. You might figure out what causes characters to behave as they do. You might note the effects that one character's words or actions have on other characters. Identifying cause and effect in fiction can help you understand a story's action and meaning.

DIRECTIONS: Complete the following flow charts to identify cause and effect in "The Rockpile."

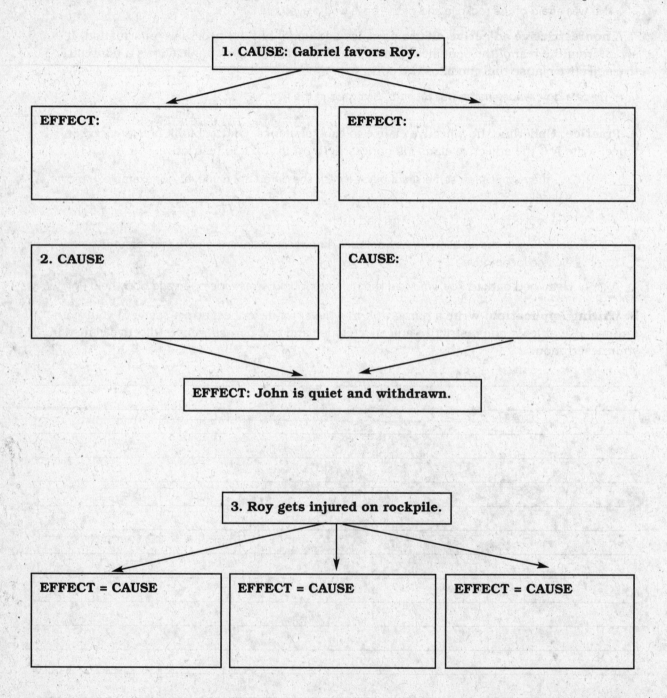

1. CAUSE: Gabriel favors Roy.

EFFECT:

EFFECT:

2. CAUSE

CAUSE:

EFFECT: John is quiet and withdrawn.

3. Roy gets injured on rockpile.

EFFECT = CAUSE

EFFECT = CAUSE

EFFECT = CAUSE

"The Rockpile" by James Baldwin

Literary Analysis: Setting

Every story has a **setting**, a particular time and place in which it occurs. The setting of a story affects how the characters feel and how they behave. Setting encompasses details that fall into several categories, such as location, weather, geography, time of day, season, and atmosphere. The social and economic conditions that prevail in a story are also an important aspect of its setting.

A. DIRECTIONS: Each of the following passages from the selection reflects a particular category of setting. Review the categories listed below. On the line before each passage, write the letter of the category (or the letters of the categories) that most applies to the passage. You will not use every category.

a. location   b. geography   c. weather   d. time of day

e. social and economic conditions   f. season   g. atmosphere

_____ 1. "At the end of the street nearest their house was the bridge which spanned the Harlem River . . ."

_____ 2. ". . . John and Roy sat on the fire escape and watched the forbidden street below."

_____ 3. "Dozens of boys fought each other in the harsh sun . . ."

_____ 4. "One Saturday, an hour before his father would be coming home, Roy was wounded on the rockpile and brought screaming upstairs."

_____ 5. "They filled the air, too, with flying weapons: stones, sticks, tin cans, garbage, whatever could be picked up and thrown."

B. DIRECTIONS: In each of the sentences in Part A, at least one word is related to a particular category (or categories) of setting. Change the setting of each sentence by replacing the word or words with your own. On the lines below, rewrite each sentence with your new words. Your new sentences can make the setting imaginative and fun.

_____

_____

_____

_____

_____

_____

_____

_____

_____

_____

_____

_____

from *Hiroshima* by John Hersey
"Losses" and "The Death of the Ball Turret Gunner" by Randall Jarrell

Build Vocabulary

Spelling Strategy Form the plurals of words ending in *z*, *x*, *sh*, *ch*, or *s* by adding *es* to the base word. For example, the plural form of the word *wish* is *wishes*. Form the plurals of words ending in *y* preceded by a consonant by changing the *y* to *i* and adding *es*. For example, the plural form of the word *philanthropy* is the Word Bank word *philanthropies*.

Using the Root -*vol*-

The Word Bank word *volition*, which means "the act of using the will," has -*vol*- as its root. You can find the root -*vol*-, meaning "to will" or "to wish," in other English words.

A. DIRECTIONS: Fill in the blanks with the most appropriate word from the following list of -*vol*- words.

volitionally	involuntary	volunteerism	malevolent

1. One _____ function of your body is the beating of your heart.

2. The charitable organization encourages _____ and donations.

3. The _____ nature of the crime was disturbing.

4. He was not influenced or pressured in any way—his decision was made

   _____.

Using the Word Bank

evacuated	volition	rendezvous
philanthropies	incessant	convivial

B. DIRECTIONS: For each Word Bank word, choose the word or phrase that is most *similar* in meaning. Circle the letter of your choice.

1. evacuated: a. departed   b. replenished   c. canceled   d. ended

2. volition: a. unwillingness   b. resolution   c. will   d. speed

3. rendezvous: a. meeting   b. dance   c. song   d. tradition

4. philanthropies: a. plans   b. attacks   c. sciences   d. charities

5. incessant: a. hopeless   b. constant   c. violent   d. clear

6. convivial: a. reluctant   b. angry   c. sociable   d. conflicting

from *Hiroshima* by John Hersey
"Losses" and "The Death of the Ball Turret Gunner" by Randall Jarrell

Grammar and Style: Transitions and Transitional Phrases

Writers often use **transitions** and **transitional phrases** to show the relationships between ideas. A transition is a single word, and a transitional phrase is a group of words. Transitions and transitional phrases show time relationships, comparisons, degrees of importance, and spatial relationships. Read the following examples:

At the time, none of them knew anything.

Before six o'clock that morning, Mr. Tanimoto started for Mr. Matsuo's house.

A. Practice: For each sentence, underline the transition or transitional phrase. Then tell whether it shows a time relationship, a comparison, or a spatial relationship.

1. " . . . just a few days before, he had heard that an influential acquaintance, a Mr. Tanaka . . . had been telling people that Tanimoto should not be trusted." _____
   _____

2. "A few minutes after they started, the air-raid siren went off . . ." _____
   _____

3. "To the south were the docks, an airport, and the island-studded Inland Sea."
   _____

4. "Like most homes in this part of Japan, the house consisted of a wooden frame and wooden walls supporting a heavy tile roof." _____

5. "Then a tremendous flash of light cut across the sky."_____

6. "He noticed as he ran that the concrete wall of the estate had fallen over . . ."

7. "There she unrolled some mats and the children lay down on them." _____
   _____

B. Writing Application: Write a paragraph based on the ideas in *Hiroshima*, "Losses," or "The Death of the Ball Turret Gunner." Use transitions and transitional phrases to show the relationships between ideas.

_____
_____
_____
_____
_____
_____
_____

from *Hiroshima* by John Hersey
"Losses" and "The Death of the Ball Turret Gunner" by Randall Jarrell

Reading Strategy: Make Inferences About Theme

To increase your understanding and appreciation of a literary work, make inferences about the **theme**, or the work's central message, as you read. You can make thoughtful inferences if you pay close attention to the writer's descriptions of events and characters, use of concrete details, and use of literary devices. These elements will often guide you toward the selection's theme.

DIRECTIONS: In the following chart, record details, descriptions of characters, and literary devices that strike you as important to the central idea of each selection. Then describe the themes in each selection and how the specific details, events and characters, and literary devices you've listed suggest these themes.

Selection	Details/Events and Characters/Literary Devices	Themes
from *Hiroshima*		
"Losses"		
"The Death of the Ball Turret Gunner"		

Name _____ Date _____

from *Hiroshima* by John Hersey

"Losses" and **"The Death of the Ball Turret Gunner"** by Randall Jarrell

Literary Analysis: Implied Theme

The **theme** is the central idea or message about life that a writer conveys in a literary work. A writer will rarely state a theme outright. Often theme is stated indirectly, or **implied**, through the writer's portrayal of characters and events, use of literary devices, and choice of details.

DIRECTIONS: Describe how the following excerpts from *Hiroshima*, "Losses," and "The Death of the Ball Turret Gunner" convey the themes of the pieces. What is implied in each excerpt?

from *Hiroshima*

1. The Reverend Mr. Tanimoto got up at five o'clock that morning. He was alone in the parsonage, because for some time his wife had been commuting with their year-old baby to spend nights with a friend in Ushida, a suburb to the north. Of all the important cities of Japan, only two, Kyoto and Hiroshima, had not been visited in strength by *B–san*, or Mr. B, as the Japanese, with a mixture of respect and unhappy familiarity, called the B-29; and Mr. Tanimoto, like all his neighbors and friends, was almost sick with anxiety.

   _____

   _____

2. The ceiling dropped suddenly and the wooden floor above collapsed in splinters and the people up there came down and the roof above them gave way; but principally and first of all, the bookcases right behind her swooped forward and the contents threw her down. . . . There, in the tin factory, in the first moment of the atomic age, a human being was crushed by books.

   _____

   _____

"Losses"

3. In bombers named for girls, we burned / The cities we had learned about in school— / Till our lives wore out; our bodies lay among / The people we had killed and never seen.

   _____

   _____

4. When we lasted long enough they gave us medals; / When we died they said, "Our casualties were low."

   _____

   _____

"The Death of the Ball Turret Gunner"

5. Six miles from earth, loosed from its dream of life, / I woke to black flak and the nightmare fighters. / When I died they washed me out of the turret with a hose.

   _____

   _____

"Mirror" by Sylvia Plath
"In a Classroom" by Adrienne Rich
"The Explorer" by Gwendolyn Brooks
"Frederick Douglass" and **"Runagate Runagate"** by Robert Hayden

Build Vocabulary

Spelling Strategy A prefix attached to a word does not affect the spelling of the original word. For example, the prefix *pre-* added to the word *conceptions* forms the Word Bank word *preconceptions*.

Using the Roots *-cep-* and *-cept-*

The speaker in the poem "Mirror" states "I have no *preconceptions*," meaning the speaker has no ideas formed beforehand. The word *preconceptions* contains the Latin root *-cep-* or *-cept-*, which means "to take, hold, or seize." Many other familiar English words contain the root *-cep-* or *-cept-*.

A. Directions: Use at least three of the following *-cep-* or *-cept-* words in a short paragraph describing one of the poets or poems in this section.

perception	exceptional	receptive	deceptive	concept

_____

_____

_____

_____

_____

_____

_____

Using the Word Bank

preconceptions	meditate	din	wily

B. Directions: For each Word Bank word, choose the word or phrase that is most clearly *opposite* in meaning. Circle the letter of your choice.

1. preconceptions:
   a. reductions   b. inventions   c. reexaminations   d. anticipations

2. meditate:
   a. act   b. reflect   c. plan   d. insist

3. din:
   a. clamor   b. silence   c. conversation   d. organization

4. wily:
   a. complex   b. angry   c. crafty   d. simple

"Mirror" by Sylvia Plath
"In a Classroom" by Adrienne Rich
"The Explorer" by Gwendolyn Brooks
"Frederick Douglass" and **"Runagate Runagate"** by Robert Hayden

Grammar and Style: Parallel Structure

Parallel structure is the expression of similar ideas in similar grammatical forms. Poets often use parallel structure to emphasize important ideas. For example, notice the parallel structure of the lines "There were no bourns./There were no quiet rooms" from Gwendolyn Brooks's poem "The Explorer" and the lines " . . . when it belongs at last to all,/when it is truly instinct, brain matter, diastole, systole,/reflex action; when it is finally won . . ." from Robert Hayden's poem "Frederick Douglass."

When items in a sentence are joined by coordinating conjunctions (*and*, *but*, *yet*, *or*) or correlative conjunctions (*either/or*, *neither/nor*), the items must be parallel. Read the following examples:

Faulty: People in the classroom were talking of poetry, hauling books, and they read aloud.

Parallel: People in the classroom were talking of poetry, hauling books, and reading aloud.

Faulty: They were either reading aloud or they listened.

Parallel: They were either reading aloud or listening.

A. Practice: Find and list four examples of parallel structure in "The Explorer" or "Runagate Runagate."

_____

_____

_____

_____

_____

B. Writing Application: Rewrite the following sentences, making the structure parallel in each.

1. The mirror is shown meditating and as a reflector of truth.

_____

_____

2. The explorer hopes for inner peace and to find a quiet place. _____

_____

_____

3. Frederick Douglass is recognized for seeing a world in which nobody is lonely and hunted and as a teacher of love and logic.

_____

_____

"Mirror" by Sylvia Plath
"In a Classroom" by Adrienne Rich
"The Explorer" by Gwendolyn Brooks
"Frederick Douglass" and **"Runagate Runagate"** by Robert Hayden

Reading Strategy: Interpret

To deepen your understanding of a poem, you must *interpret*, or search to find meaning in its words, images, and other elements. You can interpret by looking closely at a particular element such as the poem's title, the identity of its speaker, or a particular image and then deciding how the element relates to the poet's central message. You can also use your understanding of a poet's overall meaning or social context to interpret its individual elements.

DIRECTIONS: Practice your interpretation skills by answering the following questions, which are based on the poems you have read.

1. Who is the speaker in Sylvia Plath's poem "Mirror"? Use your knowledge of the identity of the speaker to interpret the following lines from the poem:

   I am silver and exact. I have no preconceptions. / Whatever I see I swallow immediately / Just as it is, unmisted by love or dislike. / I am not cruel, only truthful—

   How do the speaker's assertions in these lines relate to the poet's overall meaning?

   _____

   _____

2. How does the title of the poem "The Explorer" relate to its central message? How does the title help you to understand the poem as you begin reading?

   _____

   _____

3. One stanza in the poem "The Explorer" reads,

   So tipping down the scrambled halls he set / Vague hands on throbbing knobs. There were behind / Only spiraling, high human voices, / The scream of nervous affairs, / Wee griefs, / Grand griefs. And choices.

   How do the details presented in this stanza help you understand the poem's final lines, "There were no bourns (limits) / There were no quiet rooms."?

   _____

   _____

4. In the poem "Frederick Douglass," significant details are presented in the following line.

   Oh, not with statues' rhetoric, / not with legends and poems and wreaths of bronze alone . . .

   To what is the speaker contrasting "statues' rhetoric," and "legends and poems and wreaths"? How does this contrast relate to the poem's central message?

   _____

   _____

"Mirror" by Sylvia Plath
"In a Classroom" by Adrienne Rich
"The Explorer" by Gwendolyn Brooks
"Frederick Douglass" and **"Runagate Runagate"** by Robert Hayden

Literary Analysis: Theme and Context

Some poems contain details, images, and ideas that relate to specific events in history or to events in a poet's own life. Considering a poem's historical or biographical **context** can help you understand its **theme**, or main idea. For example, knowing that "Runagate Runagate" is a poem about the Underground Railroad should help you interpret the poem's final lines, "Come ride-a my train/ Mean mean mean to be free."

DIRECTIONS: Consider the biographical and historical context of some of the poems you've read to answer the following questions.

1. Biographical information about Sylvia Plath reveals that despite her literary accomplishments, she was often unhappy, struggling with negative emotions and negative perceptions of herself and the world around her. A great deal of her poetry shares feelings from her personal life. How does knowing this enhance your understanding of the poem "Mirror," particularly the final lines of the poem, which read,

> Each morning it is her face that replaces the darkness. / In me she has drowned a young girl, and in me an old woman / Rises toward her day after day, like a terrible fish.

_____
_____
_____
_____
_____

2. Gwendolyn Brooks was influenced by the attitudes of the Harlem Renaissance, a literary movement in which African Americans wrote works that celebrated their ethnic identity and described the realities of being treated as second-class citizens, struggling to be heard and finding choices in life. Describe how some of these ideas are reflected in the poem "The Explorer."

_____
_____
_____
_____

3. How does knowledge of African American history, particularly issues surrounding slavery and civil rights, help you understand and appreciate the poems "Frederick Douglass" and "Runagate Runagate"?

_____
_____
_____
_____
_____

"**For My Children**" by Colleen McElroy
"**Bidwell Ghost**" by Louise Erdrich

Build Vocabulary

Spelling Strategy When forming the plural of a word that ends in a consonant plus *y*, change the *y* to *i* and add *es*. The Word Bank word *effigies* is the plural form of *effigy*.

Using Related Words: *heritage*

A. DIRECTIONS: The words shown in the following list are related to the word *heritage*, which means "something handed down from one's ancestors or the past." Complete each of the following sentences with one of the words from the list.

heredity	hereditary	inherited	inheritance	inheritor

1. From her mother's side of the family, she _____ height and thick, black hair.

2. The greedy _____ did not share any of his fortune with others.

3. Some people argue that _____ rather than environment determines personality.

4. An old photograph album and a collection of personal diaries were among the items of her _____.

5. _____ characteristics appear in successive generations.

Using the Word Bank

shackles	heritage	effigies

B. DIRECTIONS: Circle the letter of the word most *similar* in meaning to each Word Bank word.

1. shackles:
   a. slavery   b. rituals   c. chains   d. ghosts

2. heritage:
   a. antique   b. ancestry   c. relatives   d. keepsake

3. effigies:
   a. alterations   b. opposites   c. melodies   d. likenesses

"For My Children" by Colleen McElroy
"Bidwell Ghost" by Louise Erdrich

Grammar and Style: Sequence of Verb Tenses

Verbs express time—present, past, and future—by means of tense. When events being described have occurred at different times, be sure to use the correct **sequence of tenses**—shift tenses to show that one event precedes or follows another. Review the different verb tenses in the following chart; then see the example of correct sequence of tenses.

Present	She **searches** for her heritage.
Present perfect	She **has searched** for her heritage.
Past	She **searched** for her heritage.
Past perfect	She **had searched** for her heritage.
Future	She **will search** for her heritage.
Future perfect	She **will have searched** for her heritage.

Incorrect: By the time she *got* home, the house *burned* to the ground.

Correct: By the time she *got* home, the house *had burned* to the ground.

In the incorrect example, both verbs are in the past tense; it is not clear if one action happened before or after the other. In the correct version, the shift from past tense to past perfect tense indicates that one action began and ended before the other.

A. Practice: Identify the tense of the italicized verbs in each of these lines, writing *present*, *present perfect*, *past*, *past perfect*, *future*, or *future perfect*.

"For My Children"

1. "I *have stored* up tales for you, my children" _____

2. "My memory *floats* down a long narrow hall,/A calabash of history." _____

3. "Grandpa *stood* high in Watusi shadows" _____

"Bidwell Ghost"

4. "It *has been* twenty years" _____

5. "She *will climb* into your car" _____

6. "Each spring now, in the grass, buds *form* on the tattered wood." _____

B. Writing Application: Write a paragraph describing the events in either "For My Children" or "Bidwell Ghost." In your paragraph, use at least three verb tenses. Use the correct sequence of tenses to make clear the relationship of the events in time.

_____

_____

_____

_____

_____

_____

"**For My Children**" by Colleen McElroy
"**Bidwell Ghost**" by Louise Erdrich

Reading Strategy: Read in Sentences

Poems can sometimes be difficult to understand, especially after only one reading. However, if you **read poetry in sentences**, rather than line by line, you can clarify confusing passages and understand a poem's literal meaning. Use the poem's punctuation as your guide through the poem. Rather than stopping at the end of a line, stop only at an endmark such as a period, question mark, or an exclamation point. Pause at a comma, colon, semicolon, or dash. Read aloud in sentences the following lines from "For My Children." How many sentences make up this six-line stanza?

> I have stored up tales for you, my children
>   My favorite children, my only children;
> Of shackles and slaves and a bill of rights.
> But skin of honey and beauty of ebony begins
>   In the land called Bilad as-Sudan,
> So I search for a heritage beyond St. Louis.

Punctuation can affect your reading of a poem. Once you read a poem in sentences to understand its literal meaning, reread the poem, pausing at line breaks to hear its rhythm. The rhythm of a poem contributes to its overall effect.

DIRECTIONS: Write answers to each of the following questions.

1. Line 2 of "For My Children" ends with a semicolon. How does this punctuation affect your reading of the first three lines—the first sentence—of the poem?

   _____

   _____

2. How many sentences are there in the following lines from "For My Children"?

   > The line of your cheeks recalls Ibo melodies
   >   as surely as oboe and flute.
   > The sun dances a honey and cocoa duet on your faces.
   > I see smiles that mirror schoolboy smiles
   >   In the land called Bilad as-Sudan;
   > I see the link between the Mississippi and the Congo.

   _____

   _____

3. In "Bidwell Ghost," every stanza but the last ends with a period. How does this punctuation affect your reading of the poem? What overall effect does this create?

   _____

   _____

4. Why do you think Erdrich chose to punctuate the last stanza of "Bidwell Ghost" as she did?

   _____

   _____

"**For My Children**" by Colleen McElroy
"**Bidwell Ghost**" by Louise Erdrich

Literary Analysis: Lyric Poetry

Lyric poetry is one of the oldest and most popular forms of poetry. Brief and melodic, a lyric poem expresses the observations and feelings of a single speaker. Unlike narrative poetry, which tells a story, lyric poetry focuses on a specific experience or subject. Another distinctive feature of lyric poetry is the creation of a single effect.

DIRECTIONS: Answer each of the following questions about "For My Children" and "Bidwell Ghost."

"For My Children"

1. What is the subject of "For My Children"?

   _____

   _____

   _____

2. What are the speaker's observations and feelings about the subject?

   _____

   _____

   _____

3. What overall effect is created in the poem? What elements or details help create this effect?

   _____

   _____

   _____

"Bidwell Ghost"

4. What is the subject of "Bidwell Ghost"?

   _____

   _____

   _____

5. What are the speaker's observations and feelings about the subject?

   _____

   _____

   _____

6. What overall effect is created in the poem? What elements or details help create this effect?

   _____

   _____

   _____

Name _____ Date _____

Build Vocabulary

Spelling Strategy The "k" sound is spelled *k*, *ck*, *ch*, *cq*, or *q*. For example, the "k" sound in the Word Bank word *bronchitis* is spelled with *ch*. When uncertain about the spelling of a word with the "k" sound, consult your dictionary.

Using the Suffix *-itis*

The suffix *-itis* means "disease or inflammation." The Word Bank word *bronchitis*, which contains the suffix *-itis*, therefore means "inflammation of the bronchial tubes."

A. DIRECTIONS: Each of the words in the following list contains the suffix *-itis*. Use the meaning of the suffix to complete each of the following sentences with a word from the list.

colitis	dermatitis	diverticulitis	sinusitis

1. The affliction of _____ inflames the derma, or skin layer.

2. Whenever the humidity rises, my _____ seems to flare up, causing pressure in the sinus or nasal cavity.

3. Uncle Max suffers from _____, which is an inflammation of the mucous membrane of the colon.

4. _____, which is the inflammation of the diverticulum, can be a serious condition.

Using the Word Bank

bronchitis	barometer	anthology	cronies

B. DIRECTIONS: Match each word in the left column with its definition in the right column. Write the letter of the definition on the line next to the word it defines.

____ 1. anthology   a. an inflammation of the mucous lining of the major air passageways of the lungs

____ 2. barometer   b. close companions

____ 3. bronchitis   c. an instrument for measuring atmospheric pressure, used in forecasting weather or finding height above sea level

____ 4. cronies   d. a collection of poems, stories, songs, or excerpts

Name _____ Date _____

"The Writer in the Family" by E. L. Doctorow

Grammar and Style: Commonly Confused Words: *affect* and *effect*

Words that sound alike, look alike, or have related meanings are often confused. Two commonly confused words are **affect** and **effect**. *Affect* is a verb that means "to influence." *Effect* is usually used as a noun that means "result." However, *effect* can also be used as a verb that means "to bring about; to cause." Look at the following examples.

Affect (verb)	How will the death of Jonathan's father **affect** (influence) Jonathan's life?
Effect (noun)	At first, Aunt Frances is pleased with the **effect** (result) of Jonathan's letters upon the elderly grandmother's spirits.
Effect (verb)	Finding the set of Great Sea Novels will **effect** (bring about or cause) a change in Jonathan's understanding of his father's youthful dreams.

A. Practice: Complete each of the following sentences by writing the correct use and form of *affect* or *effect* on the line.

1. Bronchitis _____ the mucous lining of the lung's major air passageways.

2. The full _____ of Jack's death was not felt immediately.

3. Having Harold's girlfriend to dinner _____ a positive change in Jonathan and Harold's mother.

4. A small pension would _____ the family's economic situation.

5. Jonathan felt the _____ of Harold's criticism.

B. Writing Application: Write a paragraph comparing and contrasting the influence Aunt Frances hoped for in Jonathan's letters and the actual result. Use the commonly confused words *affect* and *effect* at least once each.

_____

_____

_____

_____

_____

_____

_____

_____

_____

_____

_____

Name _____ Date _____

Reading Strategy: Judge the Characters' Actions

In Doctorow's "The Writer in the Family," Jack's death affects the lives of his wife, sons, and other relatives. Each character—Ruth, Jonathan, Harold, Aunt Frances—responds differently to his death. As you read the story, you evaluate or **judge the characters' actions** against a set of moral standards. By exploring a character's motivation or an event's impact upon a character, you can evaluate his or her behavior.

DIRECTIONS: Complete the following chart by evaluating each character's response to Jack's death. Then state the character's actions, words, or motivation that illustrates or supports your evaluation.

Character	Evaluate response to Jack's death	State supporting actions, words, or motivations
Jonathan		
Harold		
Ruth		
Aunt Frances		

"The Writer in the Family" by E. L. Doctorow

Literary Analysis: Static and Dynamic Characters

Writers use two types of characters in fiction: static and dynamic. A **static character** does not change during the course of a story. No matter what events the static character experiences, his or her personality, behavior, attitudes, and beliefs are the same at the end of the story as they were at the beginning. On the other hand, a **dynamic character** does change during the course of a story. He or she is affected by events in the story and, sometimes, learns and grows because of those events.

In "The Writer in the Family," E. L. Doctorow helps you learn about a character by what he or she does and says. A character's words and actions reveal his or her motivation and response to events. You can use a character's words and actions to help you determine whether he or she is a static or dynamic character.

DIRECTIONS: Complete the following chart, identifying whether each character listed is static or dynamic. Then support your identification with evidence—details of a character's words and/or actions—to illustrate the static or dynamic nature of each character.

Character	Static or Dynamic?
Jonathan	Type: Supporting evidence:
Jonathan's mother	Type: Supporting evidence:
Aunt Frances	Type: Supporting evidence:
Jonathan's father	Type: Supporting evidence:

"Camouflaging the Chimera" by Yusef Komunyakaa
"Ambush" by Tim O'Brien

Build Vocabulary

Spelling Strategy An English word never ends with the letter *j*, except for a few foreign derivatives, like *haj*, a Muslim pilgrimage to Mecca. If a word ends with the "j" sound, always use *ge*, as in the Word Bank word *refuge*.

Words From War

The poems "Camouflaging the Chimera" and "Ambush" feature words such as *platoon*, *grenade*, and *camouflage*, which are drawn directly from the language of warfare. Word Bank words *ammunition* and *ambush* are also words of warfare that have become part of our everyday language.

A. DIRECTIONS: Each of the words in the following list is drawn from military jargon or the language of warfare. Use each word in a sentence that illustrates its meaning. If you are unsure of the meaning of a word, consult a dictionary.

1. shell-shocked

_____

2. casualties

_____

3. foxhole

_____

Using the Word Bank

refuge	ambush	ammunition	muzzle	gape

B. DIRECTIONS: Choose a word pair that best expresses a relationship similar to that expressed in the numbered pair. Circle the letter of your choice.

1. refuge : protection ::
   a. support : defeat
   b. arrange : plan
   c. assistance : aid
   d. carefully : cautiously

2. ambush : attack ::
   a. study : analysis
   b. blueprint : plan
   c. argument : discussion
   d. surrender : retreat

3. ammunition : bullet ::
   a. utensil : fork
   b. mechanic : tool
   c. machine : operate
   d. engine : car

4. muzzle : gun ::
   a. roof : ladder
   b. door : window
   c. nose : airplane
   d. tail : fur

5. gape : stare ::
   a. whisper : talk
   b. foot : walk
   c. sleep : awaken
   d. shout : holler

"Camouflaging the Chimera" by Yusef Komunyakaa
"Ambush" by Tim O'Brien

Grammar and Style: Noun Clauses

A **noun clause** is a subordinate clause that functions as a noun in a sentence. Words that often introduce noun clauses include *that, which, what, if, how, when, where, why, whatever, whoever,* and *whether.* Read the following example from Tim O'Brien's story "Ambush":

> It was a difficult moment, but I did *what seemed right* . . .

In this example, "what seemed right" is a noun clause functioning as the direct object of the verb *did.* In some noun clauses, the introductory word *that* is implied rather than stated directly. For example:

> . . . she said "so I guess [that] you must've killed somebody."

A. Practice: For each sentence, underline the noun clause. Then identify its function in the sentence by writing above it *direct object, object of a preposition,* or *predicate noun.*

1. Vietnam War memories are what inspire many of Tim O'Brien's stories.

2. He wrote "Ambush" after his young daughter asked if he had ever killed.

3. O'Brien didn't tell her the truth because he knew it might upset the child.

4. He thought about what he should tell her in the future.

5. He hopes his stories will give her insight into why he acted as he did.

B. Writing Application: Finish each sentence with a noun clause. Try to use a variety of introductory words.

1. When he saw the enemy, the soldier did not know _____

_____.

2. He crouched in the brush and wondered _____

_____.

3. He knew _____

_____.

4. Now he cannot forget about _____

_____.

5. His hope is _____

_____.

Name _____ Date _____

"Camouflaging the Chimera" by Yusef Komunyakaa
"Ambush" by Tim O'Brien

Reading Strategy: Envision the Action

When you read a literary work, always try to **envision the action,** or form a picture in your mind of what you are reading. Writers invite readers into important moments or scenes in their work by weaving words into images. Use these images to form your own mental pictures.

DIRECTIONS: As you read the following passages from "Camouflaging the Chimera" and "Ambush," envision what the writers are describing. Picture yourself in each soldier's place. Then answer the following questions: What is the soldier seeing, feeling, or hearing? What specific images help you envision the scene? How does envisioning the scene help you understand the piece?

"Camouflaging the Chimera"

1. We tied branches to our helmets. / We painted our faces & rifles / with mud from a riverbank, / blades of grass hung from the pockets / of our tiger suits.

   _____

   _____

   _____

2. But we waited / till the moon touched metal, / till something almost broke / inside us. VC struggled/with the hillside, like black silk / wrestling iron through grass. / We weren't there. The river ran / through our bones . . . we held our breath . . .

   _____

   _____

   _____

"Ambush"

3. . . . and I remember it was still dark when Kiowa shook me awake for the final watch. The night was foggy and hot. For the first few moments I felt lost, not sure about directions, groping for my helmet and weapon. . . . The mosquitoes were fierce. I remember slapping at them . . . then looking up and seeing the young man come out of the fog.

   _____

   _____

   _____

4. The grenade bounced once and rolled across the trail. I did not hear it, but there must've been a sound, because the young man dropped his weapon and began to run, just two or three quick steps, then he hesitated, swiveling to his right, and he glanced down at the grenade and tried to cover his head but never did. It occurred to me then that he was about to die. I wanted to warn him. The grenade made a popping noise—not soft but not loud either—not what I'd expected—and there was a puff of dust and smoke—a small white puff—and the young man seemed to jerk upward as if pulled by invisible wires.

   _____

   _____

   _____

"**Camouflaging the Chimera**" by Yusef Komunyakaa
"**Ambush**" by Tim O'Brien

Literary Analysis: First-Person Narrator

A **first-person narrator** reveals his or her thoughts and feelings using the pronouns *I* and *we*. Writers use first person when they want to reveal the narrator's personality, viewpoints, and personal responses. Both "Camouflaging the Chimera" and "Ambush" use a first-person narrator. As you read, think about why first-person narration is important to these pieces.

DIRECTIONS: Answer the following questions based on the selections.

1. Komunyakaa writes that "We wove ourselves into the terrain, content to be a humming-bird's target"; "We hugged bamboo & leaned against a breeze off the river"; and "We waited . . . till something almost broke inside us." How does the first-person narration of these statements help you understand what the soldiers are experiencing?

   _____

   _____

   _____

2. Why do you think Komunyakaa writes his poem using *we* instead of *I*? What is he trying to emphasize about being a soldier?

   _____

   _____

   _____

3. In describing the moment at which he encountered the enemy soldier, O'Brien writes,

   I tried to swallow whatever was rising from my stomach, which tasted like lemonade, something fruity and sour. I was terrified. There were no thoughts about killing. The grenade was to make him go away—just evaporate—and I leaned back and felt my mind go empty and then felt it fill up again. I had already thrown the grenade before telling myself to throw it.

   How does the first-person narration in this scene help your understanding of O'Brien's situation, his reasons for throwing the grenade, and his comfort with his role as a soldier? What information would you miss if his experience were described by an outsider?

   _____

   _____

   _____

   _____

4. At the end of the story, O'Brien relives his encounter with the man. He imagines not throwing the grenade and watching the man walk away. Why are these personal reflections important to the story? What do they reveal about O'Brien?

   _____

   _____

   _____

   _____

The Crucible, **Act I,** by Arthur Miller

Build Vocabulary

Spelling Strategy When adding a suffix that begins with a vowel to a word that ends in a silent *e*, drop the *e*, and then add the suffix. For example, *ingratiate + ing = ingratiating* and *dissemble + ing = dissembling.*

Using the Root *-grat-*

A. DIRECTIONS: The root *-grat-* means "pleasing" or "grateful." Explain how the meaning of the word root *-grat-* contributes to the meaning of each of the following words.

1. gratitude _____

_____

_____

2. gratuitous _____

_____

_____

Using the Word Bank

predilection	ingratiating	dissembling	calumny
inculcation	propitiation	licentious	

B. DIRECTIONS: Match each word in the left column with its definition in the right column. Write the letter of the definition on the line next to the word it defines.

____ 1. predilection   a. charming

____ 2. calumny   b. slander

____ 3. propitiation   c. immoral

____ 4. licentious   d. instilling

____ 5. ingratiating (adj) e. appeasement

____ 6. inculcation   f. lying

____ 7. dissembling   g. preference

The Crucible, **Act I,** by Arthur Miller

Grammar and Style: Pronoun Case
in Incomplete Constructions

In an **incomplete construction**—a sentence in which a verb or a preposition is "understood"—it is sometimes difficult to decide what pronoun you need. Mentally completing the sentence will help you decide whether you need the subject or object form of the pronoun.

Abigail seems more sure of herself than *they* [do].

Without the understood verb, it is not always easy to hear that the word *they*, not *them*, is correct.

Reverend Hale is more concerned with witches than [with] *her*.

In this example, the understood word is the preposition *with*, which requires *her*—instead of *she*—as its object.

Remember that subject pronouns serve as the subject of a verb. Object pronouns are objects of prepositions or of verbs.

A. Practice: Each of the following sentences is an incomplete construction. Above each sentence write the understood word or words and use a caret (^) to show where the word or words should be inserted. Then indicate whether the italicized pronoun form is a subject or an object by writing *S* or *O* in the blank provided.

_____ 1. Mercy Lewis is concerned about Ruth as well as *her*.

_____ 2. John Proctor has loyalties to his family and *her*.

_____ 3. Reverend Hale feels more prepared than *they* to judge whether witchcraft is present or not.

_____ 4. Reverend Parris is at least as worried about himself as *her*.

_____ 5. The other girls are more frightened than *she*.

_____ 6. Betty seems in worse condition than *she*.

B. Writing Application: Circle the pronoun form that correctly completes each sentence. Remember to complete the sentence mentally to help determine the correct form.

1. Mrs. Putnam is more eager than (*they/them*) to blame the Devil.

2. Reverend Parris is as surprised as (*she/her*) that Ruth Putnam also ails.

3. Giles Corey is curious about Ruth and (*she/her*).

4. Mr. Putnam feels himself more intellectually gifted than (*he/him*).

5. Goody Putnam perhaps has more reason than (*they/them*) to believe that there is evil in the world.

6. Rebecca Nurse has a calming influence on the adults as well as (*she/her*).

The Crucible, **Act I**, by Arthur Miller

Reading Strategy: Question the Characters' Motives

Examining the behavior of characters in a story or play is always a good way to increase understanding of the plot. Specifically, to **question the characters' motives**—their reasons for acting and speaking as they do—helps alert readers to important details and ideas that are not necessarily directly stated.

In *The Crucible*, characters' motives are revealed through their actions, words, and extensive stage directions.

DIRECTIONS: Question the motives of Abigail, Mrs. Putnam, and Reverend Hale. Review each characters' words, actions, and the stage directions as you complete the table with your answers to the questions in the first column.

	Abigail	Mrs. Putnam	Reverend Hale
What motivates the character's behavior?			
Does character hide true motives? If so, how?			
Might character be unaware of true motives?			

The Crucible, **Act I,** by Arthur Miller

Literary Analysis: Drama: Dialogue and Stage Directions

Arthur Miller's **stage directions** in *The Crucible* are extensive, detailed, and full of historical information. They provide the setting, background on the situation, and information about characters' backgrounds, motives, and personalities. A reader of the play benefits from Miller's background information by gaining an understanding of the characters as people and why they act the way they do.

Still, *The Crucible* is a play. As in all plays, the **dialogue** carries the burden of communicating to the audience. From the dialogue a reader or an audience member learns how the characters think, how they express themselves, and how they feel about one another and about the situation at hand. It is only through the dialogue that the plot develops.

DIRECTIONS: Refer to dialogue, stage directions, and background information in Act I as you answer the following questions.

1. What do you learn about Reverend Parris's relationship with the community in Act I? Where do you learn this information?

   _____

   _____

2. What are Abigail's circumstances? What led her to reside with her uncle? Indicate where you find this information.

   _____

   _____

3. What relationship exists between Abigail and Proctor? How do you know this?

   _____

   _____

4. When Mrs. Putnam enters the story, how do the stage directions characterize her?

   _____

   _____

5. In what way do Mrs. Putnam's words and/or actions in Act I support her description in the stage directions?

   _____

   _____

6. Why is Mary Warren embarrassed and fearful when John Proctor enters the room? How do you know this?

   _____

   _____

Name _____ Date _____

The Crucible, Act II, by Arthur Miller

Build Vocabulary

Spelling Strategy For verbs that are complete recognizable words ending in *er*, add the suffixes *-ent* or *-ence* to form adjectives or nouns, respectively. Thus, *differ* becomes *different*, *confer* becomes *conference*, and *defer* becomes the Word Bank word *deference*.

Using the Suffix *-logy*

The most common meaning of the suffix *-logy* is "the science or study of." The suffix derives from a Greek word meaning "reason" or "word," and you can see how "science or study of" might evolve from that meaning.

A. DIRECTIONS: Use a dictionary to discover and define the root of each of the following words. Then write the meaning of the root of each, and explain how the suffix *-logy* combines with the meaning of the root to make the word.

1. psychology _____

2. ontology _____

3. entomology _____

Using the Word Bank

pallor	ameliorate	avidly	base	deference
theology	quail	gingerly	abomination	blasphemy

B. DIRECTIONS: Each item consists of a word from the Word Bank followed by four lettered words or phrases. Choose the word or phrase most nearly *similar* in meaning to the Word Bank word. Circle the letter of your choice.

1. pallor: a. ease   b. majesty   c. paleness   d. sitting room

2. ameliorate: a. nourish   b. improve   c. criticize   d. plot

3. avidly: a. rapidly   b. loftily   c. enthusiastically   d. coolly

4. base: a. degraded   b. faded   c. safe   d. planned

5. deference: a. distinction   b. citation   c. delay   d. respect

6. theology: a. study of legal issues   c. study of life forms

b. study of religious philosophy   d. study of ancient books

7. quail: a. cringe   b. subdue   c. reassure   d. seek

8. gingerly: a. hotly   b. appreciatively   c. profanely   d. cautiously

9. abomination: a. suddenness   b. mysteriousness   c. depravity   d. astonishment

10. blasphemy: a. explosion   b. illness   c. sorcery   d. sacrilege

The Crucible, **Act II,** by Arthur Miller

Grammar and Style: Commas After Introductory Words

Certain mild interjections or other interrupters sometimes introduce the rest of a sentence. In spoken language, most of us use such **introductory words** commonly: "Hey, I wish I had known that." These introductory words serve to heighten the illusion of speech in a written sentence.

When writing sentences with introductory words, use a comma to set them off from the rest of the sentence.

A. Practice: Identify which of the following sentences, some of which contain introductory interrupters, are correctly punctuated. Indicate a correct sentence by placing a *C* on the line to the left of the sentence. If the sentence is incorrect, place an *I* on the line, and correct the punctuation of the sentence.

_____ 1. "Oh, it is a black mischief."

_____ 2. "Why then it is not as you told me."

_____ 3. "Why, thank you, it's a fair poppet."

_____ 4. "What, did she do to you?"

_____ 5. "Mr. Proctor in open court she near to choked us all to death."

_____ 6. "Aye, but then Judge Hathorne say, 'Recite for us your commandments!'"

_____ 7. "Oh, the noose, the noose is up!"

_____ 8. "No, man may longer doubt the powers of the dark are gathered in monstrous attack upon this village."

B. Writing Application: Use each of the following as an introductory word in a sentence about an event or theme in *The Crucible*.

1. Oh

_____

_____

2. Yes

_____

_____

3. Well

_____

_____

4. Now

_____

_____

Name _____ Date _____

The Crucible, **Act II,** by Arthur Miller

Reading Strategy: Read Drama

When we **read drama,** we don't have the same experience as we do when we watch a play on stage. Actors interpret the lines for us. Staging and direction also shape our experience.

When we watch a play, however, we may not see exactly what the author intends. In the written play, we are shown precisely the instructions and information the author has in mind. We also get to "cast" the play ourselves. What does John Proctor look like? If you attend a performance of *The Crucible* in which John Proctor doesn't look strong enough to you, or cackles when he should be laughing bitterly, the play may not have its maximum effect. When you read drama, pay careful attention to stage directions and the text itself, even punctuation. You can get a sense of what the author wants from the actors. At the very least, you can have your own interpretation, for your imaginative mind will have a role in the creation of the play.

DIRECTIONS: Each of the following items presents a stage direction from Act II with emphasis added. What is the importance of the emphasized part of the stage direction? Write your interpretation in the space provided.

1. *The common room of* PROCTOR'S *house,* ***eight days later.***

   _____

   _____

2. *He continues on to the fireplace, . . . lifts out the ladle and tastes.* **He is not quite pleased.**

   _____

   _____

3. *. . . she takes up his plate and glass and fork and goes with them to the basin. Her back is turned to him. He turns to her and watches her.* ***A sense of their separation rises.***

   _____

   _____

4. PROCTOR, ***scoffing but without conviction***: Ah, they'd never hang—

   _____

   _____

5. MARY WARREN: I am sick, I am sick, Mr. Proctor, Pray, pray, hurt me not. ***Her strangeness throws him off . . .***

   _____

   _____

6. *It is* MR. HALE. ***He is different now—drawn a little, and there is a quality of deference, even of guilt, about his manner now.***

   _____

   _____

7. ELIZABETH, ***with great fear***: I will fear nothing. ***She looks about the room as if to fix it in her mind.***

   _____

   _____

The Crucible, **Act II**, by Arthur Miller

Literary Analysis: Allusion

An **allusion** is a reference to some well-known thing or idea. In our society, for example, people often allude to sports phenomena: "This project is the Super Bowl for us." Common allusions often take their reference from the surrounding society, so it's little wonder that the Salem Puritans allude to their religion as knowledgeably and as frequently as we allude to sports.

DIRECTIONS: Use a dictionary or other reference work to explain the italicized allusion in each of the following items.

1. At the beginning of Act II, a kind of *cold war* exists between John and Elizabeth because of past events.

   _____

   _____

   _____

2. Although an honest and strong man, John Proctor has an *Achilles heel*—his relationship to Abigail.

   _____

   _____

   _____

3. Something between a *siren* and a *harpy*, Abigail proves to be Proctor's undoing.

   _____

   _____

   _____

4. Reverend Hale brings an *ivory-tower* approach to his examination that ill fits the world he finds.

   _____

   _____

   _____

5. With the *sword of Damocles* above his head, Proctor flusters and cannot remember the Ten Commandments.

   _____

   _____

   _____

6. Even a person with the *patience of Job*, however, would grow angry at the injustice of innuendo as evidence.

   _____

   _____

   _____

The Crucible, **Act III,** by Arthur Miller

Build Vocabulary

Spelling Strategy When adding an -*ly* suffix to a word that ends in a consonant, do not double or change the consonant. The Word Bank words *deferentially* and *incredulously* illustrate this strategy.

Using Legal Terms

A. DIRECTIONS: Scenes that take place in courtrooms—whether in books, on television, or in real life—are usually full of special words and phrases that have particular meaning for the judges, lawyers, and others present. This is true of Act III of *The Crucible*. Find out what the following words mean. Then use each in a sentence about the action in Act III.

1. affidavit _____

_____

_____

2. warrant _____

_____

_____

Using the Word Bank

contentious	deposition	imperceptible	deferentially	anonymity
prodigious	effrontery	confounded	incredulously	blanched

B. DIRECTIONS: Each item below consists of a Word Bank word followed by four lettered words or phrases. Choose the word or phrase that is most nearly *opposite* in meaning to the Word Bank word. Circle the letter of your choice.

1. anonymity: a. obscurity b. fame c. solitude d. recklessness

2. blanched: a. darkened b. fair c. delayed d. eaten

3. confounded: a. established b. at risk c. angered d. clear-headed

4. contentious: a. competitive b. agreeable c. inclusive d. smoldering

5. deferentially: a. defensively b. imperceptibly c. disrespectfully d. differently

6. deposition: a. shifting b. trial c. putting in place d. informal chat

7. effrontery: a. decoration b. rearward c. politeness d. lying

8. imperceptible: a. obvious b. untouchable c. understandable d. off track

9. incredulously: a. contemptuously c. skeptically

    b. dismissively d. trustfully

10. prodigious: a. luxurious b. cheap c. bountiful d. meager

The Crucible, **Act III**, by Arthur Miller

Grammar and Style: Subject and Verb Agreement in Inverted Sentences

Whenever you write a sentence, the subject must agree with the verb in number. This means a singular subject must have a singular verb and a plural subject must have a plural verb. In most sentences the position of the subject is *before* the verb, as in this example.

      S   **V**

Mr. *Nurse announces* that the girls are frauds.

In an **inverted sentence**, the subject comes *after* the verb. The **subject and verb agreement** is sometimes difficult to "hear" in an inverted sentence. Look at these examples.

                                  V   **S**

Singular subject and verb: Critical to Elizabeth's case *is* the *credibility* of Abigail.

                                  V   **S**

Plural subject and verb: Critical to Elizabeth's case *are* the *lies* she tells about Abigail.

When you write inverted sentences, be sure not to mistake a word in the opening phrase as the subject. This can lead to errors in subject and verb agreement.

A. Practice: The following sentences are about Act III. Underline each main subject. Circle each main verb. Then identify the one sentence that contains an error in subject and verb agreement. Correct that sentence by crossing out the incorrect verb and writing the correct one above it.

1. There are many people in the vestry room.

2. Here are the husbands of the accused women.

3. Why is Proctor so stunned by Mary's behavior?

4. Continually arguing and getting in the way is Reverend Parris.

5. Hurting Elizabeth's chances are her ignorance of John's confession.

B. Writing Application: In each of the following sentences, the subject comes before the verb. Rewrite each sentence in inverted order, choosing the verb that agrees in number with the subject.

1. Abigail's behavior (*is/are*) highly persuasive.

   _____

2. Corey and Nurse (*is/are*) riled up about the treatment of their wives.

   _____

3. Mary Warren (*recalls/recall*) her confession in near hysterics.

   _____

4. Danforth (*gazes/gaze*) at Abigail in astonishment.

   _____

5. Mary desperately (*shrieks/shriek*) that John Proctor is doing the Devil's work.

   _____

The Crucible, **Act III**, by Arthur Miller

Reading Strategy: Categorize Characters by Role

When you read stories or plays with many characters, it is easy to lose track of just exactly who thinks what, who does what, and who offends whom. **Categorizing characters** according to their roles can help you keep track of any number of players. In addition, categorizing may lead you to a discovery about a character's motives or a plot development.

DIRECTIONS: Categorize the characters in Act III by answering the following questions.

1. Three different roles are played out in the court scene.

   Who are the court officials? _____
   _____

   Who are the accusers in Act III? _____
   _____

   Who are the accused in Act III? _____
   _____

2. Some characters tell the truth, and some do not.

   Who lies in Act III? _____
   _____

   Who tells the truth in Act III? _____
   _____

3. Into what other category or set of categories do the characters in Act III fit? Label the categories and list the characters in the space provided.

_____
_____
_____
_____
_____
_____
_____
_____
_____

The Crucible, **Act III,** by Arthur Miller

Literary Analysis: Dramatic and Verbal Irony

In real life, things are often different from what they seem. When this occurs—both in life and in literature—it is called **irony**. Writers and playwrights make use of two forms of irony to surprise and entertain their readers and viewers.

In **dramatic irony**, the characters think one thing to be true, but the audience knows something else to be true. This creates interest and tension in a story or play. In **verbal irony**, words seem to say one thing but mean something quite different.

DIRECTIONS: Explain the verbal or dramatic irony that exists in the following passages.

1. Upon hearing Proctor's and Mary's statements, Danforth is shaken by the idea that Abigail and the girls could be frauds. Danforth challenges Proctor with this: "Now, Mr. Proctor, before I decide whether I shall hear you or not, it is my duty to tell you this. We burn a hot fire here; it melts down all concealment."

   _____

   _____

   _____

2. Parris, to save his own reputation, is eager to support Abigail's claims and the court's decisions. He accuses several people of making attacks upon the court. Hale's response is this: "Is every defense an attack upon the court? Can no one—?"

   _____

   _____

   _____

3. Proctor reminds Mary of a biblical story about the angel Raphael and a boy named Tobias. In the story, the boy frees a woman from the devil and cures his father of blindness.

   _____

   _____

   _____

4. Hale feels there is weight in Mary Warren's deposition. He cautions Danforth about not examining it closely: "Excellency, I have signed seventy-two death warrants; I am a minister of the Lord, and I dare not take a life without there be a proof so immaculate no slightest qualm of conscience may doubt it."

   _____

   _____

   _____

5. Proctor is informed that Elizabeth has said she is pregnant. Proctor says he knows nothing of it but states that his wife does not lie. Later, when questioned about her husband's fidelity, Elizabeth lies, thinking she is protecting her husband and his reputation.

   _____

   _____

   _____

The Crucible, **Act IV,** by Arthur Miller

Build Vocabulary

Spelling Strategy Words ending in a silent *e* drop the *e* before a suffix beginning with a vowel. The rule affects these Word Bank words: *purge + ed = purged*; *tantalize + ed = tantalized*; *beguile + ed = beguiled*; *cleave + ed = cleaved*; *conciliate + ory = conciliatory*; and *retaliate + ion = retaliation*.

Using Words From Myths

Myths are fictional stories that account for natural phenomena or explain actions of gods. As English was developing, many writers and speakers were familiar with classical learning, including mythology. Thus, English includes names and stories from the myths of various cultures, and many words originate in these ancient tales.

A. DIRECTIONS: Use a dictionary or other resource to explain the mythological origins of the following words.

1. echo _____
   _____

2. volcano _____
   _____

3. Wednesday _____
   _____

4. museum _____
   _____

Using the Word Bank

agape	conciliatory	beguile	floundering	retaliation
adamant	cleave	sibilance	tantalized	purged

B. DIRECTIONS: Match each word in the left column with its definition in the right column. Write the letter of the definition on the line next to the word it defines.

____ 1. agape   a. hissing

____ 2. conciliatory   b. cling

____ 3. beguile   c. tempted

____ 4. floundering   d. purified

____ 5. retaliation   e. open

____ 6. adamant   f. charm

____ 7. cleave   g. reprisal

____ 8. sibilance   h. resolute

____ 9. tantalized   i. appeasing

____ 10. purged   j. struggling

The Crucible, **Act IV,** by Arthur Miller

Grammar and Style: Commonly Confused Words: *raise, rise*

Do not confuse the verbs *raise* and *rise*. The verb *raise* means "to lift up." The verb *rise* means "to go up" or "to get up." If a thing is going up by itself, use *rise*. If it is going up through the action of someone or something else, use *raise*. *Raise* always has a direct object, and *rise* never does.

Example: The tide *rises* with each passing hour.

Example: The surging water *raises* the boats.

The following chart summarizes the forms of the two verbs:

Verb	Present	Present Participle	Past	Past Participle
raise (takes object)	raise, raises	raising	raised	(have) raised
rise (no object)	rise, rises	rising	rose	(have) risen

A. Practice: In each of the following sentences, write the appropriate form of the verb *rise* or *raise*. For those sentences using a form of the verb *rise*, underline the subject performing the action. For those sentences using a form of the verb *raise*, underline the direct object of the action.

1. In Act IV of *The Crucible*, hopes _____ that Danforth may yet stop the injustice.

2. Reverend Hale finally _____ his voice against the proceedings at the end of Act III.

3. Although Parris _____ no objections earlier, by Act IV he might also be ready to quit the folly.

4. Perhaps it would be a wise move for Danforth somehow to stop the hysteria and chaos that are _____ in the village.

5. But if Danforth's doubts are _____, he also has a problem: what about those already executed?

6. Although Proctor would like to live, if his hopes have _____, he has given no sign.

7. As the sun _____, the pressure and suspense reach their peak.

B. Writing Application: Write a sentence using the indicated form of *raise* or *rise*.

1. (*raise*, present)_____

2. (*rise*, past participle) _____

3. (*rise*, past) _____

4. (*raise*, present participle)_____

Name _____ Date _____

The Crucible, **Act IV**, by Arthur Miller

Reading Strategy: Apply Themes to Contemporary Events

In *The Crucible*, Arthur Miller writes about a town in the grip of fear. Miller's play also refers to paranoia in America during the 1950's, when fear of communism was widespread, and even knowing a person "soft" on communism caused one to be suspected of treason.

The play also has as one of its themes the nature of belief and systems of "truth." What went so wrong in Salem in the 1690's? How could some people in the 1950's lose their good judgment? Does thinking like this still occur today?

DIRECTIONS: Write the significance of each of the following passages to the play. Comment on what it might also have meant to Americans in the times of McCarthyism in the 1950's. Finally, express what meaning the passage may have today about particular or general issues. Write your answers in the space provided.

1. They believed, in short, that they held in their steady hands the candle that would light the world. We have inherited this belief, and it has helped us and hurt us.

   _____

   _____

   _____

   _____

2. The witch-hunt was a perverse manifestation of the panic which set in among all classes when the balance began to turn toward greater individual freedom. . . . It is still impossible for man to organize his social life without repressions, and the balance has yet to be struck between order and freedom.

   _____

   _____

   _____

   _____

3. In the countries of the Communist ideology, all resistance of any import is linked to the totally malign capitalist succubi, and in America any man who is not reactionary in his views is open to the charge of alliance with the Red hell.

   _____

   _____

   _____

   _____

4. DANFORTH: In an ordinary crime, how does one defend the accused? One calls up witnesses to prove his innocence. But witchcraft is *ipso facto*, on its face and by its nature, an invisible crime, is it not? Therefore, who may possibly be witness to it?

   _____

   _____

   _____

   _____

Name _____ Date _____

The Crucible, **Act IV**, by Arthur Miller

Literary Analysis: Theme

The havoc that fear and suspicion can wreak if not countered by reason is the most obvious theme of *The Crucible*. A **theme** is a central idea or insight that a writer tries to convey in a literary work. Miller's depiction of paranoia in Salem and his references to America in the 1950's make clear his ideas on the topic.

A work of literature may have more than one theme. Miller carefully intertwines other topics and themes as well. The personal motivations of the characters, for example, contribute to their fates along with the religious issue of witchcraft. John withholds critical information about Abigail, for example, because of his past relationship with her. Hale's academic pride blinds him to hysteria's momentum for too long. How does Miller spin these threads into themes about people and how they behave? What themes does he express?

DIRECTIONS: Use the following chart to help you identify themes in *The Crucible*. In the first column are subjects or topics that Miller addresses in the play. In the second column, write a sentence that states a theme about each topic that the events in the play express. In the third column, list the events or evidence in the play that points to the theme you've identified.

Topic	Theme	Events in Play
1. Guilt		
2. Revenge		
3. Pride		
4. Intolerance		
5. Authority		
6. Integrity		